On the road to great democracy:

clear and honest
FINANCIAL REPORTS

OPERATING FUND	RESTRICTED FUNDS
Assets	Assets
<u>Debts</u>	<u>Debts</u>
NET WORTH	NET WORTH
Income	Income
<u>Expense</u>	<u>Expense</u>
NET	NET
Change in assets	Change in assets
<u>Change in debts</u>	<u>Change in debts</u>
CHANGE IN NET WORTH	CHANGE IN NET WORTH

On the road to great democracy:

clear and honest
FINANCIAL REPORTS

Including the
2006 US Government Financial Report
in a new, revised format (BETA)

Virginia Hammon, MS, TE

Library of Congress Cataloging--in-Publication Data

Hammon, Virginia 1948-

On the road to great democracy: clear and honest financial reports / Virginia
Hammon.

p. cm.

Includes bibliographical references and index.

ISBN 978-0-9786007-0-9

1. Finance, Public–United States–Accounting. 2. Democracy.
3. Political Science-Civics-Citizenship

Also available in ebook: ISBN 978-0-9786007-1-6

Published by
Great Democracy Media
greatdemocracy.com
PO Box 6440
Portland, OR 97228

Quantity discounts are available directly from the publisher:
sales@greatdemocracy.com

Dedicated to

Clifford E. Hamar and Jean S. Hamar,
unconditionally supportive parents, who taught me that if something is worth doing,
it is worth doing well–and worth making mistakes along the way.

Please join me in making the work of upgrading our democracy
deserving of the unstinting support of all our elders and mentors, and of
the gratitude of generations to come.

Contents

Part Two

Basic accounting and government accounting

Part Three

Choose Excellence!

Improvements to the U.S. Government financial reporting

⇨ TAKE OUT THE KINKS IN THE FLOW OF INFORMATION:

Chapter 9. Separate reports for separate funds

The front and center *consolidated* budget and financial report is a kink in the flow of information.

Chapter 10. Book all the assets and all the debts

Many assets and debts are off the books, which creates kinks in the flow of information and compromises effective debate.

Chapter 11. If it is income, call it income

Booking income sometimes as income and sometimes as a credit against expenses confuses people about the full cost of government and the revenue available to pay expenses.

Chapter 12. Tell the truth, the whole truth and nothing but the truth

Missing information in the financial reports, predictable spending ignored, spending hidden in footnotes, "on" and "off-budget" confusion, all contribute to keeping lawmakers and the public confused about the finances.

A popular Government, without popular information or the means of acquiring it, is but a prologue to a farce or a tragedy or perhaps both. Knowledge will forever govern ignorance, and a people who mean to be their own governors, must arm themselves with the power knowledge gives.

President James Madison, 1822

On the road to great democracy

We've got troubles. Are you afraid of multiplying dangers, angry at the dysfunctional status quo and hungry for a practical path to a sustainable future? How can we "form a more perfect Union, establish Justice, insure domestic Tranquility, provide for the common defence, promote the general Welfare, and secure the blessings of Liberty to ourselves and our Posterity"?*

With gratitude for those who have gone before us, we can come together today and practice *great* democracy. Great democracy depends on the informed participation of citizens and elected officials. To take our democracy from good to great, we need to remodel some of our decision-making infrastructure, beginning with the basic information about our nation's finances that is required for prudent, responsible and forward-looking decisions. Making key improvements to our accounting and reporting will create simple, clear and honest financial reports that will serve a great democracy.

Have you read the 2006 Financial Report of the U.S. Government? Did you hear anything in the news about it when it came out in December 2006? How many of us read this 168-page report?

---

*   The Constitution of the United States of America

At the economic conference in Waco, Texas in August 2002, President G.W. Bush said, *"The government accounting system is pretty kind of hard to explain. I've been there 18 months trying to figure it out."*

And then everybody laughed.

Let's take the joke out of our financial accounting and reporting.

Do you believe that our Representatives, Senators and President read each year's financial report and the 1000+ pages of the U.S. Government's budget before they pass spending bills? Do you believe they read all the pages in the three-foot high stacks of Omnibus Appropriation bills? If decision-makers do not read financial reports and bills personally, do you believe that the people advising them on what to promote and how to vote have your best interests at heart? What about our nation's best interests?

Are you content with a form of government where in-the-game elites make the decisions without due consideration of the issues and without a clear understanding of the financial impact of laws?

If you can answer yes to all of these questions, then you are a happy camper. You can stop reading now.

*   *   *   *   *   *

Proud to be an American only goes so far

You can be proud of your American heritage, but if you want to be proud to be an American then you have to live your heritage; you have to be an active, participating, knowledgeable, learning, voting, understanding-your-government American—to the best of your ability. We the people decide every day to act or to do nothing. We have freedom to choose and the ability to make good decisions that can put us on a path toward a healthy and prosperous future.

Call on your highest mind and look critically at leadership and at your representation. Choose to be informed. Choose to honor your nation by choosing excellence and accountability. Take action.

A path to excellence

This book and the projects at GreatDemocracy.org are for you who want a way to take an active, but not burdensome part in civic matters. They are for you who want to create a great democracy where all citizens can be active, but not necessarily activists—a government of people who can set aside a little time to give for the common good, without making political advocacy their life.

We will create tools for citizens who are willing to do a little homework, but who do not want to feel like they are getting a degree in government, social policy or finance. If you want to join with people who would like to spend some pleasurable and challenging time problem solving with their fellow citizens without rancor, hard-fought positions, and name-calling, then keep reading this book. It is a first step on the road to great democracy.

Troubled times and opportunity

Times are always troubled with shifting sets of problems because that is the nature of dynamic and chaotic life on earth. Here in America we have strong, powerful and useful bridges over troubled waters: we have the American people, we have an American commitment to democracy and we have enormous wealth. We have strong cause for optimism. We are rich in resources for making decisions that can solve problems, lead to achieving our goals, and uphold our values.

The *opportunity* to practice great democracy is a gift. Let's use it.

Why have government?

We have government whether we think we want it or need it because humans are social animals; there will always be some system for regulating our relations with each other. "Government" refers to the formal outward manifestation of this system and "culture" refers to the informal inward aspects. Both government and culture create boundaries to acceptable behavior within a given community, and create tools for working together toward shared goals. The clearer our understanding of these structures of governance and culture, the better we can use them effectively to achieve our personal and our collective goals.

How we want to live and what we value is reflected in our choice of government. In the United States, we create government to "form a more perfect union"—in order to be the best nation that we can be. Forming a democratic government assumes a higher good beyond individual self-interest.

Our government's mission:

- **Establish Justice**

- **Provide for the common defense**

- **Insure domestic tranquility and promote the general welfare**
    - Promote health care
    - Foster income security
    - Boost agricultural productivity
    - Provide benefits and services to veterans
    - Facilitate commerce
    - Support housing
    - Support the transportation system
    - Protect the environment
    - Contribute to the security of energy resources
    - Assist the States in providing education

- **Secure the blessings of Liberty to ourselves and our posterity**

(From the Constitution of the United States of America with mission details from the Financial Report of the U.S. Government)

Why democratic government?

Democracy—government of, by and for the people—offers the best tools for creating a more perfect union. There is wisdom in the community that is greater than the wisdom of any one person, or small group of people. Well-practiced great democracy can draw out this wisdom so that every public decision is the best possible decision. In a great democracy, we speak and act through government with our aggregated wisdom and collective voice for the welfare of the nation as a whole.

Great democracy means great decision-making

Great decision-making begins when all participants know where we are now. Then we can dialogue and deliberate about what we value and where we want to go next. When we know where we are now and where we want to go, we can work on the best way to get there. This is basic decision-making. We know this. We have the aptitude and the tools. We simply need to use them. With intention, we can practice great decision-making and consequently great democracy.

This book is a step on the road toward great democracy. This book is about creating tools so that each of us can bring our best mind to public decision-making. It is about how our government can serve us by giving citizens and lawmakers the simplest, clearest, and best information about our public finances so that we can make good public decisions. It is about providing tools so that we can tap into our best minds in the best way to achieve the best solutions to public issues.

What information do we need to practice great democracy?

Where are we now?

First, we need to know where we are now. We must measure what is important to us so that we know how we are doing. That is the first step in good decision-making, because we have to know where we are to make effective plans for improvement. Describing, defining and measuring where we are now is also a good place to start, because we need to start with some agreement and it is easier to agree about what is observable and measurable.

How do we know?

What is important?

How will we measure movement toward our goals?

When we are all around the same table and agree where we are now, we can decide where we want to go next. We will be set to establish what is important to each of us and to define goals and priorities. We can then look for the places in the system where change can make the most difference: close to the source of the flow of information, energy, resources and capital.

None of this can happen until we know where we are now and how we know. We need the answers, yet we have very poor systems in place to get the information that we need for public decisions. With improved systems, we will begin to have clear and simple markers about where we are now and how we are doing. We will also be able to look back one year, four years, and ten years and see how our choices have panned out. We will assess whether we are achieving our goals and be able to make timely course corrections.

Public decisions–grounded in the allocation of money

A very bright, well-educated former Hawaii State Legislator told me once, "I don't read financial reports," it was someone else's responsibility to tell him what he needed to know from such reports. I was stunned. I paid a personal and professional price for assuming that a person in his position could read and understand a basic financial report format and act on it appropriately. This lesson was one of the inspirations for this book.

Fundamentally, government decisions are about the allocation of resources. We measure, record and exchange resources in dollars, so understanding the financial situation of the U.S. Government is the foundation for making good public decisions.

A simple plan

We need a simple plan to achieve better-informed, broad-based civic participation. We need to take the kinks out of the flow of information to citizens and lawmakers. This book suggests some improvements so that we can follow the flow of our money in government.

This book is about making some simple improvements in the way we report on the financial conditions in our communities. The federal government's financial report is used as the model because federal taxing and spending choices impact every one of our lives. Federal government spending makes up **almost 20% of all the money that flows around in our economy**. Our political choices determine where this money flows.

It is important that we all know the U.S. Government's financial standing, understand the financial choices that we make and their impact. Once we have collaboratively determined a financial report format that works best for everyone, then the model can be applied at every level of government, giving us opportunities for comparison, assessment and excellent oversight.

What is our financial situation now?

What happened last year?

How much did we have to spend and how well did we spend it?

What was last year's impact on our financial situation?

If you want quick and clear information about the U.S. Government's finances, go straight to the reformatted financial report in Part I. **Part I** presents a draft format for a clear and honest U.S. Government financial report. The official 2006 U.S. Government Financial Report has been translated, with a few caveats, into a suggested format so that every citizen can understand it. The summary format fits on a drink coaster for quick and handy reference and memorable context.

If you need some additional information about basic accounting to understand the report, read Part II. **Part II** of this book includes a quick guide to accounting basics. It includes enough to give you the tools to understand the financial report and to understand why it deserves our attention first, before moving to the budget and budget reports. The current U.S. Government's financial report format and the current financial report contents are introduced.

Then, please read the suggestions for improving the financial reporting in Part III and tell us what you think. **Part III** offers specific suggestions for making our accounting, lawmaking and financial reporting simpler, clearer and more honest. These improvements will give decision-makers, including citizens, information that is critical to making good decisions. Please join the dialogue and debate at www.GreatDemocracy.org.

This book is an invitation, not a promise. The recommendations for an improved financial report are intended to be the beginning of a collaborative process with an online nexus, to perfect a financial report format of highest excellence and usefulness. With a great financial report telling us clearly where we are now, we will be ready to tackle the budget and answer the questions, "Where do we want to go? How shall we get there?"

When all able citizens understand the financial situation and the resources available for our government's mission, we will have the foundation for a great democratic practice.

We think we can and we can!

Americans are can-do people. America is rich in a tradition of striving for excellence. The American pioneering spirit is strong: we have the ability and courage to look clearly at our present situation and work hard to build safe, healthy and prosperous communities for tomorrow. Let's do it.

We share this great nation with citizens who are bright, well-educated, caring and dedicated. When we ask for specific help, most Americans will give it if they can. We are innovative people who come together and create extraordinary solutions to difficult problems. Our recent history is full of astounding developments in communication tools, warfare, transportation, pharmaceuticals, financial transactions and just-in-time production. When we recognize value in newer, safer, cleaner, more efficient, better ways of doing things, we do it. When we are greedy and lazy—claim that it just can't be done, that it is too expensive, that bureaucracy will block it, that businesses will fail, that people will lose their jobs and starve—we ignore our enormous talent for creative thinking.

Be informed

Know what you need to know to enhance your choices and consequently your freedoms. We can galvanize democratic participation and create a practical path to a sustainable future. We can create a decision-making space that welcomes all without sacrificing order, purpose and efficiency. We can give government a piece of our mind without losing ours and without losing the quality of our government. We can rally our collective wisdom and take action. When we do this, we will have a great democracy. Here is a pragmatic basis for hope and the first step on a practical path toward better decisions and better outcomes.

SMART-
Between about 1975 and 1985, most new U.S. energy-using devices—
cars, buildings, refrigerators, lighting systems, etc. –*doubled* their efficiency.
Natural Capitalism Hawkens & Lovins 1999.

STUCK-
Today the American auto industry is paying the price for balking at higher energy efficiency standards. They were unable to think efficiency AND profits, and stuck with out of date winning strategies.

We might hope to see the finances of the Union as clear and intelligible as a merchant's books, so that every member of Congress, and every man of any mind in the Union, should be able to comprehend them, to investigate abuses, and consequently to control them.

President Thomas Jefferson, 1802

Part I
The 2006 U.S. Government's Financial Report
In a simple, clear and honest, revised format

The 2006 Financial Report of the United States Government

Give credit where credit is due:

Republican President George W. Bush has been at the helm since 2001.
A Republican majority ruled Congress from 1994-2001 and 2004-2006.

INVITATION

This is a suggested format. You are invited to make suggestions for improvements online at GreatDemocracy.org. Together, we can establish the clearest format for the financial reports.

This Financial Report is available in an enriched format which includes colorful illustrations and historical information from 2002-2005 for context and comparison. Additional and increasingly accurate information is building on the website, GreatDemocracy.org.

VALUE of the DOLLAR

We measure, account for and report our financial situation in dollars.
So keep in mind the change in the value of the dollar.[1]

2002	**2003**	**2004**	**2005**	**2006**

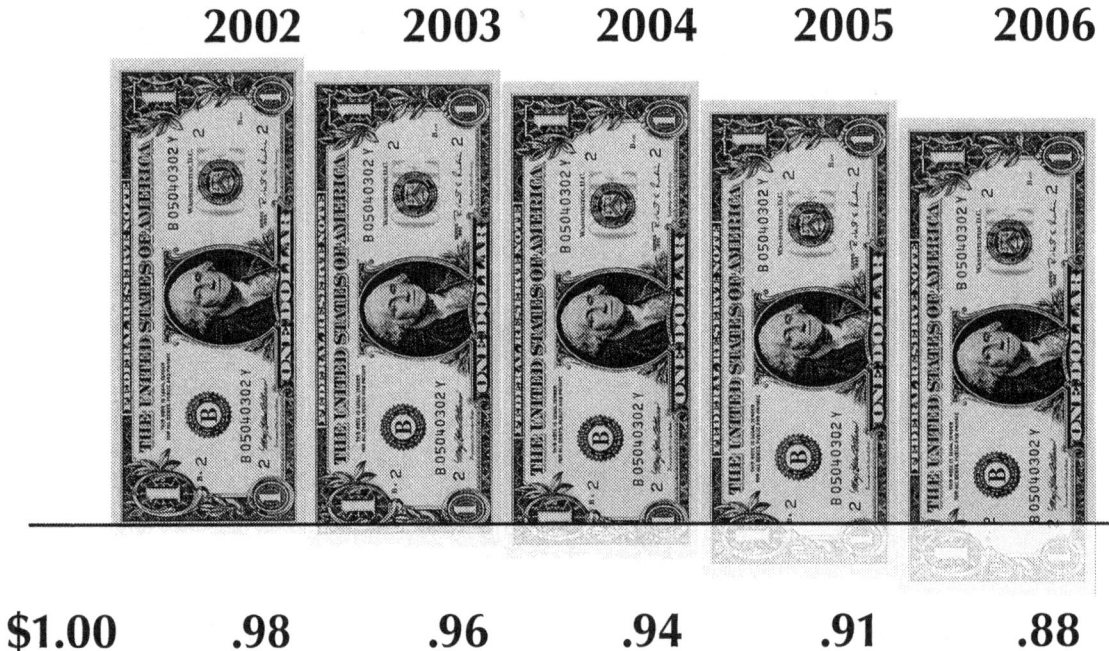

$1.00	**.98**	**.96**	**.94**	**.91**	**.88**

5 year change in the value of the dollar: - 12%

$1.00 at the beginning of 2002, was worth $ .88 at the end of 2006

1 year change in the value of the dollar: - 3%

$1.00 at the beginning of 2006 was worth $ .97 at the end of 2006

The summary on the following page fits on a drink coaster! Order vast quantities today from GreatDemocracy.org and distribute at all your favorite restaurants and bars. When every citizen understands this summary information, we will have our discussions about the details in context and we can begin to make better decisions.

Summary

Bold=billions

OPERATING FUND

What is our situation now?

Assets	**1,289**,000,000,000
Debts	**10,625**,000,000,000
Net worth	$ - **9,336**,000,000,000

What happened last year?

Income	**1,611**,000,000,000
Expense	**2,233**,000,000,000
Net	$ - **622**,000,000,000

Change in assets	- **28**,000,000,000
Change in debts	**373**,000,000,000
Change in net worth	$ - **401**,000,000,000

RESTRICTED FUNDS

What is our situation now?

Assets	3,865,000,000,000
Current debts and liabilities	3,446,000,000,000
Net long term liabilities for current participants	44,147,000,000,000
Net worth	$ - **43,728**,000,000,000

What happened last year?

Income	1,514,000,000,000
Expense	1,342,000,000,000
Net	$ **172**,000,000,000

Change in assets	*not enough information, yet*
Change in debts	"
Change in net worth	$ **172**,000,000,000

The OPERATING FUND

The Operating Fund includes all the money available for general operations–all other monies are collected for specific purposes, restricted in their use to those purposes, and tracked in separate fund accounts.

It is important to have an historical perspective on spending, so that patterns are clear. The historical data for 2002-2005 is best guess data because there is no data available on the funds separately. For this next page and the historical summary of restricted funds on page 27, the numbers have been extrapolated using proportions comparable to 2006. These historical numbers **may or may not be accurate.**

Please focus on the usefulness of the format.

Detailed information on the sources of information and the steps taken to arrive at all of these numbers can be found in the notes.

2002-2005 are adjusted for the
decline in the value of the dollar:
%*= percent of income

2002 - billions

Assets	906
Debts	8,789
Net Worth	- $ 7,883

Income	1,311	
Expense	1,799	
Net	- $ 488	137%*

Change in assets	$
Change in debts	$
Change in Net worth	$

:-(

2005

Assets	1,317
Debts	10,252
Net Worth	- $ 8,935

Income	1,404	+ 15%
Expense	2,342	+ 12%
Net	- $ 962	169%*

Change in assets	5	0%
Change in debts	356	+ 4%
Change in Net worth	- $ 351	- 4%

:-(

2003

Assets	1,328
Debts	9,352
Net Worth	- $ 8,024

Income	1,179	- 10%
Expense	2,012	+12%
Net	- $ 894	176%*

Change in assets	422	+ 46%
Change in debts	563	+ 6%
Change in Net worth	- $ 141	- 2%

:-(

2004 Election Year

Assets	1,312
Debts	9,896
Net Worth	- $ 8,584

Income	1,221	+ 4%
Expense	2,000	- 2%
Net	- $ 820	167%*

Change in assets	- 16	- 1%
Change in debts	544	+ 6%
Change in Net worth	- $ 560	- 7%

:-(

2006 OPERATING FUND

What is the situation now?		Change in 1 yr	4 years
Assets	1,289,000,000,000		
Debts	10,625,000,000,000		
Net Worth	**- $ 9,336**,000,000,000	- 5%	- 18%

What happened this year?			
Income	1,611,000,000,000	+15%	+ 23%
Expense	2,233,000,000,000	- 6%	+ 24%
Net	**- $ 622**,000,000,000	139%	of income

Change in assets	- 28,000,000,000	
Change in debts	+ 672,000,000,000	
Change in Net worth[3]	**- $700**,000,000,000	- 5%

:-(

5 year average: spending = 158% of income

Thousands, Millions, Billions, Trillions

It is very difficult to grasp the difference in the magnitude of thousands, millions, billions and trillions. It might help to compare it to time:

If

$ 1	=	1 second
One thousand $ 1,000	=	17 minutes
One million $ 1,000,000	=	12 days
One billion $ 1,000,000,000	=	32 years
One trillion $ 1,000,000,000,000	=	31,710 years

2006 U.S. Government
OPERATING FUND

What is our situation now?

STATEMENT of NET WORTH

Assets

Property, plant, and equipment, *net*[4]	688,500,000,000
Inventories and related property	281,300,000,000
Loans receivable	220,800,000,000
Accounts and taxes receivable	68,800,000,000
Other assets	42,700,000,000
Cash & other monetary assets	-12,800,000,000
Total Operating Fund Assets	**$ 1,289**,300,000,000

Debts & Liabilities

Debt held by the public and accrued interest	4,867,500,000,000
Debt held by the restricted funds and accrued interest[5]	3,657,600,000,000
Other[6]	1,669,900,000,000
Environmental and disposal liabilities	305,200,000,000
Accounts payable	58,400,000,000
Total Operating Fund Debts & Liabilities	**10,625**,000,000,000

NET WORTH

Subtract debts from assets. Net worth is a negative $ 9,336 billion ($9.3 trillion)

$ - 9,336,000,000,000

OPERATING FUND ASSETS

2006 is the only year for which there is enough information in the financial report for an informed guess about what assets belong to the Operating Fund and what assets belong to the restricted funds. For 2002-2005, a formula was applied based on the ratio of apparent operating and restricted fund assets reported in the 2006 consolidated financial report. Please view this as a desired format for a future report that is close to accurate, but not totally so.   Formulas are available on GreatDemocracy.org.

CHANGE IN ASSETS

There is currently no meaningful point in looking at the change in assets over time (even if we had accurate numbers). The big increase in assets in 2004 is because the Department of Defense finally booked some of its assets (about $330 billion at one time). Since they have not completed the job, and a significant portion of our assets are simply "off the books," the change in assets is of minimal significance.

It *will be useful* to look at the change in the value of our assets WHEN we have all of our assets on the books. Support this improvement by letting the President, and your senator and representative know that it is important to you.

ASSETS *NOT* ON THE BOOKS

All federally owned land that is set aside for the use and enjoyment of present and future generations and land on which military bases are located. This means that as this land is sold, there is NO readily accessible record of this loss in assets.

Water, gas, oil and mineral wealth on or under public land. There is no readily accessible record of their depletion.

National transportation, communication, health and education infrastructures paid with federal dollars.

All heritage and cultural assets (e.g. museum collections, libraries).

"Brand America"– Increasingly, businesses are giving a monetary value to the intangible value of their brand. Since our entire faith-based monetary system rests on the goodwill of the world, it might be useful to give it a value on the books, and note when it deteriorates.

As the above assets deteriorate or disappear, their passing goes unnoticed, since we have not yet made an effort to catalog them. How can we make good decisions, if we do not know what we own collectively?

OPERATING FUND DEBTS, LIABILITIES & POTENTIAL LIABILITIES
NOT ON THE BOOKS

Veteran's projected disability benefits are not on the books. Currently about 20% of all Iraqi War Veteran's are qualifying for disability (probably about 400,000 over time)

Deferred maintenance on all government property

Federal Deposit Insurance Corporation (FDIC), Insurer of last resort for banks (remember the savings and loan debacle?)

Crop failure subsidies to private insurance

Flood insurance

Pension Benefit Guaranty Corporation guarantees

Guarantees for terrorism insurance payouts

Guarantees for Fannie Mae and Freddie Mac mortgages

Estimates for the liabilities left OFF the books range from $6-10 trillion, 5-10 times the debts and liabilities that you see ON the books, rendering any reports of increase or change of very minimal usefulness.

2006 U.S. Government
OPERATING FUND

What happened last year?

INCOME & EXPENSE STATEMENT

Forfeited Income - "Tax Expenditures"[7]

Preferential tax exemptions	**1,277**,000,000,000	79%

Income

Individual income taxes	1,046,000,000,000	65%
Corporate profit tax	350,000,000,000	22%
Marketplace sales & services[8]	85,000,000,000	5%
Federal Reserve receipts[9]	30,000,000,000	2%
Estate and gift taxes	27,000,000,000	2%
Custom duties	25,000,000,000	1.5%
Excise taxes	25,000,000,000	1.5%
Other taxes and receipts	13,000,000,000	1%
"unreconciled transactions"	11,000,000,000	0%
TOTAL OPERATING FUND INCOME	**1,611**,000,000,000	100%

Expense

LEGISLATIVE BRANCH[10]	5,000,000,000	0%
JUDICIAL BRANCH	7,000,000,000	0%
EXECUTIVE BRANCH:		

Off the top:
Legally
mandatory >

Morally
mandatory >

INTEREST on debt held by public	222,000,000,000	14%
INTEREST on debt held by restricted funds	185,000,000,000	12%
DEFENSE Past-Veterans Affairs	130,000,000,000	8%
DEFENSE Present & Future	678,000,000,000	42%
Health & Human Services*	350,000,000,000	22%
Agriculture	127,000,000,000	8%
Education	124,000,000,000	8%
Energy*	79,000,000,000	5%
Homeland Security/FEMA	77,000,000,000	5%
Housing & Urban Development	51,000,000,000	3%
Justice	29,000,000,000	2%
Treasury[11]	22,000,000,000	2%
NASA-National Aeronautic & Space	21,000,000,000	1%
State Department	18,000,000,000	1%
Labor*	16,000,000,000	1%
Interior*	16,000,000,000	1%
USAID-International Development	13,000,000,000	1%
Transportation*	11,000,000,000	1%
Commerce	10,000,000,000	1%
EPA-Environmental Protection	9,000,000,000	1%
National Science Foundation	7,000,000,000	0%
Executive Office of the President[12]	7,000,000,000	0%
SBA-Small Business Administration	2,000,000,000	0%
General Services Administration	1,000,000,000	0%
US Nuclear Regulatory Commission	1,000,000,000	0%
FCC-Communications Commission*	1,000,000,000	0%
All other entities	14,000,000,000	1%

TOTAL OPERATING FUND EXPENSES % of income   **2,233**,000,000,000   139%

Net overspending $ **622**,000,000,000

PREFERENTIAL TAX EXEMPTIONS are both income and expense. If these preferential exemptions did not exist the revenue would be there, so it is important to see what proportion of income we forego for special purposes.   When we decide that certain people will not have to pay a tax that others are paying under similar circumstances, we are choosing to forfeit income for a purpose, so forfeiting income due is also another form of spending.   2002-2004 are estimates made by the GAO. More current information is not available from the GAO, so 2005-2006 are an extrapolated average.

MARKETPLACE SALES & SERVICES are revenues earned in the marketplace. This is a fuzzy category in government accounting and includes things like fees for parks or patents, the sale of assets like minerals and land (though not all these sales are recorded here), the rights to our airwaves, and miscellaneous sales to the public. This total of $85 billion is the sum of the $17.1 billion given in the current official report under income, plus the estimated Operating Fund share of the $226 billion total in "earned revenue" that is credited on the expense side of the current report, leaving a "net expense."

UNRECONCILED TRANSACTIONS are corrections for sloppy accounting.

EXPENSE NUMBERS do not match the official financial report numbers because they are the gross expenses and include an estimated allocation of the $344 billion in intragovernmental transfers (which are primarily the social insurance payments for government employees).

SOME AGENCIES have not been included in this Operating Fund report because they function as independent, self-funding agencies, and generally do not draw from the general operating fund: United States Post Office, Tennessee Valley Authority, Federal Deposit Insurance Corporation (FDIC), Export-Import Bank of the U.S. The reports for these agencies will be given in a supplemental report in this proposed model.

 * These agencies in the expense list manage restricted funds that make up more than 10% of their spending reported in the official consolidated report. The agency expenses listed here do not include the spending of the funds that they manage. See pages 28-33 for the separate reports on the restricted funds.

2006 Operating Fund OUTCOME

Total revenue available (may include the sale of assets)	1,611,000,000,000
Total spending	2,233,000,000,000
Net overspending	$ **622**,000,000,000
	139% of revenue
Total assets sold to cover overspending*	not enough information yet
Total borrowed to cover overspending	$ 622,000,000,000
2006 average interest paid on US debt[13]	4.7%
Estimated **annual** future interest cost of **2006** debt	* $ 29,200,000,000

*An amount greater than all but the 5 biggest government agencies!

In 2006 we had 298,000,000 citizens.
Roughly 100,000,000 had taxable income.
Individual taxpayers paid 65% of the tax burden in 2006 and corporations paid 22%.

If you are one of the 100 million taxpayers, at current average interest rates, your share of 65% of the $29 billion in extra interest cost for overspending in **just 2006**, which you will be paying each and every year for at least the next 30 years short a miracle, will be **$189.**

In 2006, your share of the *gross debt* went up **9%** to **$170,000** per American, or **$440,000** per household.

---

* Wouldn't it be nice to have these numbers?

Restricted "Trust" Funds

What is a restricted "Trust" fund?

WE the people have decided that the purposes funded by the following funds are so important and so critical to our nation's well-being that we must collect money in a unique way, according to distinct fairness principles, and set up a separate fund for each of these specific purposes.

The use of these specially collected funds is ***restricted by law to specific activities***. When these funds are set up, we effectively create a covenant with ourselves to collect and spend the money for a specific and restricted purpose. These funds have been referred to as "Trust Funds," and beginning in 2006 as "earmarked funds." A restricted fund receives specifically identified revenue and other financing sources that

(1) remain available over time,

(2) are required by statute to be used for designated activities, benefits, or purposes, and

(3) must be accounted for separately from the government's general revenues.

When these restricted funds collect more money than they need in a given year, they are also required by law to loan the "surplus" to the Operating Fund. They receive a Treasury Security IOU in return. Nearly all of the assets on the restricted funds' books are investments in these Treasury Securities. In this report format, this is visible in the Operating Fund Debts & Liabilities as the "Debt held by the restricted funds and accrued interest." In the current official consolidated financial report and budget report summaries, this sum is net out and vanishes from view. In 2006, this total debt was $3,658 billion.

To understand an entity's financial situation it is critically important to see separate accounts for separate funds. Combining funds designated for restricted purposes with funds in the general operating fund leads to misunderstanding the full cost of government and the full revenues, because huge amounts of intragovernmental exchanges disappear from view.

Summaries for the sixteen largest restricted funds follow the consolidated summary.[14]

2002

Assets $
Debts $
Net Worth $

Income $
Expense $
Net $

Change in assets*   + $ 237
Change in debts
Change in Net worth $
☺

2005

Assets $
Debts $
Net Worth $

Income $
Expense $
Net $

Change in assets*   + $ 203
Change in debts $
Change in Net worth $
☺

2003

Assets $
Debts $
Net Worth $

Income $
Expense $
Net $

Change in assets*   + $ 204
Change in debts $
Change in Net worth $
☺

2004

Assets $
Debts $
Net Worth $

Income $
Expense $
Net $

Change in assets*   + $ 227
Change in debts $
Change in Net worth $
☺

2006 RESTRICTED FUNDS

What is our situation now?

Assets	3,865,000,000,000
Current liabilities	3,446,000,000,000
Long-term liabilities*	44,147,000,000,000
Net worth	**$ - 43,728**,000,000,000

What happened last year?

Income	1,514,000,000,000
Expense	1,342,000,000,000
Net	**$172**,000,000,000
Change in assets**	not enough info
Change in debts	not enough info
Change in net worth	**not enough info**

HISTORICAL 2002-2005. There is currently not enough information in the financial reports to complete the summaries for 2002-2005. If it would be useful to you, then you must ask for it.

*This report includes the long-term liabilities of the restricted funds *on* the balance sheet. The official financial report leaves them *off* the balance sheet.

** The change in assets only includes the increase in Treasury Security debt held by the restricted funds. This gives you an idea how much money the Operating Fund has been borrowing from the restricted funds each year. The restricted funds have other assets that may have changed. These numbers have been adjusted for the declining value of the dollar.

2006 U.S. Government
RESTRICTED FUNDS - SUMMARY

What is our situation now?

STATEMENT OF NET WORTH

Assets

Investments in US Treasury Securities*	3,554,800,000,000
Other federal assets	102,800,000,000
Non-federal assets	96,500,000,000
Fund balance with Treasury	87,000,000,000
Cash and other monetary assets	23,700,000,000
Total Operating Fund Assets	**$ 3,864**,700,000,000

Debts & Liabilities

Current liabilities due and payable to beneficiaries	3,349,800,000,000
Long-term social insurance responsibilities*	44,147,000,000,000
Other liabilities	95,700,000,000
Total Restricted Fund Debts & Liabilities	**$ 47,593**,000,000,000

Net worth	**$ - 43,728**,000,000,000

What happened last year?

It is most useful to see the major restricted funds individually to see which ones are adequately or inadequately funded and which ones have been building up significant assets in U.S. Treasury Securities and now drawing substantial percentages of their operating income from interest that must be paid by the Operating Fund. Note the importance of "interest on Treasury Securities" to each fund's operations.

---

*   These are the IOUs from the Operating Fund. Note that we have a paltry $311 billion in relatively "hard assets" to offset $47,593 billion in debts and liabilities.

FEDERAL OLD-AGE & SURVIVORS INSURANCE TRUST FUND also known as "Social Security"

42 United States Code (U.S.C.) § 401

Funded by payroll and self-employment taxes (86%), interest on investments in Treasury securities (14%).

To provide a basic annuity to workers to protect them from loss of income at retirement and provide a guaranteed income to survivors in the event of the death of a family's primary wage earner.

Administered by the Social Security Administration.

Assets	1,817,000,000,000
Current debts & liabilities	46,000,000,000
Long term debts & liabilities	6,449,000,000,000
Net worth	**- 4,678**,000,000,000 ☹
Income	629,000,000,000
Expense	452,000,000,000
Net	**176**,000,000,000
Increase in assets	179,000,000,000
Change in debts*	2,000,000,000
Increase in net worth*	**177**,000,000,000

*Not counting any changes in long-term liabilities.

FEDERAL HOSPITAL INSURANCE TRUST FUND also known as "HI-Medicare Part A"

42 U.S.C. §1395i

Funded by payroll and self-employment taxes (92%), interest on Treasury securities (8%).

To provide the cost of inpatient hospital and related care for individuals age 65 or older who meet certain insured status requirements, and eligible disabled people.

Administered by Department of Health & Human Services.

Assets	329,000,000,000
Current debts & liabilities	41,000,000,000
Long term debts & liabilities*	11,290,000,000,000
Net worth	**- 11,002**,000,000,000 ☹
Income	207,000,000,000
Expense	186,000,000,000
Net	**21**,000,000,000
Increase in assets	+ 26,000,000,000
Change in debts	not enough information
Change in net worth	not enough information

SUPPLEMENTAL MEDICAL INSURANCE TRUST FUND
aka "SMI-Medicare Part B & D"

Part B: 42 U.S.C. §1395t, Part D: 42 U.S.C. §1395w-116

Funded by the Operating Fund (Department of Health & Human Services) and premiums (99%-breakdown not available), interest on Treasury securities (1%).

To provide supplementary medical insurance for enrolled eligible participants to cover physician and outpatient services not covered by Medicare Part A (Part B) and to obtain qualified prescription drug coverage (Part D).

Administered by the Department of Health & Human Services.

Assets	86,000,000,000
Current debts & liabilities	44,000,000,000
Long term debts & liabilities*	21,015,000,000,000
Net worth	**- 20,973**,000,000,000
Income	184,000,000,000
Expense	151,000,000,000
Net	**33**,000,000,000
Increase in assets	34,000,000,000
Change in debts	not enough information
Change in net worth	not enough information

CIVIL SERVICE RETIREMENT & DISABILITY FUND

5 U.S.C. §8334-8348

Funded by Federal civilian employee's contributions, agencies' contributions on behalf of employees, appropriations, and interest on investments in Treasury Securities (44%).

To provide retirement and disability benefits to federal civilian employees.

Administered by the Office of Personnel Management.

Assets	700,000,000,000
Debts	1,292,000,000,000
Net worth	**- 592**,000,000,000
Income	83,000,000,000
Expense	126,000,000,000
Net	**- 43**,000,000,000
Increase in assets	29,000,000,000
Increase in debts	72,000,000,000
Decrease in net worth	**- 43**,000,000,000

MILITARY RETIREMENT FUND

10 U.S.C. § 1461-1467

Funded by Department of Defense contributions and general appropriations (76%), and interest on Treasury Securities (24%).

To provide retirement benefits for Army, Navy, Marine Corps, and Air Force personnel and their survivors.

Administered by the Department of Defense.

Assets	208,000,000,000
Debts	967,000,000,000
Net worth	**- 759**,000,000,000 ☹
Income	52,000,000,000
Expense	113,000,000,000
Net	**- 61**,000,000,000
Increase in assets	11,000,000,000
Increase in debts	72,000,000,000
Decrease in net worth	**- 61**,000,000,000

FEDERAL DISABILITY INSURANCE FUND

42 U.S.C. § 401

Funded by payroll taxes (90%), and interest on Treasury Securities (10%).

To protect against the loss of earnings due to a wage earner's disability by providing money payments.

Administered by the Social Security Administration.

Assets	207,000,000,000
Debts	24,000,000,000
Net worth	**183**,000,000,000 ☺
Income	100,000,000,000
Expense	93,000,000,000
Net	**7**,000,000,000
Increase in assets	9,000,000,000
Increase in debts	1,000,000,000
Increase in net worth	**8**,000,000,000

HIGHWAY TRUST FUND

42 U.S.C. § 9503

Funded by taxes on gas, other fuels, certain tires, initial sale of heavy trucks and highway use by commercial vehicles. Gas taxes are at a rate set in 1993.

To promote domestic interstate transportation and to move people and goods.

Administered by the Department of Transportation.

Assets	16,000,000,000
Debts	4,000,000,000
Net worth	**12**,000,000,000
Income	39,000,000,000
Expense	37,000,000,000
Net	**2**,000,000,000
Increase in assets	5,000,000,000
Decrease in debts	8,000,000,000
Increase in net worth	**13**,000,000,000

Just maintaining our bridges would cost about $75 billion every year.[15]

UNEMPLOYMENT INSURANCE TRUST FUND

42 U.S.C. § 1104

Funded by taxes on employers (94%) and interest on investments in Treasury Securities (6%) and supplemented by appropriations from the Operating Fund during periods of high and extended unemployment.

To provide temporary assistance to workers who lose their jobs.

Administered at the federal level by the Department of Labor and through a unique system of partnerships with the States.

Assets	69,000,000,000
Debts	2,000,000,000
Net worth	**66**,000,000,000
Income	44,000,000,000
Expense	32,000,000,000
Net	**12**,000,000,000
Increase in assets	12,000,000,000
Decrease in debts	60,000,000
Increase in net worth	**13**,000,000,000

AIRPORT & AIRWAY TRUST FUND

26 U.S.C. § 9502

Funded by taxes on air transport, fuel and international departure taxes (96%) and interest on Treasury Securities (4%).

To provide for airport improvement and airport facilities maintenance, fund airport equipment, research, and a portion of the Federal Aviation Administration's administrative operational support.

Administered by the Department of Transportation.

Assets	8,600,000,000
Debts	2,200,000,000
Net worth	**6,400,000,000**
Income	11,000,000,000
Expense	12,000,000,000
Net	**- 1,000,000,000**
Decrease in assets	2,000,000,000
Decrease in debts	1,300,000,000
Decrease in net worth	**1,000,000,000**

RAILROAD RETIREMENT TRUST FUND

45 U.S.C. § 23 and 45 U.S.C. § 231n-1

Funded by taxes on railroad employers, employees and an indecipherable "other" (84%), interest on investments in Treasury Securities (16%).

To provide annuities and survivor benefits to eligible railroad employees and their survivors, and to provide disability annuities based on total or occupational disability.

Administered by the National Railroad Retirement Investment Trust.

Assets	34,400,000,000
Debts	4,600,000,000
Net worth	**30,000,000,000**
Income	11,000,000,000
Expense	10,000,000,000
Net	**1,000,000,000**
Increase in assets	2,000,000,000
Increase in debts	20,000,000
Increase in net worth	**2,000,000,000**

MEDICARE ELIGIBLE RETIREE HEALTH CARE FUND

10 U.S.C. § 1111, 10 U.S.C. § 1116, and 10 U.S.C § 1117

Funded by the Department of Defense (DOD) (87%) and interest on investments in Treasury Securities (13%).

To finance and pay the liabilities under the DOD retiree health care programs for Medicare-eligible beneficiaries.

Administered by the Department of Defense.

Assets	85,400,000,000
Debts	538,900,000,000
Net worth	**- 453**,500,000,000 ☹
Income	32,000,000,000
Expense	8,000,000,000
Net	**24**,000,000,000
Increase in assets	24,700,000,000
Increase in debts	500,000,000
Increase in net worth	**24**,200,000,000

FOREIGN SERVICE RETIREMENT & DISABILITY TRUST FUND

22 U.S.C. § 4042 and 22 U.S.C § 4045

Funded by contributions from active participants and their U.S. Government agency employers (36%), appropriations, and interest on Treasury Securities (64%).

To provide pensions to retired and disabled members of the Foreign Service.

Administered by Department of State.

Assets	14,100,000,000
Debts	14,300,000,000
Net worth	- 200,000,000
Income	1,200,000,000
Expense	1,500,000,000
Net	300,000,000
Increase in assets	500,000,000
Increase in debts	800,000,000
Decrease in net worth	200,000,000

HAZARDOUS SUBSTANCE SUPERFUND
26 U.S.C. § 9507

Funded by fines, penalties and cost recoveries from responsible parties (18%), appropriations from the Operating Fund (75%), and interest on Treasury Securities (7%).

To address public health and environmental threats from spills of hazardous materials and from sites contaminated with hazardous substances.

Administered by the Environmental Protection Agency.

Assets	3,000,000,000
Debts	600,000,000
Net worth	2,400,000,000
Income	1,600,000,000
Expense	1,400,000,000
Net	200,000,000
Increase in assets	640,000,000
Increase in debts	560,000,000
Adjustment to books from '05–'06?	104,000,000
Increase in net worth	184,000,000

NATIONAL SERVICE LIFE INSURANCE FUND
38 U.S.C §1920

Funded by the public and veterans (.1%) and by investments in Treasury Securities (99.9%).

To provide life insurance for policyholders who served during World War II.

Administered by the Department of Veteran's Affairs.

Assets	10,800,000,000
Debts	10,500,000,000
Net worth	300,000,000
Income	1,000,000,000
Expense	1,000,000,000
Net	6,000,000
Decrease in assets	500,000,000
Decrease in debts	500,000,000
Change in net worth	6,000,000

BLACK LUNG DISABILITY TRUST FUND

26 U.S.C. § 9501

Funded by excise taxes on coal mine operators (58%) and investments in Treasury Securities (.03%), AND *loans from* the Operating Fund (42%).

To provide disability benefits to coal miners who are totally disabled due to pneumoconiosis (black lung disease) and death benefits for the eligible survivors of those miners who die from the disease.

Administered by the Department of Labor.

Assets	50,000,000
Debts	9,650,000,000
Net worth	- **9**,600,000,000
Income	600,000,000
Expense	1,000,000,000
Net	- 400,000,000
Increase in assets	3,000,000
Increase in debts	400,000,000
Decrease in net worth	- 400,000,000

LAND & WATER CONSERVATION FUND

16 U.S.C. § 4601-11

Funded by an annual transfer of $903 million from the Minerals Management Service, Department of Interior program, the majority of which are royalties from Outer Continental Shelf oil deposits.

To create and maintain a nationwide legacy of high quality recreation areas and facilities.

Administered by the Department of Interior.

Assets**	15,000,000,000
Debts	0
Net worth	**15**,600,000,000
Income	900,000,000
Program expenses	0
Unspecified "transfer" out of fund	400,000,000
Net	500,000,000
Increase in assets	500,000,000
Change in debts	0
Increase in net worth	500,000,000

* Total assets of the Land and Water Conservation Fund consist of a fund balance with Treasury of $14,836,000,000. There is no investment income for this fund; it has $15 billion "in the bank" earning no return. Expenditures appear to be less than the $50 million it would take to register in the consolidated USFR Financial Report. Odd that we have no land and water that needs conserving.

SECOND LOOK – Our Priorities

OPERATING FUND + RESTRICTED FUND SPENDING

AFTER looking separately at the funds we made available for operations and the funds that we collected for restricted purposes, we have a clear idea of what was available and how it was spent.

NEXT, it would be useful to look at how we spend by purpose. This requires putting together what we are spending from the Operating Fund with the funds we have set up for a specific purpose. For example, the Department of Transportation manages two major restricted funds for highways and air transportation. In 2006, these restricted funds represented $54 billion (87%) of the department's consolidated net spending. Only $8 billion (13%) of the Department's funding came from the Operating Fund. To see the total government spending for maintaining an effective transportation system, we have to combine the spending from the Operating Fund and the spending from the restricted funds.

Many sources create pie charts of federal spending using the expense numbers from the budget report, which currently combines the Operating Fund with restricted funds. These charts are useful for looking at proportions. However, there is a problem with these charts: they use the cash-based and consolidated numbers. For example any report that shows $499 billion for the 2006 Department of Defense spending is using a budget number that leaves out all the spending commitments for future spending which bring the total to $658 billion, and the DoD expenses for its employees' payroll costs, which brings the grand total to about $678 billion (2006). That's roughly half again as much spending–a $179 billion difference.

A BALLPARK MODEL

For a ballpark look at the proportion of spending for each general purpose the chart opposite uses the consolidated net costs from the current financial report. Remember that these numbers net out the payroll tax costs for the employees in each of these departments (and all other spending between departments). These additional costs would likely make most of the balls proportionately larger, so this is a ballpark approximation of our relative spending priorities.

A representation of the interest to the restricted funds has been added to make it possible to clearly see the size of our interest payments in proportion to the rest of our total spending from the Operating Funds and the restricted funds. After Defense (including Veterans Affairs), Health & Human Services (which includes Medicare), and Social Security, the next largest priority appears to be to provide a candy jar for investors to whom we must pay substantial interest on our debt. That is what happens when you borrow to operate.

DEFENSE

HEALTH & HUMAN SERVICES

SOCIAL SECURITY

INTEREST

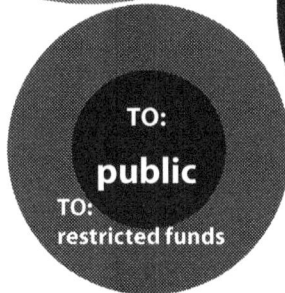

TO:

public

TO: restricted funds

AGRICULTURE

EDUCATION

TREASURY

TRANSPORTATION •••••

HOMELAND SECURITY

HOUSING & URBAN DEVELOPMENT

NASA

STATE DEPARTMENT

AID: AGENCY or INTERNATIONAL DEVELOPMENT

ENVIRONMENTAL PROTECTION AGENCY

EXECUTIVE OFFICE OF THE PRESIDENT

ENERGY

LABOR

JUSTICE

INTERIOR

COMMERCE

NATIONAL SCIENCE FOUNDATION

For a stunning and elaborately detailed presentation of the consolidated net costs from the cash-based budget go to TheBudgetGraph.com

DISCLAIMER
The numbers in this report may not be reliable.

FIRST, the numbers may be unreliable because they are from the Financial Report of the United States Government, issued December 15, 2006, and freely available online from the Treasury Department. The Comptroller General of the United States, David M. Walker, in the Government Accountability Office (GAO) is tasked with auditing the Report. Mr. Walker reports that the financial report of the United States Government cannot yet be audited.[16]

The Comptroller General, David M. Walker, "disclaims" any ability to render an opinion on the financial reports. Here's what he says: There are still three major obstacles to even having enough information to perform an adequate audit:

1. Serious financial management problems at the Department of Defense;

2. The federal government's inability to adequately account for and reconcile intragovernmental activity and balances between federal agencies; and

3. The federal government's ineffective process for preparing the consolidated financial statements.

He says, "As a result of these limitations, readers are cautioned that amounts reported in the consolidated financial statements and related notes may not be reliable." ("This means that the data could not be satisfactorily audited and may be incorrect, perhaps materially so.") Mr. Walker goes on to describe inconsistencies of tens of billions of dollars and how they "affect the reliability...[of] information used to manage the government day to day and budget information reported by federal agencies."

Out of 24 agencies required since 1997 to meet the standard of an audit, only 19 government agencies have achieved success. The five remaining unsuccessful agencies represent approximately $790 billion, or 27%, of the federal government's reported net cost, and $797 billion or 53% of the federal government's reported total assets for fiscal year 2006 (including both the Operating Fund and restricted funds).

Treasury made $.8 billion in adjustments to make agency accounts balance with Treasury accounts. Then the GAO listed $11 billion in "unreconciled transactions." Federal agencies estimate that they make more than $45 billion in improper payments (GAO-3/07). Only 8 out of 24 major agencies in the U.S. Government have more money to spend than that $45 billion in improper payments.

The Department of Defense, which spends 42% of the Operating Fund revenue, cannot pass an audit. The Department of Defense accounts are the primary reason that the whole government's accounts cannot yet be audited. How long are you going to accept this level of performance from your lawmakers and administration?

SECOND, this format makes significant changes to the federal consolidated report format. The U.S. Government's financial reports come in a consolidated format, so separating the Operating Fund's income and expenses from the restricted funds' is difficult. For the first time, in 2006, the official report shows the separate income for the Operating Fund and the restricted "Trust" funds–though not in any of the summaries. It does not yet show the same breakdown for expenditures. Without the aid of Rumpelstiltskin, it is impossible to fully separate the restricted funds' expenses from those of the Operating Fund. Given that Treasury cannot reconcile the "intragovernmental activity," it is impossible to accurately state the full cost of each department. This report here achieves the broad outlines—and is probably not off by any more than the tens of billions of dollars of discrepancies in the official reports (for other reasons). So, take it all with a grain of salt.

The format in this book makes the following improvements:

1. It uses the Financial Report numbers, which are actual income and expense, instead of the Budget numbers. VERY IMPORTANT and worth repeating: the Financial Report numbers are accrual-based accounting. This means that they present an accurate picture of what we actually spent *and* what we committed by contract to spend—even if the bill has not come in yet. The Budget is cash-based and only presents the actual cash out the door, so every year the budget leaves out from $202 billion (2006) to $441 billion (2005) in spending commitments that we make that will fall due in the future.

2. This report separates the Operating Fund from the restricted "Trust" funds. This is the only way to get an accurate picture of the financial situation. In consolidating the Operating Fund and restricted funds all of the money that is received, paid, borrowed and owed between the government funds drops out of sight. So, in the 2006 "consolidated" Financial Report summaries, $344 billion in general expenses to the Operating Fund and income to the restricted funds drops out of sight, as does $185 billion in interest paid by the Operating Funds to the restricted "Trust" funds, seriously distorting our understanding of the cost of government, the revenue to cover this cost and our financial situation. This distortion has been corrected in this draft report format.

3. In the following report, all the income is counted as income. The current official financial report puts most of the income that the government charges and receives for services in the marketplace as a credit on the expense side of the ledger. This means that about $226 billion in government receipts and expenses disappear from view in the consolidated summaries, giving everyone a false picture of real income and real expenses.

The numbers that you see in the previous report are not the numbers you usually see because:

- **This report is accrual-based (from the financial report), instead of from the cash-based budget reports. It includes all our commitments, past, present and future.**

- **The Operating Fund and a summary of the restricted funds are reported on separately, so that the full cost of government operations is clear.**

- **All income is booked as income so that you can understand the full resources available to government and the full cost of programs.**

- **The long-term liabilities for the social insurance programs are on the books.**

We can further improve the reports until every single taxpayer and voter in the United States can understand them, and vote for people who improve our financial situation. Read on, for the road to this greater democracy:

Knowledge is Power

Sir Francis Bacon, 1561-1626

*You can only be free
when you are
informed. . .*

Part II
Basic accounting &
Government accounting

Part II:
Basic Accounting and Government Accounting

Accounts require three statements that answer two basic questions:

Where are we now?
    1. Net worth statement

What happened last year
    2. Income and expense statement
    3. Changes in net worth statement

There are three basic kinds of accounting.
It is very important that you understand the difference:

Cash
Accrual
Fund

Useful things to know about government finances:

How is the government keeping track of our money?
How is it reporting to Congress and to citizens?
History of government accounting
Good and bad news
The information pipeline
Too many funds

Chapter One

Where are we now?
What happened last year?

Remember the first time you sat down at your own kitchen table with a stack of bills and your paycheck and said, "How am I going to make this work?" Paying attention to your financial situation is a milestone in growing up.

It is time we all sat down at our public kitchen table. Most government decisions are about how our nation's wealth is distributed. We keep track of money distribution by keeping accounts. To offer your best mind, your best thoughts and best voice to public decision-making, you must understand the financial report so that you can put decisions in their financial context. When all citizens in our democracy can sit down together to figure out how we are going to make it work, our democracy will have grown up a notch.

Here is what you need to know so that we can get it done:

Basic Accounts

Accounts are designed to answer two basic and important questions at the end of a year about our financial situation:

> **Where are we now?**
> **What happened last year?**

For a quick check on how we are doing, all the details can be simply and clearly summarized in these nine numbers:

Where are we now? What do we have?

---

1.   Assets—what we own
2.   Debts—what we owe
3.   **Net worth**

☺ or ☺ or ☹

What happened last year?

---

4.   Income
5.   Expense
6.   **Net (income or loss/cost)**

7.   Change (increase or decrease) in assets
8.   Change (increase or decrease) in debts
9.   **Net change in net worth**

☺ or ☺ or ☹

Where are we now?

We have one primary financial report that tells us what are financial situation is at a point in time–usually the end of the year. The net worth statement tells you what you are worth. When you subtract what you owe from what you own, your net worth is what is left. This is the snapshot of your financial situation at that time.

Net Worth Statement

We answer, "Where are we now?," by keeping a list of our **assets** (cash and the cash value of things that we own), and a list of our **debts and liabilities** (the money that we owe and the money that we are obligated to pay in the future). We subtract what we owe from what we own to get our **net worth**, or net assets. (This is sometimes called a "Statement of Financial Position."

NET WORTH – Our financial situation NOW

+	Assets, I own
-	Debts and liabilities, I borrowed and owe
=	**NET monetary worth**

Assets

Assets are the things that you own that can be converted back to cash or that will earn you new money. This will include income producing real property, investments and the tools and equipment that are purchased to make a product. It may also include your investment in training and education.

Most assets lose value over time. To make sure that an asset and debt statement is an accurate record of net worth each year, the value of assets must be reduced as time goes by. This is called depreciation. There is no sure way to get a totally accurate current value—short of selling the asset—without getting an expensive appraisal every year. Since this would just run up your expenses, there are accepted formulas for reducing the value of assets that can be expected to drop in value. These depreciation schedules determine how long an asset can be expected to be useful. For example, tools, equipment and real properties lose value over time, so their asset value is depreciated—over 3, 5, 10 or 20 years. If a business figures that the asset will last ten years, then every year for ten years one tenth of the cost is subtracted from the asset column, and the same amount is counted as an expense—out the door gone forever.

Deciding how to depreciate an asset requires taking many factors into consideration.

Every business has to decide what it is going to count as an expense and what it will count as an investment in an asset. Sometimes the line between expenses and assets is fuzzy. For example, is software, which is usually outdated in a few short years, an asset, or an annual operating expense? Many businesses base their decision on the size of the purchase. If you are a multi-billion dollar business and you buy a $5,000 software operating system, it will be expensed. It is not worth the trouble to put it in assets and then have to show that its value depreciates every year. If you are a home business, then it may very well be worth the trouble to count a $5,000 software operating system as one of your assets. Often the tax code determines whether spending is booked as an asset or an expense for businesses.

In government accounts, we do not need to be concerned about tax considerations, so we can opt to put spending in the categories that make the most sense. It would be useful to have a public dialogue about what criteria we want to use for determining whether spending is for an asset that we will keep on the books, or an annual expense. (See Chapter 10)

Debts and liabilities

Debts and liabilities are sometimes counted as the same thing because you are on the line for this money, one-way-or-another. More specifically, debts are money that you borrowed and owe by contract to others. Liabilities may be any obligation that you have incurred. For example, if you own a property and have been dumping poison into your soil, the law may hold you liable for cleaning up after yourself and you would need to book the projected cost of this cleanup as a liability.

Promises to make payments in the future are also liabilities. If you sign a purchase agreement, the payments due in the future are accounts payable and counted as a debt. If you are promised a pension by contract, then that pension is a liability on your employer's books. When the U.S. Government commits to paying pensions for retired government employees, this is a liability on the government's books.

Net worth

Subtract your debts from your assets and the difference is your net worth. If you sold off all of your assets, and you could pay off all your debt and have some cash left over, then you have a positive net worth. Or, if you could only pay off part of your debts, then you have a negative net worth. The statement of net worth states your financial position at a specific point in time–usually end of year.

What happened last year?

There are two parts to answering "What happened last year?"

    1) What happened in operations?
    2) What was the impact of operations on net worth?

1. OPERATIONS: Income and Expense Statement

We answer, "What happened in operations last year?," by keeping a list of all the *new money* that came in and all the money that went *out the door-gone forever,* and call these lists income and expense. We subtract our expenses from our income to get the year's operating net:

OPERATIONS – INCOME & EXPENSE

    +   Income - new money that came in

    -      Expense - money that went out forever

    =   **NET - the difference**

Income

Income is only your *new* money coming in. Money can come in for several reasons: operating income (new money), repayment of money that people borrowed from you, or the sale of an asset. Only the money coming in from operations is counted as "income" because it is the only *new* money. Income is also called "revenue."

When someone pays back a loan, they are returning money that came in before and that you loaned out. This returned money is not reported in your income. It is an exchange of assets; an I-am-owed asset becomes an I-have-cash asset; you do not have new income. So your income column will not have any information about the returned loan—the information is in the asset account.

If you sell your property assets for cash, this, too, is not counted as income. You are exchanging a property asset for a cash asset. The value of the asset or the cash that was required for purchase was already counted as income when the money or the asset first came to you. When you sell an asset, you may now have more money to spend, but it is not new money coming in (income). When you sell an asset for more than you paid for it, the difference is counted as income, because it is new money to you.

Expenses

Expenses are money that is out the door and gone forever. Money can go out the door for several reasons: for operating expenses (out the door and gone forever), or to buy an asset, or to pay off a debt. Not all money going out the door is counted as an expense—only the money that is going out the door-forever for the first time is counted as an "expense." Expenses are also called "costs."

If you spend your money on a house that can be converted back to cash then the money is *not* out the door and gone forever. It moved from a cash-on-hand asset to a house/property asset.

When you take cash and pay off some of your own debt, this debt repayment is not counted as an expense because you already spent the money

When we-the-government sell off public land assets to finance operations, this information about the source of cash flow would not appear in "income," it would be an exchange of land asset for cash asset in the asset account.

That is, IF & WHEN we book all of our assets. Most of our public land assets are **not yet booked as assets,** they are labeled "Stewardship Assets" and kept off the books.

This means that when these assets are sold and gone forever, the information is not clearly on the books at all. (See Chapter 10)

on something and recorded that expense when you made the commitment and borrowed the money. It is down on your books as debt. When you are repaying a debt with your cash, your *cash asset* is used to reduce a *debt.* Neither transaction shows up in income and expenses. However, the interest that you are paying on your debt is new out-the-door-gone-forever spending and so interest payments are counted as expenses.

You have to look at your net worth statement and changes in net worth to get the full picture of the money coming in and going out. This is why the income and expense statement is only a partial answer to "What happened last year?"

Net

Subtract your out the door and gone forever spending from your new income and you have the net. This net may be a net operating loss, or a net gain, depending on whether you spent more than you took in, or saved a bit of your income. This number tells you how well you did in your operations in the last year. The net will *not* tell you how your assets, liabilities and net worth fared over the past year—*only how well your operations went.* You will have to look to the asset and debt statement and statement of changes in net worth to understand the impact of last year's operations on your total financial situation.

2. THE IMPACT—Change in Net Worth Statement

How did the year's operations change our financial situation? So far we have statements of net worth and income and expense. We know where we are at the end of the year, and we know how our operations did for the year. We still need to know what impact last year's operations had on our net worth. Did our net worth go up or down as a result of last year's operations? Did our assets increase or decrease? Did our debts increase or decrease?

While our net worth statement tells us where we are at the end of the year, it will not tell us how we got into this position. To answer the

In business the net is usually referred to as the "net profit" or "net loss." In government, consistently spending more than our income is referred to as the "net operating cost."

"Cost" is a term with neutral connotation, unlike "loss" or "overspending."

By using "net operating cost" instead of "net loss" or "net overspending," our current government reports whitewash reality for us. This contributes to poor understanding of our financial situation.

question, "How did last year's activities alter our financial position?," we need a third statement, changes in net worth, to show how our assets and debts changed in the last year.

NET CHANGE in NET WORTH

Net increase or decrease in my assets

Net increase or decrease in debts and liabilities

NET change in net worth

The statement of changes in net worth is **the number one most important bottom line for holding our managers accountable.** It is an important summary document. It tells us:

- Are we worth more or less at the end of the year?

- Have our policies increased our assets and reduced our debts?

- Are we investing in assets or spending out the door and gone forever money on impulse buying, pork-barrel kiss-up?

- If we are going into debt, is the borrowed money going for investments in the future or going out the door and gone forever, placing a burden without benefit on our children and grandchildren?

- Are we selling off our assets to pay for annual operations?

- Are taxing and spending policies leading to a healthier financial situation and greater net worth?

These three statements, 1) net worth, 2) income & expense, and 3) changes in net worth, give us the summary financial information that we need to begin making good choices for our future.

You need all three of these statements, to have a whole picture of how we are doing. When you look at any one of these statements, you only have a part of the picture and may not be seeing critical information.

These three statements give us a framework for filling in the details and at the same time keeping a clear and simple overview for good decision-making. In a good accounting system there will also be lots of specific and useful detail to back up these three summary statements. Details are important. And, it is easier to find the details that you need when the summary is simple, clear and comprehensive; you know which file drawer to open and it should be easy to find every detail in a flash.

CASH FLOW STATEMENT
–an extra for the money flow managers

A cash flow statement puts all these elements together. It includes all the spending, whether it is expense, spending to buy an asset or spending to reduce a debt. It includes all of the income, whether it is operating income, income for a debt repaid, or income from the sale of an asset.

A cash flow statement is a money manager's tool for determining how the individual or business will manage the in and out flow of cash. You may make a great sale and need to wait six months for the money. You may be expecting plenty of money, but have a shortage of cash for a big bill coming due. A cash flow statement shows how you *manage the flow* of money over a year. It is useful and often used as a cash flow *projection,* showing how you will juggle your incoming and outgoing monies over the next year.

In an ordinary business, managers will need a cash flow projection statement to see when all the monies are actually flowing in and out of the cash box, to make sure that they always have the means to keep the lights on, pay wages and keep tax payments current. In government, we hope that we can leave that aspect to the professionals in the Treasury Department.

Summary

Here is the summary that you and your lawmakers need..... Just nine simple numbers can give managers a good summary of the current situation and the past year's activity:

Where are we now?

1.   Assets
2.   Debts and liabilities
3.   **Net worth**

        ☺ or ☺ or ☹

What happened last year?

4.   Income
5.   Expense
6.   **Net income or net loss/cost**

7.   Change (increase or decrease) in assets
8.   Change (increase or decrease) in debts
9.   **Net change in net worth**

        ☺ or ☺ or ☹

Chapter Two

Keep track
Cash, accrual and fund accounts

Imagine sitting at your kitchen table checking over last year's income and expenses. You have ledgers tracking your money in and your money out. You want to plan how you will stretch your $46,000 annual salary to meet your goals for good living in the coming year. You are puzzling over why you end up needing to borrow to make ends meet. As you sort through your accounts, you have an "Ah ha!" moment. You realize that your list of expenses has never included any of your credit card purchases—they are literally off the table. You have only been keeping track of your *cash* income and *cash* expenses. The increasing interest and principle payments on your credit cards have blind-sided your good intentions.

Can you make wise plans for the new year if you continue to ignore what you charge on credit and must pay for in the future—including interest! What if you were charging half again as much as you make—charging another $23,000 on your credit card *every year.* How long could you stay afloat?

Solely keeping track of the actual cash going in and out of the door is one legitimate form of accounting. It simply is not useful for all purposes. It is particularly inadequate for long-term prudent financial planning.

There are three basic kinds of accounting. It is critically important that you understand these basic kinds of accounting to understand federal accounting and reporting. A simple and easy explanation of cash accounts, accrual accounts, fund accounts and U.S. Government accounts follows.

Cash Accounts

Remember the "Treasurer's Report" from school. Someone stood up and said, "We've raised $100 from our Big Event and we collected $50 in dues, for a total income of $150. We spent $120 on party supplies. We have a balance of $30 in our checking account." That is simple cash accounting.

Your checkbook register is a simple cash account. In cash accounting you record money coming in *when it comes in* as an increase in your cash. You record money going out, *when it goes out,* as a decrease in your cash account. This is basic, simple accounting and works just fine for an individual with simple and basic needs.

SIMPLE CASH ACCOUNT

Income - Expense	In or out	Balance
Salary Bonus	+ $ 10,000	$ 10,000
Hawaii vacation	- 5,000	5,000
Loan to bro'	- 1,000	4,000
Pay credit card	- 1,000	3,000

"Double entry bookkeeping" adds a little bit of complexity that is useful when you want to keep track of the *kinds* of income and expenses that you have. In double entry bookkeeping, every single transaction is entered in your books in two places to show "What did I pay for?" and "How did I pay for it?" This sounds more complicated than it is. Say you are keeping cash accounts. If you paid $10,000 cash for a Hawaiian Cruise, you would take $10,000 out of your cash asset account and you would record $10,000 as a vacation expense.

HOW did I pay?	Cash	- $10,000
WHAT did I pay for?	Vacation	+ $10,000

These two entries constitute "double entry" bookkeeping. The plus and the minus of these two entries cancel each other out. This is called balance. If you forget to enter one or the other, your books will be out of balance. We are lucky to have software today that does all the thinking for us about what to debit and what to credit in double entry bookkeeping—remembering for us what to plus and what to minus. Double entry cash accounting works well for your personal checking, or if you have a small business with a relatively steady pattern of income and expense.

A set of cash accounts is also sometimes used by businesses of all sizes for annual budgeting and planning. It can be helpful for management to look at how much money they expect to have and how much they plan to spend for the coming year. A cash-based budget keeps it simple because it just looks at the actual money coming in and going out, and ignores contracts for revenue or contracts to pay in the future.

Cash-based budgeting is narrow-focus budgeting, not big-picture budgeting.

Accrual Accounts

All discussions about government taxing and spending require that you understand the difference between cash and accrual accounts.

☞IMPORTANT!

Accrual accounting is more sophisticated than cash accounting and gives you additional information. Accrual accounting adds the money you are obligated to *pay in the future* and the money that people are obligated to *pay you in the future.*

Say you are paying for your $10,000 Hawaiian vacation in 10 monthly payments and you have signed a contract that obligates you to this purchase. You want to keep a record of this future obligation. Cash accounting will not do it for you; cash accounting only records the money as you spend it—$1,000 each month for 10 months.

In September 2006, a $448 billion defense appropriation was passed by Congress. This is a *cash-based* appropriation.

The Department of Defense's *net** spending on an *accrual-basis* and adjusted for the decline in the value of the dollar has been:

2001- $ 777
2002- $ 420
2003- $ 562
2004- $ 672
2005- $ 704
2006- $ 658

Is it responsible to only consider cash-based expenditures when the actual, accrual-based spending is so much higher?

*Net of all expenses paid to restricted funds and net of "earned revenue."

In accrual accounting you record an expense *when you commit by contract to spend the money.* So, you would record $10,000 as a vacation expense, the day that you sign the contract, and you would enter the $10,000 as a debt that you owe (accounts payable). Your cash is as yet untouched. However, you have recorded your future obligations; the commitment to pay is "on the books."

Each month when you pay $1,000 on your vacation commitment you would take $1,000 out of your cash and reduce your debt by $1,000, until you have paid it off. In any month, a quick look at your accounts will tell you how much you still owe—the balance remaining.

In accrual accounting you also record income when you enter a contract to receive money. It will show up in your records as income and as an asset (account receivable) until you actually receive the money. When the money comes in, your cash balance goes up and the money people owe you (assets) goes down.

Accrual accounting gives a much clearer picture of your finances because it shows what you owe in the future and what money you can expect to come in. Accrual accounting is used by most large businesses because it is *the only way to get a realistic financial picture of yesterday, today and tomorrow.*

Leadership at the top—boards of directors and chief executive officers—must see accrual-based financial reports to fulfill their long-term oversight responsibilities. Public companies must produce accrual-based financial reports for their investors, because without accrual accounts, investors would have no idea what obligations were on the books.

The choice of cash or accrual accounting will make a difference at tax time for a business. Many businesses do not want to pay taxes on revenue that they may be owed, but that they have not yet received. On the other hand, they may want to count expenses that they paid for on credit. Businesses can choose to file cash-based or accrual-based tax returns.

When it comes to government's planning for the future, there is a global trend toward using accrual-based accounting for budgets as well as financial reports. Accrual-based budgeting is a more sophisticated and accurate way to plan because it keeps past and future commitments on the table in plain sight. You can plan for the future better when you know what the future holds, and accrual-based budgeting is the only budgeting format that gives you full information.

A cash-based budget, because it is simpler and more focused on the here and now, continues to be used by managers who want to focus on one year or one department at a time.

Fund Accounts

All discussions about government taxing and spending require that you understand fund accounts.

☞IMPORTANT!

Let's say that your grandmother is willing to set up a fund to pay for your vacations for your lifetime. She is going to give you $10,000 each year, but it can only be spent for vacationing, not for your ordinary bills. If you blow it on a hot car, the gift stops. She wants to see an accounting of her gift each year. This requires a separate account just for the money that she gives you. It will show her gift as income and you will write in all your vacation costs as expenses. To keep your grandmother's trust, you will keep the vacation funds and the vacation account separate from your ordinary income and expenses.

My basic accounts	Vacation Fund
Assets	Assets
Debts	Debts
Net Worth	**Net Worth**

My basic accounts, cont.	Vacation Fund, cont.
Income	Income
Expense	Expense
Net	**Net**
Change in assets	Change in assets
Change in debts	Change in debts
Net change in Net Worth	**Net change in Net Worth**

Fund accounting is used when you have to keep track of money for more than one purpose and at least *one purpose is restricted.* Most nonprofit organizations are required by funders to use fund accounting because they often have an operating account and special accounts for special purposes. For example, a school may have an operating account that keeps track of tuition and operating expenses. The school might also collect donations that are restricted for use as scholarships or restricted for use on special equipment or new buildings. If you donate $1 million for a building, you want to be assured that the money goes to pay for the building and not for teacher salaries, field trips to Hawaii or building maintenance.

If you are reviewing a school's accounts and want to know how the school year went, you will need to see separate accounts for the operating fund and the scholarship or building fund accounts. It might be a terrible year for operations: low enrollment and the boiler broke. It might be a great year for restricted scholarship donations. So, the school might get a $1 million donation for scholarships and not be able to use a penny of it for a new boiler.

School Operating Fund		Scholarship Fund	
Income	$ 1,000,000	Income	$ 1,000,000
Expense	1,500,000	Expense	100,000
NET	**$ - 500,000**	**NET**	**$ + 900,000**
	☹		☺

Fund accounting is no more complicated than cash or accrual accounting. Think of it as a bundle of separate ordinary accounts that have the same basic components: assets, debts, **net worth**, income, expense, **net**, change in assets, change in debts, **net change in net worth**. You can look at each fund as an independent account.

Fund accounting then adds one additional layer: the consolidated or unified total. A consolidated total is important. It is a sophisticated and accurate way to present the complete financial picture for a complex entity *to people who can read past the summary numbers.* Here is what the consolidated income and expense summary would look like for the school above:

Consolidated Income and Expense	
Income	$ 2,000,000
Expense	$ 1,600,000
NET	**$ + 400,000**
	☺

The consolidated income and expense summary gives a very different picture from the separated fund reports. Information is lost. While the consolidated total is an important tool for *financial* managers, all by itself a summary of the consolidated report is *next to useless to the business managers and planners.*

For anyone running a business and making management decisions, the useful information is in the **separate fund account reports**.

Did we have net revenue or a net loss in operations? Did we increase our restricted funds?   In the consolidated report above, with the $1 million donation to the scholarship fund, the report shows a $400,000 net income for the year, which looks great. However, the operating fund was half a million in the hole and that is likely to be a total disaster. Leadership and management need to see separate accounts for each fund, since each fund is restricted to its own income and expenses. No one can make good decisions with only the consolidated report—you are deciding blind if this is the only information that you have.

To effectively manage more than one fund, you have to be able to see and to work with the funds separately.

The U.S. Government keeps separate fund accounts, but reports to management (Congress and citizens) with a *consolidated* accounts report. This leads to poor decisions. We cannot possibly make good management decisions with the consolidated totals as our primary point of reference (See Chapter 9).

Nearly every tax and spend advocacy organization uses the numbers from the government's *consolidated cash-based budget* for promoting their positions. Everyone is off base because enormous sums have disappeared from view. In the consolidated U.S. Government Financial Reports and Budgets, there is nearly as much money off the table as there is on the table, and that is no way to argue a point or to make good decisions. It is also simple to remedy. In Part III you will find some simple changes to U.S. financial reporting that can give us the information that we need to make good decisions.

Cost accounting

Cost accounting is a way to figure the cost of one particular mission, project, objective or contract that may be fulfilled by multiple agencies or accounting units. It can be useful when we all have a basic understanding of the overall financial situation and we are ready to look at particular federal government mission objectives and the cost of current strategies for achieving our goals.

Matching method to purpose & intent

Management succeeds when it matches the most useful kind of accounting and reporting to its intention, purpose and values. Accounts and their reports fulfill two basic functions:

> **1. TO UNDERSTAND where we are now and how we got here.** A *report* on past activities provides this information.

> **2. TO PLAN and decide what we shall do in the future.** How much income do we expect? How much do we plan to spend in each area? For planning, we create a *budget*.

For each function (understanding the past or planning) you have two choices: cash-based or accrual. You can choose cash-based or accrual-based accounting for keeping track and reporting, and you can choose cash-based or accrual for budgeting. You can choose when you budget whether you just want to know what cash will come in and go out, or whether you want to include the commitments that you make to spend in the past, present and future. Your reports will reflect whether you chose to know just what happened last year, or chose a report that includes all your past and future commitments. Your choice will reflect your values and the outcome that you intend.

If your purpose and intention is only to track the now, you will choose cash-based accounting, produce a budget that is cash-based and an end of year report that matches the cash-based budget to the cash-based accounts. If your purpose includes tracking and planning for long-term fiscal health, then you must choose accrual-based accounting, budgeting and reporting.

60 days after the 2006 U.S. Government Financial Report was issued, Google had not one single reference to it except the government sites where the report is available for download.

In 2005 the overspending reported in the cash-based budget was $319 billion and $760 billion in the accrual-based financial report– a difference of $441 billion.

For the United States Government, we choose cash-based accounting for the Budget before the year begins, cash-based appropriation bills, and a cash-basis for the Budget Report at the end of the year. We choose accrual-based accounting for an additional financial report that is given almost zero attention in the public arena. Past and future expense commitments account for a big difference between the bottom line in the cash-based budget and budget reports and the accrual-based financial reports.

In 2006, the Budget Report said that we spent $248 billion more, in cash, than we took in. This was called a $248 billion "deficit." The accrual-based Financial Report said that *we spent $450 billion more than we took in* and it was mostly ignored. The consolidated difference in net cost between the Budget Report and the Financial Report was $202 billion. Total consolidated reported income was $2,186 billion, which means that commitments representing more than 20% of total available income were ignored in the budget process.

What does this say about our purpose and intention in keeping government accounts? Are we managing our resources for today, or managing for tomorrow? Are we best served when we choose a cash-based budget and budget report?

Remember intention and purpose in evaluating our government's use of standard (and not-so-standard) accounting practices.

For a basic understanding of the financial situation, here's what you need to know about accounting:

- **Cash accounts**—simple and basic NOW information.

- **Accrual accounts**—add information about FUTURE and PAST commitments.

- **Fund accounts**—let you keep track of money collected for RESTRICTED purposes.

- **Consolidated accounts**—provide financial managers with information about the integrity of the accounting, but summaries of consolidated accounts strip out information that is *crucial to management.*

- **Cost accounting**—provides information of the costs of specific objectives that may be fulfilled across accounting units.

Cash, accrual and fund accounting are *not* equally useful for all purposes. It is helpful to understand the increasing value they offer when keeping complex finances, simple, clear and honest. And, it is important to consider the purposes for which accounts are kept:

- **BUDGET**—What shall we do?
  Cash-based budget: What shall we do *next* year?
  Accrual-based budget: How will next year's plans fit into our long-term commitments and strategic plans?

- **FINANCIAL REPORT**—How did we do?
  Cash-based financial report: How much cash came in last year and how much went out?
  Accrual-based financial report: How did last year's performance impact our long-term fiscal health?

Chapter Three

Government Accounting
Shameful, bad, good, better–best

We've had over 200 years to achieve excellence in our government's financial accounting and reporting. We're not there yet. In fact, our financial accounting and reporting systems still have so many problems, the accounts cannot be audited to determine whether or not the numbers are accurate. That is inexcusable and shameful. There is an ongoing effort to remedy the situation, and in the past ten years significant improvements have been made. However, it is not yet enough. You and I must speak up loudly and demand accurate accounts and reports; make excellence, not just a top priority, but an absolute deal-breaker. If your person in Congress is not demanding accuracy, integrity, honesty and excellence in financial reporting throughout government, funding the staff necessary, and holding all agencies to the highest standards, then vote someone else into office. Your life depends on it.

Here's the story on U.S. Government financial accounting and reporting:

The Treasury Department, an executive branch agency, keeps track of our money—our income and expenses, assets and debts. At the end of a fiscal year the Treasury Department produces a financial report that is given to the Office of the Comptroller General of the United States, Head of the Government Accountability Office (GAO), a legislative branch office, for audit. Executive branch Treasury and legislative branch GAO are intended to provide a check and balance. Sadly, the GAO cannot yet do its job, and Congress does not seem to be paying attention.

The fiscal year (FY) for the United States Government runs from October 1st to September 30th, and is described by the ending date. The FY 2006 began on October 1, 2005 and ran to September 30, 2006. The report for FY 2006 was issued on December 17, 2006, giving the government about two months to prepare it.

A goal to get the previous year's financial report out before the budget for the following year (which generally comes out at the beginning of February) was first met in 2004. That is helpful to decision-makers who take the time to read it; they know how the previous year went before making plans for new spending. And for the *first time ever* our lawmakers had that option in *2004*.

The Comptroller General has noted in each of the ten financial reports to date that Treasury staffing is inadequate; heroic and dedicated effort is required to deliver the reports. Adequate staffing to keep excellent track of your tax dollars is clearly not yet a funding priority of Congress.

☞IMPORTANT!

Congratulations to department chief financial officers, to the Treasury and to the GAO! We owe them a debt of gratitude for their dedication and perseverance in improving the timeliness and quality of the federal financial reports. Thank you! Thank you to Treasury and GAO staff for hard work under difficult circumstances, and for the continuing dedication to improving our government's financial accounting and reporting.

Slow improvements...

The evolution of government accounting has been a continuous process with tiny increments of improvement occurring every year. This summary skims over the highlights:

1776

From 1776 to 1921 the United States Government used simple cash accounting. Government taxed and spent what it collected. The U.S. Government kept a cash-based account of taxing and spending. It had no budget, no accrual-based financial report, and no way to gauge either short-term or long-term effectiveness.

1921

It took 150 years to decide that a formal budget and a little oversight was a good idea. The Budget and Accounting Act of 1921 required the first cash-based budget. It set up the Office of Management and Budget (OMB) in the executive branch under the President. For legislative branch oversight, this law set up the General Accounting Office* (GAO) to "investigate, at the seat of government or elsewhere, all matters relating to the receipt, disbursement, and application of public funds." The law required the GAO to report to the President and to Congress with "recommendations looking to greater economy or efficiency in public expenditures." (Sec. 312(a), 42 Stat. 25. June 10, 1921)

From 1921 to 1945 the GAO used what is called "voucher checking," to audit government accounts. This meant a huge staff of clerks checked every government transaction to assure that written authorization and justifying receipts were present. The focus was on the trees not the forest.

From 1921 to 1997 the U.S. Government had a budget and a report on whether the budget was met—a list of departments and their spending. The GAO also produced miscellaneous reports on government spending. Our government now had a way to gauge short-term accountability—did we tax and spend according to procedure and according to the budget?

1945-1954

During the years from 1945 to 1954, the GAO began to shift toward a more comprehensive look at government finances, focusing on methods and standards of accounting. These methods and standards were put into practice with the Government Corporation Control Act (1945) which

---

* In 2004, the name of the GAO was changed to the Government Accountability Office to better reflect their full mandate.

authorized the auditing of wholly owned government corporations and mixed ownership corporations. The methods and standards that were developed and then put into practice on government corporations were made law in the Budget and Accounting Procedures Act (1950).

In 1952, the GAO pulled four different task groups together to create a Division of Audits. This division continued to develop the manuals and systems for financial oversight, but continued to limit its auditing to government corporations–shrubs, a few trees, but not yet the whole forest.

1970s

In 1973, nearly 200 years after our nation's founding, Congress decided it would be a good idea to know what we have committed to pay in the future and what we have committed to pay in the past, but have not yet paid. Congress decided that an accrual-based financial report would be useful in addition to continuing to use a cash-based budget for planning and simple accountability.

A prototype financial report that consolidated all of the agency reports was initially produced by the private accounting firm of Arthur Anderson for fiscal years 1973 and 1974. In 1975, the U.S. Department of Treasury took over and produced its first Prototype Financial Report for 1975. These early reports used a "relatively simple" format.

These reports were not audited, *"though Treasury hired private firms to conduct independent reviews of source data and collection procedures."*
2004 USFR, p. 27

1990s

The 1990s saw major improvements to the content and format of the U.S. Government's financial accounting and reporting. Several laws were passed that made significant changes, including the Chief Financial Officers (CFO) Act in 1990, the Government Management Reform Act of 1994, and the Federal Financial Management Improvement Act in 1996. Here are the improvements that these laws introduced and required:

Professionally prepared and audited statements

> *Most importantly, the CFO act "...for the first time required annual, audited financial statements for the United States Government and its component entities."*
> 2001 USFR

Financial reports prepared by professionals and audited—a brave and bold concept whose time came in **1990**.

Audits

The 1990s laws required that the consolidated financial reports be audited. An audit is a standard business procedure requiring someone other than the people keeping the accounts to check that controls are in place and practiced to assure that the numbers are accurate and honest.

Since 1984, the Government Accountability Office (GAO) had been auditing the financial statements for various federal agencies, including the General Services Administration and the Departments of Agriculture, the Air Force, Housing and Urban Development and Veterans Affairs. Evidently, to our lawmakers' surprise, *"These audits improved the quality of agency financial information and identified significant problems in agency financial operations and reporting."* 2003 USFR

So, six years later, in 1990, Congress decided it might be a good idea to require financial statements and audits from all the major government departments and agencies, and to require a consolidated financial statement for government as a whole. It gave agencies seven more years to figure out how to do it.

A Comptroller General, Chief Financial Officers

To achieve professional, annual, audited financial statements, the 1990 law created the positions of Comptroller General of the U.S. in the Government Accountability Office (GAO) and Chief Financial Officers for 24 major government agencies—some departments with more money to spend that most countries and many big businesses.

The CFO Act recognizes that,

The lack of a cadre of highly qualified financial management professionals has long hampered effective federal financial management operations.

So, the CFO Act took steps to bring qualified financial management professionals into government. Good thinking in 1990!

Controls

Every business with more than one employee has to establish systems and procedures for keeping track of money coming in and going out. These systems and procedures are called controls. Effective controls assure the integrity of transactions, accounts and reports.

The new CFOs were tasked with establishing control systems and procedures, and with monitoring compliance to assure fiscal integrity.

Accounting Standards

These 1990s laws created the Federal Accounting Standards Advisory Board (FASAB) to professionalize, standardize and monitor government accounting procedures, as government accounting differs in some ways from standard business accounting.

Putting the plan into action

The CFO Act set up a schedule for pilot projects whereby certain agencies took a shot at preparing agency wide financial statements for specific years. For example the IRS was required to present a financial statement and audit by 1992.

It took several years to develop the standards and several years to get departments started with the new system of accounting and reporting. The first comprehensive financial report came out on schedule in 1997, moving from prototype to official report.

The degree of accuracy and integrity in the financial reporting of the United States government has improved significantly since the CFO Act put Chief Financial Officers in each of the 24 main government departments, established the position of a Comptroller General to oversee the comprehensive U.S. financial reporting, and created a body to monitor and set government accounting standards. No surprise.

Useful financial information
The CFO Act requires that 24 main government agencies be able to:
> *...generate timely, accurate, and useful financial and management information, including reporting performance results, to make decisions and monitor government performance every day.*

Good and true financial reports are the bedrock of great decision-making. When transactions are made with integrity, and we have accurate and trustworthy reporting, we have a foundation for great democracy.

1994
In 1994 Vice President Al Gore initiated National Performance Review, which focused in part on modernizing and "integrating" federal financial management systems, and improving financial reporting, cost accounting and performance measurement. The Bush II administration has continued to promote these reforms, however adequate staffing has not yet been funded in his budgets or by Congress.

1997- 1st Consolidated Financial Report
For the 1997 first ever comprehensive financial report, few of the individual agencies could pass an audit with an "unqualified" distinction. Because of serious deficiencies in the accounting at some agencies, the consolidated financial report as a whole could not be audited. But, we were on our way!

From the 1921 Budget Act, it took 75 years to get citizens and lawmakers an audit-attempted, accrual-based consolidated financial report. Remember, an accrual-based financial report is a critical tool for leadership and for oversight. Sadly, up until now the U.S. Government Financial Report has garnered little public attention, and it is certainly not used as the reference for dialogue, debate and decision-making. No one is focusing on the Big Picture, yet.

1997
1st!

U.S. Government
Financial Report

2003

In 2003 FASAB began reclassifying what assets must be booked and included in the financial report, and what can be called "Stewardship" responsibilities and described in supplemental notes to the financial reports. This reclassification process is ongoing and is intended to portray a more accurate reflection of our national assets on the balance sheet. It has a long way to go (see Chapter 10).

2005-2006

In 2005, another improvement was made: the Statement of Social Insurance was reclassified as "a basic financial statement" and now requires a full audit status as part of the total financial report. In 2006, for the first time a Statement of Social Insurance was reported and audited as a principal financial statement and included in the Financial Report.

In 2006, for the first time, the revenues collected for the restricted "Trust Funds" were distinguished from the funds collected for the Operating Fund. This was a major milestone towards clarity.

TODAY

Good News

Our government accountants are on a slow roll. In the past sixteen years significant improvements have been made to the financial reports of the U.S. Government. We are on the path toward excellence in our financial reporting and accountability. We can continue to choose to make improvements.

Each of the government departments has been working to get their financial report out in time to be of use in planning for the next year. In 2005 all of the 24 major federal agencies were able to issue financial reports on or before November 15th.

In 2005 for the first time, the total number of agencies demonstrating an "ability to use timely and accurate financial information to make decisions about program management" increased to six agencies (out of 24). In 2006, the number increased to eight agencies. Grindingly slow progress, but I guess that's good news.

The financial accounts of the major restricted funds can all pass an audit, and these restricted funds represent more than half of all government financial commitments.

Most of the Operating Fund agencies can pass an audit, too.

Bad news

While most of the 24 individual agencies can pass an agency audit, **the agencies that spend the bulk of the money cannot.** Consequently, the consolidated financial report of the U.S. Government **cannot yet be audited,** so passing an audit still lies in the future. In 2006, for the tenth consecutive year, "material deficiencies" prevented the GAO from "expressing an opinion" on the federal governments consolidated financial statements. They "disclaimed" an ability to do the audit. We are at *the beginning* of achieving exemplary accounts that serve all stakeholders, and do our nation proud.

Disclaimed

One can attempt to do an audit, and then find that there is inadequate information or inadequate systems in place to perform the audit. In this case, the auditor will "disclaim" an ability to do the audit. The comptroller General of the United states has issued a disclaimer for *every year to date* on the consolidated U.S. Government Financial Reports. Shame!

Another 15 years after the 1990 law, only 73% of government net spending can pass an agency audit. The government departments that spend more than 50% of all the Operating Fund tax dollars *cannot yet be audited— let alone get a clean audit report.* In 2006 four agencies still received "disclaimers of opinion" on their financial statements: Department of Defense, State, Homeland Security and NASA. A "disclaimer" means that the accounts are so bad an audit cannot be performed—pass or fail cannot be determined. The Department of Energy could be audited, but it could not *pass* its audit.

2006
The CFO
Act agencies
that received
DISCLAIMERS of
opinions on ALL of
their fiscal year 2006
financial statements:
Defense
Homeland Security
NASA
State

Qualified "unqualified"

In 2005, of the 24 accounts that were audited, only one got a totally "clean," green light designation from both the Government Accountability Office and the Bush II Administration. Seventeen agencies were given an "unqualified" rating, which should mean that they get a gold star without qualifications. However, in the words of David M. Walker, Comptroller General of the United States, they were *"able to obtain unqualified audit opinions only by expending significant resources to use extensive ad hoc procedures and [by] making billions of dollars in adjustments to derive financial statements months after the end of a fiscal year."*

Ad hoc procedures mean that the auditors decided the numbers were mostly accurate but that the systems that provide the checks and balances were inadequate. For instance, it might mean that there is no system to record that inventory reportedly purchased has been delivered and is in the warehouse without going out there and physically counting each and every item at the time of the audit. The final count might match, but the "ad hoc" procedure requires heroic and expensive effort. Or, that heroic and expensive effort might find that there is waste and fraud. In some cases, we simply do not know, because we are not making the heroic effort required.

The 2006 report states that auditors for 17 of the 24 CFO Act agencies reported that the agencies' financial management systems did not substantially comply with one or more significant legal requirements:

> *As a result, the financial management systems at the majority of federal agencies are still unable to routinely produce reliable, useful, and timely financial information, and the federal government's capacity to manage with timely and objective data is limited, thereby hampering its ability to effectively administer and oversee its major programs.* 2006 USFR, p.156

Significant "adjustments" to balance the books

Nearly every single agency has line items making sizable adjustments to reconcile their accounts. This is the same thing you might do if your checkbook balance did not reconcile with your bank statement. "Billions of dollars in adjustments" certainly does not sound worthy of an "unqualified" hurrah for an audit.

To make the 2006 consolidated financial statements balance, Treasury made an adjustment to the books of $11 billion. The Financial Report called it "Unmatched transactions and balances." For the first time the source of these "unmatched transactions"–primarily intra-agency errors– was included in the Supplemental Information of the Financial Report (on page 144). Thanks GAO/Treasury for some new and useful information!

For our government, what does an $11 billion error/adjustment mean? Well, that $11 billion is more than we spend to protect our environment ($9 billion), and more than we spend on maintaining healthy commerce ($10 billion). It would represent a 7-10% increase in the budget of all but Defense and Health & Human Services. It is a significant amount of slop, even though it only represents .3% of the combined income of all funds.

I'm curious. What standard of accuracy do the big banks set? Do big businesses on the planet accept accounting errors of this magnitude? Is this acceptable to our lawmakers? Is it acceptable to you? If you find this standard too low, then what are you doing about it?

At least our government accountants are pointing out this inadequacy now, which gives us hope for continuing improvement.

Material control weaknesses

Every year, Comptroller General David M. Walker points out that there are "pervasive and generally long-standing material weaknesses." He goes on, and continues for about 7-15 pages explaining why he cannot do the job he is tasked with—auditing the consolidated financial report. One of the pages he takes to explain these deficiencies is included on the following page.

He explains that,

> *"A material weakness is a condition that precludes the entity's internal control from providing reasonable assurance that misstatements, losses, or noncompliance material in relation to the financial statements or to stewardship information would be prevented or detected on a timely basis.* 2006 USFR, p. 27

Restatements the following year

The Comptroller General also noted in 2004, 2005 and 2006 that there is a disturbing trend of agencies to restate the previous years numbers. In 2005 six agencies went back and restated the previous year's reports, which suggests that they are struggling in a big way with getting it done right, or willing to ENRON the books a bit to look better while the public is paying attention. Who knows?

From the 2006 FR, Statement of the Comptroller General, p. 27 and p. 150 (a composite):

Our report on the U.S. government's consolidated financial statements for fiscal years 2006 and 2005 is enclosed. ...

A significant number of material weaknesses related to financial systems, fundamental record-keeping and financial reporting, and incomplete documentation continued to (1) hamper the federal government's ability to reliably report a significant portion of its assets, liabilities, costs, and other related information; (2) affect the federal government's ability to reliably measure the full cost as well as the financial and nonfinancial performance of certain programs and activities; (3) impair the federal government's ability to adequately safeguard significant assets and properly record various transactions; and (4) hinder the federal government from having reliable financial information to operate in an economical, efficient, and effective manner. We found the following:

- Certain material weaknesses in financial reporting and other limitations on the scope of our work resulted in conditions that, for the 10th consecutive year, prevented us from expressing an opinion on the federal government's consolidated financial statements. About $797 billion, or 53 percent, of the federal government's reported total assets as of September 30, 2006, and approximately $790 billion, or 27 percent, of the federal government's reported net cost for fiscal year 2006 relate to 5 of the 24 Chief Financial Officers (CFO) Act agencies' fiscal year 2006 financial statement that were disclaimed on or not audited.

- The federal government did not maintain effective internal control over financial reporting (including safeguarding assets) and compliance with significant laws and regulations as of September 30, 2006.

- Our work to test compliance with selected provisions of significant laws and regulations in fiscal year 2006 was limited by the material weaknesses and scope limitations discussed in our report.

DISCLAIMER OF OPINION ON THE CONSOLIDATED FINANCIAL STATEMENTS

Because of the federal government's inability to demonstrate the reliability of significant portions of the U.S. government's accompanying consolidated financial statements for fiscal years 2006 and 2005, principally resulting from certain material weaknesses, and other limitations on the scope of our work, described in this report, we are unable to, and we do not, express an opinion on such financial statements.

As a result of these limitations, readers are cautioned that amounts reported in the consolidated financial statements and related notes **may not be reliable.**

(Emphasis added, because it is stunning, jaw-dropping astounding for this to be true of our U.S. financial accounting and reporting.)

Department of Defense

The Department of Defense is highlighted every single year as the primary cause of the poor state of our government's financial accounting and reporting. What they do poorly has a big impact because they spend over 42% of the total operating fund income. In 2006, on an accrual basis, Defense spent $658 billion (out of $1,611 billion)—plus their payments to the restricted funds (roughly $20 billion in FICA and unemployment insurance for their employees, which net out and disappear from view in the consolidated report as income to the restricted funds and expense to the DoD).

In every single one of the ten financial reports, the Comptroller General notes how very far the DoD has to go before their accounts meet basic business accounting standards.

> *...the Federal government was unable to support significant portions of the total net cost of operations, most notably related to DoD.* 2006 USFR, p.161

> *The largest and most challenging impediment to rendering any opinion on the U.S. government's consolidated financial statements continues to be serious financial management problems at DoD.* 2004 USFR, p. 3

The 2001 Auditor's report for the Department of Defense stated,

> *We reported that DoD processed $1.1 trillion in unsupported accounting entries to DoD Component financial data used to prepare departmental reports and DoD financial statements for FY 2000. For FY 2001, we did not attempt to quantify amounts of unsupported accounting entries to the financial data.*

The auditor probably regretted making the statement in 2000 about "$1.1 trillion in unsupported accounting entries." This statement has been widely reported in the alternative media and poorly understood. So in 2001, they simply refused to attempt to quantify unsupported accounting entries. This $1.1 trillion number has been floating around the web ever since they printed it, with many people interpreting it to mean that the Department of Defense (DoD) lost and/or cannot account for $1.1 trillion in one year.

Is it that bad? The entire accrual-based Defense budget in 2001 was $777 billion, and they had something to show for their spending, so how could they have half again as much in unsupported accounting entries? Unsupported means that there is inadequate paperwork to confirm the transactions are legitimate. It may mean that as they purchased, then inventoried, then shifted goods and services from one department to another, and perhaps sold items, that the paperwork was never done properly. For example, it could mean that Defense paid for materials, accepted delivery and moved them around a lot without keeping good controls. One item might account for several unsupported accounting entries. And, without the audit trail, it is impossible to know if the money was actually spent, well spent, poorly spent or simply stolen.

Given the amount of money represented in these unsupported transactions, it is clear that the Department of Defense is not doing a prudent and responsible job of financial oversight. One can justifiably say that $1.1 trillion in unsupported entries—more than the total budget of the department at the time—represents remarkable incompetence or egregious malfeasance.

In the National Defense Authorization for FY 2002 (Public Law 107-107), Congress threw up their hands on auditing the Department of Defense and decided to *"minimize the resources used to prepare and audit financial statements with unreliable data, and redirect those resources to improving financial management policies, procedures, and internal controls."* In other words, they acknowledged that the systems were so bad at the Department of Defense, there was no way an audit could be done. Instead of wasting money trying to massage a bad system, it was time, again, to put the money into creating a new good system.

This bill gave the Department of Defense until 2006 before they had to submit to an audit. Our Congress seemed to think that from 1990 to 2006–sixteen years– was a reasonable amount of time to get a functioning, credible accounting system in place. So how did they do in 2006. They were disclaimed, again. What are your Senators and Representative doing about this? Make it a deal breaker.

When does imprudent and irresponsible become criminal when you are responsible for other people's money?

Where does responsibility lie, if the President and the Congress are consistently failing to fund adequate financial oversight staff?

With you and your vote.

Given the size of the Defense Budget, it is fair to assume that by holding the DoD to a standard of excellence that eliminates waste and fraud, we could free up enormous sums for more productive use. If the Pentagon is blowing 5% of their money through waste and fraud, in 2006 that would have been about $33 billion—more money than *the total department budget for 2/3 of all the other departments.* For example, the Environmental Protection Agency—charged with protecting the air and water upon which our lives and our children's futures *depend absolutely,* has a budget of $9 billion—petty change for the DoD and well within their margin of error.

The level of waste and fraud in the DoD is likely to be considerably higher than 5%, considering the billions going into the Iraqi occupation, running at $5-$12 billion per month for more than four years. In 2003, President George W. Bush appointed Paul Bremer as Director of Reconstruction and Humanitarian Assistance and Head of the Coalition Provisional Authority (CPA) in Iraq. Bremer then gave a tiny firm in San Diego (with a private residence address and no credentials as Certified Public Accountants), the contract to keep the records for over $20 billion in Iraqi Oil revenues destined to pay for the reconstruction of Iraq.[17] When auditors were installed *two years into the occupation,* the CPA auditors found that $8.8 billion of the funds were spent with "inadequate stewardship" and big chunks just went out the door without paperwork. Giant C-137 cargo planes were used to haul tons of cash to Iraq, cartons of cash were handed over to ministries still under our control, where in one instance 72,000 security personnel were paid, and the auditor could find only 604 names on the payroll. In the last weeks before handing over control to a new Iraqi government, the CPA had contractors bring duffle bags to collect their payouts in cash. Little paper work was done.

War and emergency action are used as the excuse—as if the United States is some backwater republic that cannot muster adequate staffing and oversight. You can put a decent system of accounts into place with a $100 software purchase. You can easily assemble a crackerjack team of accountants, purchasing experts and auditors to supervise processing and data entry. Two years and more than $20 billion in spending without a

---

Read ***Imperial Life in the Emerald City*** by Rajiv Chandrasekaran (2006) or ***Fiasco*** by Thomas E. Ricks (2006) to understand the extraordinarily high–impeachable, if not criminal– incompetence in the Bush II administration's execution of their occupation of Iraq, and Congress's total failure to meet their Constitutional responsibility for oversight and accountability.

Legal fiduciary trustee of $20 billion fails to keep track of $8.8 billion (44%).

This is criminal negligence.

professional team of accountants and auditors is incomprehensible and surely criminal negligence, by all standards of honor, decency and law.

How can we know whether we are spending wisely or just spending a lot when the department that spends nearly all of the available discretionary cash in the operating fund is unable to produce accurate financial reports? It is difficult to address increasing safety *and* wise defense spending when the accounts cannot be audited. For example, in 2003, many people were puzzled that then Secretary of Defense Donald Rumsfeld was unable to find enough cash in hundreds of billions of dollars in allocations to buy adequate armor in a timely manner for our combat troops.

We can only have a productive discussion about *any* taxing or spending *when* we have an accurate report of the Department of Defense spending.

If we really want to tax and spend wisely, then the Department of Defense is the place where truthful, trustworthy, and wise spending will have the greatest impact. If we want to talk about cutting expenses so that we can responsibly cut taxes, then we must have the courage to talk about creating efficiencies and reducing costs in the Department of Defense– and shifting some of our global problem solving to less costly alternative strategies with higher cost-return ratios.

The Department of Defense gets away with sloppy accounting because leaders and lawmakers stir up fear for our safety, which triggers our primitive brain functions. In our child brain we can only think, "Daddy, Do whatever it takes to keep me safe." When we call on our higher brain functions, we know that we have enough resources to defend the country, spend efficiently and wisely, AND keep accurate accounts. Anyone who thinks otherwise does not belong in a leadership position. (When we call on our higher brain functions, we also know that using the military to solve global political problems is the most costly solution in dollars, lives and error impact of any potential strategy.)

It is puzzling why it seemed necessary to Congress in 2002 to give the Department of Defense another four years to get up and running with accurate and auditable accounting, when they had already been given 12 years to accomplish the task. Now that this additional time is up and the DoD still cannot be audited, and the CFO at the DoD is still holding her job, we must ask how much longer this administration and Congress are going to enable inadequate performance at the DoD.

Sixteen years–and still counting–of less than mediocre accounting at the DoD is a long way from the excellence we should expect on a platinum budget. How about a little tough love for department heads and financial officers in the Department of Defense? Meet an audit in 2008 or lose your job. Meet an audit in 2008 or lose funding in any failing department and everyone in the department is out of a job. Our leadership should set a zero tolerance for sloppy accounting, make it a priority, issue the ultimatum and *fund enough staff* to make a clean audit of every government agency a reality. Why haven't they done it? You must insist; ask the Presidential candidates for 2008 if they will commit to a high standard of accounting excellence, oversight and accountability with a zero tolerance policy.

The Executive Office of the President

The buck stops here. Minimizing and blocking oversight appears to be a deliberate and intentional policy of the Bush II administration. They have doubled the money going to private contractors (to $400 billion, which is roughly one fourth of the revenue available for operating expenses in 2006). The number of government employees issuing, managing and auditing contracts has barely grown.[18] For example, the State Department has increased its spending on private contractors from $1 billion to $4 billion per year. They have 17 contract officers to oversee the 2500 contracts this requires, which is 147 contracts with an average value of $235 million *per officer.* Even if each one of these officers is costing $200,000 (including long-term health and retirement benefits–which is just a guess), these 17 officers are only costing $3.4 million, less than 1/10th of 1% for compliance. Is this prudent and responsible? Would any business operate with this miniscule level of oversight? When does a failure to build in prudent oversight become criminal negligence of a fiduciary responsibility? When so many of the no-bid contracts are going to friends who make big contributions to your campaign,[19] and when the incompetent execution of their contracts put the nation at risk,[20] at what level does this become high treason?

The Bush II administration's failure to put oversight in place as it commenced programs, and its stonewalling against the efforts of others to do so in a timely way leads to the conclusion that the criminally negligent care of billions of Iraqi and U.S. taxpayer dollars was (and continues to be) deliberate. President George W. Bush confirmed this conclusion when he awarded Mr. "Inadequate Steward of $8.8 billion-Bremer the Presidential Medal of Honor for what he termed, "exemplary service." Further confirmation came in March 2006, when with White House direction, the DoD was still stonewalling putting on-site auditors into the Iraqi Operations, and the Republican-controlled Congress, the branch of government responsible for oversight, aggressively supported this choice. President George W. Bush has given us plenty of evidence that he is satisfied with inadequate and irresponsible fiscal management practice.

In 2004, reflecting the values they practice, the Republican controlled Congress gave the Executive Office of the President *direct* control over another $18 billion in Iraqi Reconstruction funds provided by American taxpayers. This sum appears unheralded in the fifteen fold increase in the budget[21] for the Executive Office of the President from an historical average of around $400 million ($.4 billion) to $6,000 million ($6 billion). It was critical to our national security and to "winning the war" in Iraq to contract the reconstruction with speed, efficiency, transparency and integrity. President, G.W. Bush already had executive authority over a host of agencies, including USAID (with hundreds of staff in place and nearly 50 years of experience) who could have stepped up to this plate–as could the Army Corps of Engineers. How can we account for the Executive Office of the President's willful grab for more direct control over the process? Was the ability to shield spending from public and Congressional scrutiny a factor? Given the record of President G.W. Bush to that date, your Congressmen could have predicted that oversight would continue to be minimal and obstructed, and that the primary beneficiaries would be the corporate friends of the White House. Are you OK with that? If you vote again for a Senator or Representative who went along, you are signalling your acceptance of this standard, and your willingness to foot the bill–in dollars and lives.

In 2007 we are learning from the Special Inspector General for Iraq Reconstruction that much of this spending has been mismanaged with little oversight by people whose primary qualification for the job was loyalty to the President.[22] The magnitude of the irresponsibility moves beyond well intentioned incompetence. When a President "at War" creates or negligently allows wiggle room for his friends' war profiteering at the expense of national security, this is treason. The disdain for the Iraqi people whose assets were in our care, for the American taxpayer who must shoulder the burden of recompense, and for the soldiers who must deal with the blowback is surely criminal negligence and, when the buck stops where it should, it is surely an impeachable offense. We will continue to get poor performance as long as we are unwilling or unable to hold people in government accountable.

The Inspector General's reports do not bode well for a high standard of fiscal responsibility and accountability *anywhere* in the Bush II administration. Shame! It is past time for all lawmakers to value honesty, require accountability and insist on oversight.

It is perfectly reasonable to demand that only government agencies that can handle money in a professional way get money to spend. However capable your lawmakers are, if they are not insisting on accurate accounts, they are abdicating their responsibility to oversee the spending of your tax dollars.

There are no good excuses for sloppy accounting at the Treasury and in the departments of the government of the United States of America in the year 2007. We must demand the highest level of accountability *all* the time from our government.

Other deficiencies worth mentioning

The reporting GOAL is currently less than 100%

All the financial reports of all government agencies are not included in the financial report. It is difficult to ascertain exactly what is not included. The Judicial and Legislative Branches of government show up in the budget reports and in the financial reports as simple line items because they are *not required by law to submit comprehensive financial statements of information to Treasury.* They have provided what they choose to provide. How can we know what is being left out? Who is

Do your lawmakers value honesty and require accountability?

Have they called for investigations and for people to be held accountable?

Ask them.

Hold them accountable. Fire the enablers at the 2008 election.

providing oversight if not Treasury, GAO or citizens? How is the check and balance of power provided, when there is no oversight? As a concerned citizen, I would like to see an audited report, please.

Other agencies that are off the books because they are privately owned, but that expose the federal government to considerable liability, include the Federal Reserve System, the Federal Home Loan Banks, the Federal National Mortgage Association, and the Federal Home Loan Mortgage Corporation. Should we agree to keep these liabilities off the books and out of sight? Are we willing to carry a public burden of risk for entities that keep proprietary secrets, make unknown private investors wealthy, and refuse full public oversight? Why would we want to do this?

Improper payments

In 2002 Congress passed the Improper Payments Information Act. It requires that federal agencies annually review all programs and activities to identify where improper payments may have been made, and then make an estimate of how many improper payments are being made, so that there is a benchmark for making improvements. This is a work in progress and the Office of Management and Budget projects that most of the programs designated high-risk will be reporting a national improper payment estimate by 2008.

> Examples of improper payments include payments made for services that are not rendered, or payments made to beneficiaries of government programs who do not qualify.

Federal agencies' estimates of improper payments based on available information for fiscal year 2004 exceeded $45 billion.[23] This dropped by $6.5 billion to $37 billion in 2005—an improvement. However, these improper payments only included estimates for about 30 out of 57 programs that are at high risk, and this amount is still equivalent to more than the budgets of all but the largest ten (out of 24) government agencies.

Demand excellence.

It is interesting that the government has determined that roughly $1.5 trillion out of $2.5 trillion dollar total federal spending consists of high-risk programs where improper payments might be made. The remaining $1.0 trillion (approximately) that was deemed not to be risk susceptible is made up of compensation, contractual services, and net interest on the public debt. Considering that the missing $8.8 billion in Iraq was for compensation and contractual services, one has to wonder how far we have to go to get to accurate and accountable financial management.

Information security

In 2002 Congress passed a Federal Information Security Management Act and the Cyber Security Research and Development Act.

> *Although progress has been made, serious and widespread information security control weaknesses continue to place federal assets at risk of inadvertent or deliberate misuse, financial information at risk of unauthorized modification or destruction, sensitive information at risk of inappropriate disclosure, and critical operations at risk of disruption.* 2006 USFR, p. 167

The GAO has been reporting information security as a high-risk area in *every one of the ten financial reports.* (In updating the quote above from one year to the next, all I had to do was change the date and the page number.) It took public reporting on major breaches of security and massive confidential data file losses in 2006, to get Congress to pay *any* attention to securing our government's vital and confidential accounts.

Why is that? What accounts for the inexcusable gap between warnings of danger and administrative or Congressional action? You. You have to be willing to hold your Representative and Senator accountable. Liking them personally or feeling loyal to them for years of service is nice, but by itself creates a system that is ripe for abuse. Your inner child wants your papa-president and papa-congressman to always be right and righteous. Put this inner child down for a nap, call on your inner adult and demand excellence and accountability. Excellence and accountability can lead to great democracy and a better future.

Ask yourself: Do you want to be represented in Congress by people who are content to spend your tax dollars *without* accurate and audited accounts?

Shameful

It is astonishing that the government only passed a law to present audited financial statements in 1990. It is shameful that in 2006, our government accounts **cannot yet be audited** so that we even know whether they would pass or fail. An audit is a standard business process: an independent accountant checks that you are adding and subtracting correctly; checks that if you say you spent or received money, you can prove it; checks that if you bought equipment, you have it in a verifiable inventory; and checks that you have adequate accounting and control measures to assure that the books are not cooked.

Up until 1997, our lawmakers had no simple and clear way to see the big picture—a comprehensive financial report for the U.S. Government. Today they still have no assurance that the numbers they see are accurate, or that spending is free of fraud and waste.

Any discussion of taxes and spending is severely handicapped when everyone's numbers are off by tens of billions of dollars. Any discussion of taxes, spending and finance is significantly less useful and productive when you do not know if the numbers are reliable. An audit is an important tool. It tells you if your numbers are accurate and if the tracking systems have integrity. Very basic stuff.

If you started voting before 1990, you have been voting for tax collecting and tax spending lawmakers that did not feel they needed an annual, audited financial statement for the U.S. Government. If you began voting after 1990, check to see whether your lawmakers were satisfied with a 40% success rate and 16 years to get the Department of Defense up to speed.

If you have a Senator or Representative that was in office for any length of time before 1990, doubt his or her financial savvy and common sense. If your lawmaker has been around for a long time and did not work for decent financial reports, consider that your lawmaker may lack financial savvy, integrity and/or the courage to fight for transparent, honest and accountable government.

Lawmakers who have been in office a long time may have the seniority to bring home the bacon to your state, but you can be sure that ultimately all of us are paying a premium for that pork because these lawmakers do not understand the financial impact of their decisions. It is puzzling how lawmakers could ever feel good about their decisions without the fundamental information provided by an audited financial statement.

The value of chief financial officers, professionally prepared and audited financial statements, and accounting standards has been understood for decades, if not centuries, by our best and brightest. President Thomas Jefferson saw this information as essential for government and the governed.

Because every culture will have people at all levels of maturity in every realm, including financial intelligence, it is a good idea to choose law-makers at the highest levels of our collective cultural wisdom. They can pull the rest of us up and help us reach for the best that is within our culture. Since that does not appear to be the case at present, we must speak up for excellence, collectively, loudly and clearly.

TOMORROW

In a great democracy, an easy to understand, full financial report must be available to every citizen. Rather than waiting another 30 years for the next big improvement in federal financial reporting, let's begin now.

We tend to assume that those in power are on top of the fundamentals. This is a false and dangerous assumption and why we enshrined checks and balances of power in our Constitution; broad based and balanced power leads to the best decisions and to a more mature democracy.

The President and Congress have over $1,600 billion of our dollars to spend in the Operating Fund alone. They can honor our hard-earned contributions by setting aside enough of our dollars to assure that the monies are cared for at the highest level of accountability, NOW.

You, the informed citizen, have an important part to play in insuring the integrity of our decision process.

Call your lawmakers and let them know that excellence in accounting–full integrity–is very important to you and to the nation.

The past few financial reports have said that the personnel at Treasury have *"excessive workloads that required an extraordinary amount of effort and dedication to compile the consolidated financial statements."* There are simply not enough people to do the job well. When there is a potential to save tens of billions of dollars in slop money, it is difficult to justify the penny pinching that keeps the government accounting departments understaffed. Penny-wise and pound-foolish. Let's grow up and begin to spend wisely by first choosing to spend for adequate financial oversight.

We are can-do people with a wealth of financial expertise in our marketplace. If the President, every Senator and every Representative asked, "What will it take to get all government spending audited, and all departments able to **pass an audit by next year?**," and, if they listen to the professionals keeping the accounts and work collaboratively to make it happen, it will happen! And, I guarantee that it will cost pennies to the dollars that will be saved by having accounts that meet the highest standards of excellence and integrity.

Recap

1776 –	Simple cash accounts
1921 –	A budget and an oversight agency
1945 –	Begin to standardize methods, control systems and produce first agency audits
1970s –	A prototype comprehensive financial report
1997 –	The 1st Consolidated, accrual-based financial report, audit attempted
Today –	U.S. Government consolidated accounts CANNOT YET be audited, primarily because of inadequacies in the accounts of the Department of Defense.
Tomorrow:	Hold your elected officials accountable.

<u>YOU</u> MUST DEMAND EXCELLENCE!

Chapter Four

The pipeline—
Taxing, spending and reporting flow

To understand the federal accounts you need to understand a little bit about the planning, taxing and spending process—in part because each step of the process currently has its own peculiar set of accounts. The format of the accounts changes along the route from planning, through authorizing, appropriating, spending and reporting.

Here is the pipeline:

1. Budget: The President's plan for your tax dollars
President's Office of Management and Budget (OMB)

As the name indicates, OMB is the administrative branch agency concerned with financial planning, budgeting and overseeing the implementation of taxing and spending once Congress has approved a plan.

> *OMB's predominant mission is to assist the President in overseeing the preparation of the federal budget and to supervise its administration in Executive Branch agencies. In helping to formulate the President's spending plans, OMB evaluates the effectiveness of agency programs, policies, and procedures, assesses competing funding demands among agencies, and sets funding pri-*

orities. OMB ensures that agency reports, rules, testimony, and proposed legislation are consistent with the President's Budget and with Administration policies. www.whitehouse.gov/omb

OMB submits a plan, a *cash-based* Budget

A budget is a planning document about how the administration would like to spend government money. The Budget is a mammoth document of 1000+ pages.

The Budget of the United States Government is a collection of documents that contains the budget message of the President, information about the President's budget proposals for a given fiscal year, and other budgetary publications that have been issued throughout the fiscal year. Other related and supporting budget publications, such as the Economic Report of the President, are included, which may vary from year to year. (OMB)

2-4. Congress passes laws

- Budget Resolution to authorize the revenue and spending parameters

- Authorization Bills to authorize specific spending

- Appropriation Bills to appropriate specific funds to specific departments

BUDGET RESOLUTION: Congress sets boundaries

The President sends the cash-based budget of "on-budget" accounts to Congress. Congress reviews the President's Budget and then passes a budget resolution that sets the *parameters* for spending—total revenue collection, total spending, and total borrowing. Basically they are saying here's the total amount we are going to spend, tax for and borrow. The Budget Resolution is not binding law.

The Post Office and the Old Age, Survivors and Dependents Trust Fund (a.k.a. OASDI or Social Security Trust Fund) are both "off-budget," so the income and expenses for these two entities are not part of the budgeting, authorizing and appropriation process.

AUTHORIZATION BILL:
Congress issues "licenses" to spend

Many agencies and programs in our government are subject to annual re-authorization.   For example, Congress first has to pass a bill that says that the Department of Transportation can continue to exist and spend tax dollars, before Congress can appropriate or set aside money for the Department of Transportation.

Every program has to first be authorized by Congress before money can be appropriated.   Authorization is the "Mother may I?" stage.   Forget to ask, and your bill goes nowhere. In November 2004, the Republican-controlled House spent days objecting to appropriations bills that had not yet been *authorized*. Since the Republicans controlled the House, it seems fair to hold them responsible for assuring that authorization bills were in place before calling the appropriation bills to a vote. They failed to do so, and wasted an astounding amount of time. This is an example of very poor decision-making leadership.

APPROPRIATION OR TAX BILL:
Congress sets aside the money

Within the parameters of their own Budget Resolution, and after authorizing expenditures, Congress then passes appropriation bills for spending, and tax bills for collecting money that specify the detailed taxing, spending and tax waiving (called "tax expenditures"). Once the appropriation bills are passed, money for the spending that the bills identify is made available to the specified departments.

Congress can authorize or appropriate money for one-year—use it or lose it, or it can designate funding as multi-year, or place no time restrictions on the spending. They must then find ways to fit multi-year commitments into a cash-based budget format. This turns our reporting and budgeting into elaborate Rube-Goldberg contraptions that stymie quick and clear understanding. What an extraordinary headache for the accountants!

A list of the appropriations bills, their status and links to their content is available at Thomas Legislative Information on the Internet. Go look at one of the bills and let us know how long it takes you to figure out how much is being spent on what. If you can find any way to figure this out in less than 15 minutes let us know, please, at GreatDemocracy.org.

CONFUSION: authorized and/or appropriated?

In October 2006 Congress passed an authorization bill for a $7 billion fence along the Mexican border.

"It's one thing to authorize. It's another to actually appropriate the money," said Senator John Cornyn (R-Texas)

Also note that programs can be *authorized* and then NOT funded. Politicians sometimes use confusion over authorization and *appropriation* to mislead their constituents. They can blow their horn for authorizing a program and then refuse to appropriate funds. For example, on March 31, 2004, Washington Post columnist George F. Will wrote an article echoing the administration's defense against accusations of unpreparedness on 9/11; he credited the Bush II administration for "authorizing a quadrupling of spending for covert action against al Qaeda" before 9/11. In fact no additional funds were appropriated for anti-terrorism activities until *after* 9/11.

Ask your Congressperson to be clear and honest about authorizations and appropriations. Ask your favorite media to take the pledge to be clear in financial reporting, to clearly identify when money is authorized or appropriated, and to remind their audience of the difference every time they mention a bill so that everyone is clear.

5. Treasury credits accounts

Money is credited to Treasury Department accounts for each of the government departments receiving appropriations. The money appropriated by Congress is credited to one of about 30 major accounts, and several hundred lesser accounts at the Department of Treasury. Treasury, which falls under the administrative branch, serves as the master accountant.

6. Agencies spend & report

The President and all of the departments and agencies in the administrative branch of government are responsible for implementing taxing and program spending. Each department keeps its own set of accounts and Treasury acts as master banker, keeping another set of accounts for them.

Government departments can obligate the money by signing contracts, then actually write the checks over several years. There is a rush of contract writing in September before the end of the fiscal year, encouraged by the annual cash-based budgeting and reporting process.

Department comptrollers or private companies audit the books of each department and the audited books go to Treasury a few months after the end of the year.

7. Treasury consolidates and reports

The Treasury department gathers each agency's audited financial statements. Treasury reconciles each agency's reports with its own accounts for each agency, and then consolidates them into a consolidated financial report. To date, the reconciliation process requires billions of dollars in adjustments to make them match. ($11 billion in 2006 out of a combined total revenue of $3,125 billion– a .3% margin of error.)

Sometimes the agencies use their own unique report format that may take extra work to reconcile with Treasury's account format. There is work underway to create a standard set of accounts so that interdepartmental transfers will match up and so that Treasury accounts will match agency accounts. In 2002 this good idea was made into law and the effort funded–at what must be an inadequate level, since they are still working on it.

8. GAO audits and reports

All the agencies and Treasury fall under the administrative branch. As a check and balance on the administration's authority to handle the money, Congress has oversight authority, through the Government Accountability Office (GAO). As the investigative arm of Congress, it is charged with examining all matters relating to the receipt and disbursement of public funds.

The GAO is tasked with auditing the annual financial report of the U.S. Government in cooperation with Treasury and submitting the report to Congress.

The Financial Report is then published with statements from the Secretary of the Treasury, including *Management's Discussion and Analysis*, followed by the *Consolidated Financial Report*, and the *GAO's Audit Report* prepared by the Comptroller General. The Financial Report also includes sections on unaudited *Stewardship Information*, *Notes to the Financial Statements*, and some supplemental information. It all takes up about 170 pages.

GAO: The Government Accountability Office

The Budget and Accounting Act of 1921 (31 U.S.C. 702) established the GAO to independently audit Government agencies. Over the years, the Congress has expanded GAO's audit authority, added new responsibilities and duties, and strengthened GAO's ability to perform independently.

In 2004 the name was changed from the General Accounting Office to the Government Accountability Office, keeping the acronym, GAO.

The Comptroller General of the United States is the head of the GAO. The President with the advice and consent of the Senate appoints him for a term of 15 years. David M. Walker is our current Comptroller General. President Clinton appointed him in 1998 so he will serve until 2013. The Comptroller General has issued many interesting reports on the finances of the U.S. Government. Go to the GAO website at www. GAO.gov and click on Truth and Transparency or any of the Sustainability articles. One is titled, *"Facing Facts about America's True Fiscal Condition and Fiscal Outlook; the outlook is grim and will get worse unless we act soon."* Mr. Walker must feel like a dying canary in a coal mine because the media, the Congress and the public are not paying much attention to his observations. Let's change that.

9. Report to citizens

A simple, clear and comprehensible report to citizens is next to come. Let's take the kinks out of the flow of information on taxing and spending—from the budget through to the financial report.

Just a few simple changes can make an enormous difference; more people will understand the financial reports and our financial situation, and our public decisions can be grounded in good sense. It's easy. And, even if some of it is difficult, we can do it. We are a clever bunch.

The pipeline; taxing, spending and reporting flow:

1. The President submits a budget.

Congress passes laws:

2. **Budget Resolutions** set the parameters for tax collecting and spending.

3. **Authorization bill**s give permission to spend.

4. **Appropriation bills** provide the money.

5. **Treasury credits agency accounts** with their appropriation.

6. **Agencies spend and report** back to Treasury.

7. **Treasury reconciles** agency reports with its own accounts, consolidates all accounts and prepares a financial report.

8. The **GAO audits** (so far, it has only been able to attempt an audit) and prepares an audit report to accompany the Financial Report prepared by Treasury.

9. **The U.S. Government Financial Report is issued and presented to Congress and to the citizens.**

Recommendations for improvements follow in Part III.

Chapter Five

! IMPORTANT !

↓

More than one fund

You can understand our federal fiscal situation only when you understand fund accounting. The U.S. Government uses fund accounting to keep track of over 400 different funds. We set up a separate fund when there is a specific purpose for money collected in a distinct way.

Here are the major funds that require our full attention:

The Federal Operating Fund

The Federal Operating Fund is our annual spending money for government operations and for long-term investments in our infrastructure. First, the Operating Fund must cover mandatory previous spending commitments like interest payments, and other legal, contractual commitments. Then, the Operating Fund covers spending programs set up by law, such as food stamps. These programs count as "mandatory spending" because the number of people who qualify for payouts determines how much money must be spent. We are committed to a certain level of spending unless or until the laws that determine who and for what people qualify are changed.

However, unlike interest owed to the public, which is a legally binding contractual obligation, these "mandatory" spending commitments can be changed by new laws.

The remainder of the Operating Fund is for Congressional spending for annual operations and capital expenditures. When Congress has a choice about how much to spend without making or changing a law, spending is called "discretionary."

Operating Fund Income

Individuals who pay taxes to the federal government know that the federal government collects taxes from them in two major ways: income tax and payroll taxes. These taxes are collected on an individual's gross income (less a slew/slough of deductions). Personal income taxes and business profit taxes go into the Operating Fund and payroll taxes go to the Social and Medical Insurance Trust Funds (restricted funds).

Amounts are from the 2006:

2006 – 65%

Previous 4-year
Average – 70%

Trend: down

Individual income taxes - $1,046 billion

Sixty-five percent of the income for the Operating Fund comes from individual income taxes. Individuals are taxed on their gross income after taking deductions when they can. Income taxes are collected based on an elaborate code that takes about 30,000 pages to define. Now that is kinky—but, a topic for another discussion.

2006 – 22%

Previous 4-year
Average – 15%

Trend: up

Corporate profit taxes - $350 billion

Corporations also pay "income" taxes and now contribute 22% of the Operating Fund. Corporations are taxed on their net income, not their gross income. This means that they deduct all their expenses before they calculate their "income" tax obligations. Calling it a corporate profit tax, instead of a corporate income tax is more accurate and honest. Honesty builds understanding and leads to better decisions.

According to the GAO,[24] in 2003, 60% of U.S. corporations were doing so poorly that they were unable to contribute any share at all to support the national infrastructure—they simply paid no taxes whatsoever to the federal government. These corporations enjoyed the benefits of our tax-paid infrastructure for free. Some corporations even juggled the tax laws to net income *from* the federal government.

Of the corporations who did pay taxes, only 6% were doing well enough to contribute more than 5% of their profits. That means that, according to their tax returns, only 2.4% of *all* corporations were doing well enough that they contributed more than 5% of their *profits* in taxes. However, in November 2003, Business Week reported that "Corporate profits are on a tear; results soared in the 3rd quarter." This mismatch of market success with the dribble of corporate tax returns suggests that tax laws are overly friendly to corporations and/or that there is some degree of duplicity, dishonesty and an absence of civic virtue in the corporations who avoid tax contributions while reaping generous profits.

Marketplace sales and services–"Earned revenue"- $85 billion

In addition to income from taxation, another 5.3% comes in from government sales and fees for services in the marketplace. This revenue from marketplace transactions is called "earned revenue" by government departments and agencies. National Park Service fees, patent fees, and the sale of excess inventory (property, plant, equipment and land), broadband and offshore drilling leases are examples of marketplace transactions that are counted as "earned revenue."

2006 – 5.3%

Previous 5-year average – 4.9%

Trend: up

In 2006, total earned revenue was $244 billion (roughly $85 billion belongs to the Operating Fund and the remainder to restricted funds). Marketplace revenue is the third largest source of income for the Operating Fund. Some of this income is booked as income and some is booked as a credit on the expense side of the ledger. In 2006, for the first time in the "Table 1" of the Executive summary, the income that is booked as "earned revenue" on the *expense* side of the ledger appeared with income. That is helpful! Thanks Treasury/GAO. The proposed format in this book combines the earned revenue from the expense side and the earned revenue already on the income side, and includes them both as income–money coming in– since that is what it is. (Chapter 11)

Federal Reserve receipts - $30 billion

2006 – 1.9%

Previous 4-year average – 1.8%

Trend: down, then up

The Federal Reserve is a privately owned corporation with a unique relationship to our federal government.[24] Private parties own the shares in this central bank and they are guaranteed a fixed 6% return on their investment. Unlike shares in most businesses, shares in the Federal Reserve Bank cannot be used for collateral or traded on the open market. Also, shareholders do not have any say in the running of the Bank. Bank management is selected through a political process. Because of these anomalies, the Federal Reserve Bank states that it is *not* privately owned. This obfuscates a fundamental truth, which is that private parties are first at the profit trough of the central bank of the U.S. (Canada has a richly informative central bank website that puts the U.S. Federal Reserve's website to shame, and it notes that shares in the central bank of Canada are owned by the Canadian people–rather than private parties, as in the U.S.)

After private shareholders take their guaranteed cut, the U.S. Government receives the remainder of the profits made by the Federal Reserve Bank on its Operations.

Estate and gift taxes - $27 billion

2006 – 1.7%

Previous 4-year average – 2.1%

Trend: down

Less than two percent of the Operating Fund income comes from estate and gift taxes. Estate taxes tax *the inheritance* of a very tiny percent of the public—the offspring of people at the very top of the wealth range, who are asked to make a contribution in keeping with the extraordinary wealth dropping into their laps by virtue of their parentage. The people inheriting this wealth are being taxed *for the first time* on this income, which is coming to them, not on the basis of merit or hard work, but because of their parent's efforts. The sad picture of the small family farm on the auction block because of the "double taxation" of "death taxes" is a myth clothed with a scary name, used to manipulate gullible people into supporting the elimination of taxes on the *estates* of the ultra-rich.

Custom duties - $25 billion
The U.S. Government charges custom duties on the importation of various goods and services. This extra cost is passed on to retail buyers. The expectation is that higher duties will make foreign goods more expensive and that this will help protect American businesses in these markets from foreign competition.

2006 – 1.5%

Previous 4-year average – 1.7%

Trend – up, then down

Excise taxes - $25 billion
Another 1.5% of the Operating Fund comes from excise taxes– $24.5 billion in 2006. These are taxes on production (like tobacco, alcohol and firearms), and taxes on imports. (Another $49.6 billion in excise taxes were collected for restricted funds, and I have included them in the restricted fund accounts.)

2006 – 1.5%

Previous 4-year average – 2%

Trend – down

Other taxes and receipts - $13 billion
This category includes fines, penalties, interest and miscellaneous income.

2006 – .8%

Previous 4-year average – 1.2%

Operating Fund fairness principles
Individual income and corporate profit taxes, the primary sources of operating fund income, are based on fairness principals that, in theory, increase the percent of the share paid the greater your wealth. These tax schedules place a heavier burden on the wealthy—both as a flat number and as a proportion of their income and wealth. This fairness principle reflects a value encouraged by most world religions; give more when you have more; carry a heavier burden when you have a fleet of wagons and give the family on foot a helping hand.

2006 Operating Fund Income

	BOLD= billions	
Individual income taxes	**1,045**,700,000,000	65 %
Corporate profit taxes	**350**,000,000,000	22 %
Marketplace sales & services	**84**,800,000,000	5 %
Federal Reserve receipts	**29**,900,000,000	2 %
Estate & gift taxes	**27**,400,000,000	2 %
Custom duties	**24**,700,000,000	2 %
Excise taxes	**24**,500,000,000	1 %
Other taxes and receipts	**12**,900,000,000	1 %
"Unreconciled transactions"	**11**,000,000,000	0 %
TOTAL INCOME	$ **1,610**,900,000,000	100%

The Federal Restricted "Trust" Funds

The federal restricted funds are monies that are collected and used for specific purposes and which must be accounted for separately by law. Social Security, Medicare, Medicaid, Unemployment Insurance, Highway, Airway and government employee retirement pension accounts are all restricted funds, many bearing the name "Trust Fund." The money for these funds comes through specific taxes like FICA, unemployment, and the gas tax, or as program expenses like retirement benefits for government employees.

The Social Security Trust Funds (Old-age and Survivors Insurance Trust Fund and Disability Trust Fund–OASDI) and the Medicare Trust Funds are the largest of the restricted funds. They are funded primarily through payroll taxes. Payroll taxes are the 7.65% that comes out of the first $94,200 of your wages. Your employer is paying another 7.65% on top of your contribution, making the total of payroll taxes equivalent to 15.3% of your wages up to $94,200 (2006). Payroll taxes are paid into the restricted fund accounts for Social Security (12.4%) and Medicare Part A (2.95%).

Some of the revenues for other restricted funds are based on fees for use or premium rate tables. For example, taxes on gas and fuel fund the Highway Trust Fund and these taxes are flat rates per gallon of gas.

Restricted "Trust" Funds—fairness principles

The basic fairness principles underlying the restricted funds are quid pro quo and social contract insurance. Using the principle of quid pro quo, those who use the service, pay according to their use. Taxes on gasoline are an example of a simple use-based fairness principle; the more you use, the more you pay. Everyone pays a "fair share" regardless of their *ability* to pay; taxes on gasoline are simply part of the cost of driving a car.

The fairness principles of the social insurance funds, which are primarily funded through the collection of payroll taxes (FICA) are more complicated, reflecting our confusion about our goals, values and their purpose. In theory, social contract insurance principles dictate that in a given pool of people (in this case, wage income earners because people who earn income on investments do not contribute), the payout potential is divided between participants. For our social insurance funds, we do this dividing according to ability to pay (the size of your income), but put a cap on your taxable income. You pay a flat percentage (proportionate share) on your income up to a cap ($94,200), and all income thereafter is free of these taxes. This means that people making less than $94,200 contribute *proportionately* more.

The rationale is that benefits paid out for the Social Security portion of the FICA tax are also capped; once eligible, everyone collects Social Security benefits, regardless of need, on a graduated scale, based on what they put into the system. The leading principle is that you should get out according to what you contribute–quid pro quo–with a smattering of proportionality and a smattering of according to need. While the Old Age & Survivors Insurance Trust Fund started out as a those who have, pay, and those who need, draw benefits, it has increasingly become a quid pro quo (I get out according to what I put in) system. This is a step backward in terms of human moral development.

People who earn up to $94K per year in wages pay 7.65% of their wages into the Social Insurance Trust Funds. When your wages surpass $94K, you do not contribute any percent of the wages over $94K to FICA. An executive making $10,000,000 is paying 7.65% on the first $94,200 of his wages - $7,206. He pays nothing more, so his total FICA burden is $7,206, the same as the person making a total of $94K per year. The man earning $10,000,000 is paying .07% while everyone making under $94,200 pays 7.65% of his or her wages.

In Finland, your fine for speeding more than 15 miles over the limit is according to your income. A Nokia executive paid $102,000 USD for a speeding ticket.

If we consider the purpose of fines punitive, then this makes sense. However, proportional equality is a more difficult concept than a flat "fee" for speeding that is paid by all, regardless of income.

Quid pro quo rationale does not apply to Medicare, Medicaid, hospital and drug benefits, which, if you meet requirements, are not subject to a cap (although specific services may be). We collect the Medicare, Medicaid and Hospital Insurance portions of our payroll taxes on a scale that is capped, but pay out according to need. This means that the people paying the full 7.65% on an income under $94K are paying a proportionately higher share of their income for these government services to the needy (and to those who qualify, but who are not really needy).

On a continuum of cognitive development, it is easier to consider fairness in terms of quantitative equality. It is more difficult to understand proportionate equality. On the scale of moral development the concept of quid pro quo comes earlier than the concept of giving according to your ability to those according to their need. That's why the world's religions work hard to teach the more mature concept of sharing your wealth–encouraging people to grow beyond self-interest.

The confusion in the values and principles underlying the social insurance restricted funds, reflects our general confusion about who we are as a community and the purpose of these funds. Are we a caring community that wants to provide safety nets for the needy, funded by those who are able to contribute? Is self-reliance our ultimate value, and everyone should look out for themselves? Should the government be in the business of operating a national pension fund or an insurance program?

Many more funds

There are 210 restricted and/or "Trust Funds" that are designated as significant funds by the agencies who manage them. In total there are about 400 funds tucked away into the consolidated report—impossible to see simply and clearly by form or function. There are about 270 federal funds whose spending is mandated or restricted, about another 70 whose funds are partially mandatory and another 31 funds, whose spending is completely discretionary. I have not yet found a simple list of all of the funds, their purpose and a simple, straightforward financial report for each. If you can find this, please let me know. This book can only address them in principle and take a look at the primary funds in a little more detail.

Summaries of the sixteen largest restricted funds are given in the U.S. Government Financial Report as of 2005 (and given for 2006 in Part I of this book).

Excellent leadership and management need to know whether these funds are collecting money for their mandated purpose and spending it as covenanted, or whether they are collecting more than they need and feeding the Operating Fund, or whether they are underfunded by their special funding mechanisms and drawing substantially from the Operating Fund. This information is lost when the funds are bundled with the financial reports of the agencies who manage their activities.

U.S. accounts track many funds:

- The general **Operating Fund** gets most of its revenue from individual income taxes, corporate profit taxes and sales and services in the marketplace. A share of the Federal Reserve Bank's profits, estate and gift taxes, excise taxes and custom duties each contribute less than 2% to the kitty.

- Hundreds of distinct funds collect specific revenues for restricted purposes. This book recommends calling these funds, "**restricted funds**."

Somebody scoffed, "Oh, you'll never do that
At least no one ever has done it"
But she took off her coat and she took off her hat
And the first thing we knew, she'd begun it. ...

You are the person who has to decide,
whether you'll do it or toss it aside;
You are the person
who makes up your mind,
whether you'll lead
or will linger behind,
whether you'll try
for the goal that's afar,
or just be contented
to stay where your are.

Edward A. Guest
(mostly)

Part III
Choose Excellence!
Improvements to the US government Financial Reporting

Part III:

Suggested Improvements to the U.S. Government Financial Reports

Take out the kinks:

- Remember that the greatest asset of the U.S. Government is the ability of taxpayers to contribute to the nation, not the government's power to tax its citizens.

- Use a consistent format for the budget and financial report or pay attention first to the financial report and second, the cash-based budget.

- Provide separate reports for separate funds.

- Book all the assets and all the debts.

- If it is income, book it as income.

- Tell the whole truth in the budget and tell the whole truth in the financial reports.

- A stand-alone financial report comes first.

- Be consistent.

Widen the pipes and increase the information flow:

- Note the change in the value of the dollar.

- Provide simple and comprehensive summaries.

- State the cost of borrowing.

This section explains these simple improvements that can take our reporting to clear, honest and comprehensible, and take our democratic practice from mediocre to great. Remember, if you disagree, say so at GreatDemocracy.org, so that together we can perfect a report format for citizens. If you agree, tell your lawmakers, today.

Chapter Six

Take the kinks out
of the information pipes

The opportunity of democracy lies in the flow of ideas from citizens to government and the flow of information back. The quality of this flow defines the quality and maturity of a democracy. We've got a lot of kinks in our information pipes that compromise the decisions that we make, compromise our democracy, and drain our resources. Some improvements are simple; they require a decision to make improvements—the intention to improve our democracy—and simple changes to our information systems. All the changes presented in the next few chapters are well within the scope of our skill sets—easy to do when we decide that improvements are important.

Imagine a factory with a big boiler that heats up water and then pipes the hot water into different parts of the factory for a manufacturing process. Your assignment is to reduce the amount of energy that the company is using so that costs are lower and profits are higher.

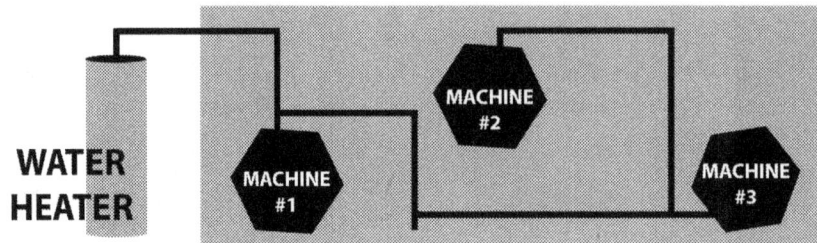

You might begin by checking each of the machines to see that they are properly maintained to use the hot water efficiently. You might check the insulation on the machinery to be sure that the water in the machines is staying hot. Each correction and efficiency out on the end use of the water will make a difference, but it will be a small, localized difference. If you improve the efficiency of one machine that uses 20% of the hot water piped into the factory by 10%, you get a total 2% improvement (10% of 20% equals 2%)—a little, but not a lot of improvement.

The biggest use of energy is the power used to heat the water and pump it through the factory. The greatest energy savings is possible at the front end of the factory's energy use. If you take the kinks out of the pipes at the source of the flow, and reduce the amount of energy needed to pump the water into the factory by 10%, you save the full 10%. If you shorten the distance between the water heater and the machines, you might save another 10% off the top.

When you are able to make change as close as possible to the beginning of a work flow, the change has the biggest impact. Eliminating the obstacles to flow and shortening the distance of travel, saves energy, saves money and increases profits.

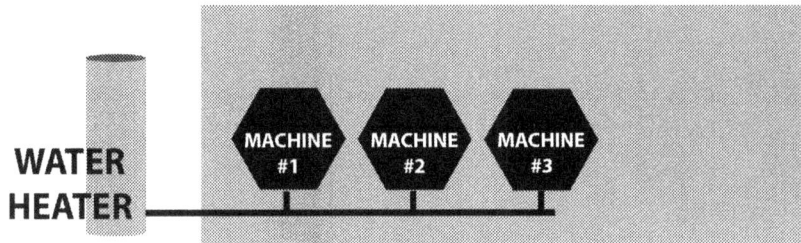

The closer you are to the source of the flow with your improvements, the greater the savings and greater the gain.

It is time to take the kinks out of our information pipes in public decision-making and lawmaking. Everyone gets busy advocating change out on the end of the decision-process—putting out what they see as fires. We argue that we are spending too much or too little on defense, on education, on environmental protection. When someone's throwing water on your ideas or projects, you turn up the heat. We end up with a lot of fire and water activity on specific issues that drains the energy out of our democracy.

When we focus on the points where information comes into the decision-making and problem-solving process, we can make dramatic change and reduce the amount of energy wasted in getting to good solutions. Let's take the kinks out and bring the information closer to citizens and lawmakers. Let's take the kinks out and make the information that we need to practice great democracy simpler, clearer, more honest and trustworthy. We can do it.

The biggest obstacle may just be habit. There is a classic story told at countless business seminars about the holiday ham. A young woman watches her father fixing the holiday meal. He takes the ham and slices the end off, puts it in his pan, adds the secret family sauce and sticks it in the oven. The daughter, who wants to learn the family recipes, asks why he cuts the end off the ham. Dad says that he does not know, but that is the way his mother did it, so that is the way he does it. The grandmother comes for the holiday dinner and dad and daughter ask her why she always cut off the end of the ham. She stares blankly for a moment and than says, "Because that is the only way it would fit in my roasting pan."

The lesson is that we often continue to do things out of habit or tradition, when they made sense at the time the tradition began, and may make no sense at all now. This is clearly true of our government financial systems.

Kinky financial information pipes

The financial reports of the United States Government are chock full of kinks in the path to clear, simple and honest communication. Some of these kinks in the path may have made sense when they were initially instituted. Some are the results of efforts to correct errors by adding caveats and explanations instead of getting to the root of the problem.

Today, if you read the 170 pages of the 2006 U.S. Government Financial Report, you will have some of the information that you need, you may also have some significant misperceptions about the state of the finances and the year's activities. Certainly, you will have a lot of questions. To fully understand 2006, it may help if you wait for the 2008 budget, which will have the actual budget numbers for 2006, read the 177 pages of this 2008 Budget, the 424 pages of Analytical Perspectives, and the 336 pages of Historical tables that accompany the President's Budget. However, you will need to keep in mind the difference between the accrual-based financial report and the cash-based budget. And, unless you are a wizard of government finance, you will still be scratching your head in some confusion about the state of our financial situation in 2006.

A significant chunk of the information accompanying both the financial report and the budget documents goes like this: We have this many apples. They are not really apples because they are orange citrus fruit that some people call oranges. We are calling them apples because we are required by law to do so. And, while we say they are in this basket, the "apples" are really in another basket, and for this section of the report we will call them "fruit," similar but not distinct from the "round objects" that we call them in another section. And, here are 10 pages that reconcile some of the differences that show up as you read through the reports, because we totaled the apples up as "apples" for one set of reports and totaled the "apples" up as oranges for another set of reports.

Here are a few samples...

> *Some of these (user charges) are collected by the Federal Government by the exercise of its sovereign powers and conceptually would appear on the receipts side of the budget, but are required by law to be classified on the spending side as offsetting collections or receipts.* 2006 Budget: Analytical Perspectives, p. 303

> *There is no substantive difference between trust funds and special funds or between revolving funds and trust revolving funds. Whether a particular fund is designated in law, as a trust fund is, in many cases, arbitrary.* 2006 Budget Analytical Perspectives, p. 372

> *The unified budget of the Federal Government is divided by law between on-budget and off-budget entities. The off-budget Federal entities conduct programs that result in the same kind of spending and receipts as on-budget entities. Despite its off-budget classification, this spending channels economic resources toward particular uses in the same way as on-budget spending. Off-budget spending and receipts are discussed in the following section on off-budget Federal entities.* 2006 Budget: Analytical Perspectives, p. 377

> *In the private sector, when costs exceed revenue it is called a loss; in the Federal accrual world, we call this the net Operating Cost.* (2005 USFR, p. 4)

I'm going to guess that half of the material in the 1,000+ pages of budget and financial report is explanation (that is certainly needed) of the bizarre and inconsistent definitions (kinks in the flow) of what could be clear information. Every time there is a kink in information flow that

Kinks in the flow of information make understanding exponentially more difficult.

takes several pages of explanation, understanding is made exponentially more difficult. When lawmakers and citizens make decisions without understanding the financial consequences, we are in trouble; our lives and livelihoods are at stake.

In 2005, The Government Accountability Office (GAO) added a 30 page supplement to the Financial Report called, *"Understanding the Primary Components of the Annual Financial Report of the United States Government"*—bringing the total number of pages up to 173 that year. This is a useful addition to the existing financial reports. They are to be thanked and commended for this effort to make the Financial Report easier to comprehend. However, the chart on page 28 of this supplemental report which maps *"How the Federal Government's Financial Statements Relate to One Another,"* (reproduced on the opposite page) shows how formidable keeping it simple can be.

We live in a sound bite world, so the press and pundits—and probably most of our lawmakers—grab a few of the numbers that stand out in the first tables and run with them. Public policy debate is not grounded in any real understanding of either our current financial situation or in the annual activities that change our financial situation. Lawmakers make decisions a bit as if they are evaluating a fashion designer's work by checking the attractiveness of her dry cleaner. With every hurdle to understanding, people, who might have solution ideas if they only knew the real nature of the problem, drop out.

In Spring 2005, Paul Volker, a former Chairman of the US Federal Reserve and Undersecretary of the Treasury, warned that there was a 75% chance of a major market crash within the next five years. At the same time, David M. Walker, Comptroller General of the United States, and an accountant by training, warned,

"I think the greatest threat to our future is our fiscal irresponsibility."

How the Federal Government's Financial Statements Relate to One Another

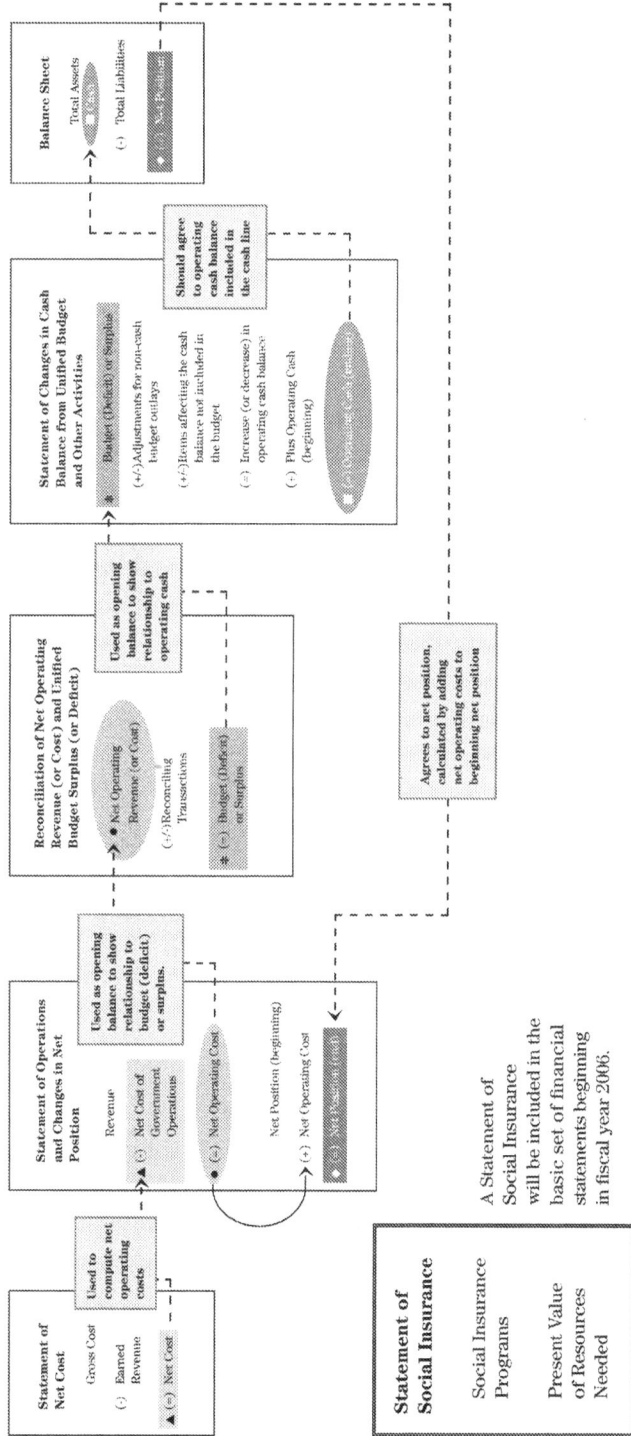

Statement of Net Cost

Gross Cost

(-) Earned Revenue

▲ (=) Net Cost

Used to compute net operating costs

Statement of Operations and Changes in Net Position

Revenue

(-) Net Cost of Government Operations

(=) Net Operating Cost

Net Position (beginning)

(+) Net Operating Cost

● (=) Net Position (end)

Used as opening balance to show relationship to budget (deficit) or surplus.

Reconciliation of Net Operating Revenue (or Cost) and Unified Budget Surplus (or Deficit)

● Net Operating Revenue (or Cost)

(+/-) Reconciling Transactions

= (=) Budget (Deficit) or Surplus

Used as opening balance to show relationship to operating cash

Statement of Changes in Cash Balance from Unified Budget and Other Activities

= Budget (Deficit) or Surplus

(+/-) Adjustments for non-cash budget outlays

(+/-) Items affecting the cash balance not included in the budget

(=) Increase (or decrease) in operating cash balance

(+) Plus Operating Cash (beginning)

■ (=) Operating Cash (ending)

Should agree to operating cash balance included in the cash line

Balance Sheet

Total Assets

(-) Total Liabilities

● (=) Net Position

Agrees to net position, calculated by adding net operating costs to beginning net position

Statement of Social Insurance

Social Insurance Programs

Present Value of Resources Needed

A Statement of Social Insurance will be included in the basic set of financial statements beginning in fiscal year 2006.

Source: GAO.

Mr. Walker went on to assert that 2004 may have been the most fiscally reckless in the history of our Republic. And, 2005 was worse. 2006 got a tiny bit better, but not enough to correct our path or to celebrate.

Fiscal responsibility requires understanding the financial situation and the financial impact of decisions. All of us can continue to argue positions—out there on the limbs of understanding—and some of these positions may be good ideas and some bad ideas. But, their value will be sheer chance, because until now very few arguments are grounded in any real comprehension of the financial situation of the U.S. Government and in the impact of each year's activities on the next year's financial position. It does not need to be this way. When we make the changes at the process and system level, we reduce the amount of effort, energy, cost and confusion that derail our decision-making. Creating simple, clear and honest financial reports is the first powerful change we can make that will have system-wide value.

Can do—tackle the numbers bugaboo

Many people take one look at numbers and head in the opposite direction. It does take a unique kind of mind to love a comprehensive and detailed financial report. The rest of us need the numbers presented in a useful format that suits our purposes.

Accountants, managers and leaders each look for different kinds of information from accounts.

Accountants and financial managers need a certain kind of information from financial reports; they need to know that all the entries are accurate, that the summaries include all transactions, and that safeguards prevent fraud and dishonesty. Accountants focus on the integrity of the numbers; they want to know if the numbers are true and trustworthy. It is not their job to attend to whether the management decisions that result in the numbers are good decisions.

Leadership and management look for a different kind of information from financial reports; executive management wants to know if the decisions that resulted in the current financial situation were the right choices and a strategic and functional fit with the intended goals. A CEO *starts* with relying on accurate and trustworthy numbers, and then focuses on what the numbers mean in relation to policy decisions. Executive management looks to understand whether actions have led to more or less success—have the goals been achieved with efficiency? This interpretation of the finances goes beyond the responsibility of the accountants and looks at the numbers from a different point of view.

Good professional leadership and management learn how to read formal financial reports; they learn to extract the information that they need to understand the financial situation so that they can make good decisions for the future. (We have CEOs who are paid gazillions annually, but claim that they do not understand the financial reports and activities of their own companies. However, these are examples of our worst, not our best corporate leadership.)

In a democracy, as citizens we are the board of directors that hires, fires and supports the management team. Since most of us are not professional accountants, how can we provide oversight and a check and balance on government? How can we understand the 170 page financial report and the 1,000+ pages of budget of the U.S. Government with any degree of comprehension? It is extremely difficult.

What can we do? Up until now, if you could not read and understand the lengthy reports, you were out of luck. Nearly all books, organizations and advocacy websites that aim to educate the public about taxing and spending priorities use the *cash*-based *consolidated* budget report summary, which is useful to an accountant, but not particularly useful to lawmakers and citizen managers. So all their hard work is built on a foundation that is off base because it leaves out a critical level of detail. And that confuses as much as it helps.

This book offers an alternative: a simple, honest and clear opportunity for every citizen to understand the numbers. It will also help those in Congress and in the executive branch who currently rely on someone else's understanding of the numbers because the full reports are too big, too boring and too difficult to comprehend.

Caveats

This book is as much about the questions as the answers.

Many books are the work of experts who have answers to share with the public. This book is about how to frame the questions and the answers, so that the answers are true, trustworthy, and fit our decision-making needs. Though I have extensive experience keeping small business accounts, framing productive discussion around contentious issues, and a handy background in the Montessori approach to teaching mathematics, I am not a certified public accountant.

The Financial Report in this book is a draft format. Add your comments and questions on the website greatdemocracy.org

This book contains a new draft format for the U.S. Government's financial report and some simple additions to the budgets and bills. The numbers in this book are mostly accurate, but not completely accurate for two reasons:

1) The numbers are from the U.S. Government's financial report, and the finances cannot pass an audit. The best that the Government Accountability Office (GAO) can do is to say that the numbers are mostly accurate, but may be "significantly and materially unreliable."

2) The format used in the report in Part One **separates** the Operating Fund from the restricted funds because that is the best way to give citizens and lawmakers the information they need to manage well. While this might be a simple, mouse-click task for government accountants, it is a formidable task for anyone who has to pick through thousands of pages of departmental reports to tweeze out the restricted funds from the Operating Funds. The 2006 Financial Report took a significant step toward making separate fund account activity clear, but I have still had to cut and paste from different sections of the financial report. So errors are possible.

Together we can collaboratively perfect the report format so that it will be in the best format for all of us. We can enroll enough citizens and lawmakers who care about honesty and clarity in government financial reporting to make simple, clear and honest reporting a reality.

In addition to the continuously improving consolidated format that serves our professional financial monitors in the GAO and Treasury Departments, we can have a simple, clear and honest format that serves leadership, lawmakers and citizens best.

In the meantime, the website, GreatDemocracy.org, invites citizens to track down the details tucked away in department reports and collaboratively we can build a totally accurate and comprehensive report in a format that is most useful to us. Let's build a website that makes it easy to find just the details that you want and to see them in full context.

Simple Improvements—big difference

The following section presents two basic types of improvements—improvements that take the kinks out of the information pipes, and improvements that widen the pipes so that information can flow more effectively. These improvements can give us clear and useful financial reports. Most of these improvements are easy to make and can transform our discussions about how to increase and preserve our national wealth.

These may not be the best improvements. You may know more or have better ideas. Please go to GreatDemocracy.org and weigh in. Add your thoughts to the collective memory and workspace on the website. When we have perfected the description of the improvements that we need in order to understand the finances fully, we can make it happen.

When we improve the way that we make decisions, all decisions will get better and outcomes will improve.

Chapter Seven

☞ **KINKY THINKING:**
"The power to tax is government's greatest asset" ☞

⇨ **TAKE OUT KINK #1:**

Think asset = ability to pay

We have a big kink in our thinking. A simple and powerful assumption is derailing effective decision-making: the idea that government's greatest asset is its power to tax. We will look for smarter solutions, make better public decisions and get better results when we recognize that the *ability* of taxpayers to contribute a fair share to the nation is our greatest asset. Changing the focus from power to tax, to ability to pay will be profound.

Thinking that power is our greatest asset leads to bigger equals better, and attention to growth and size. Thinking that our ability to pay taxes is our greatest asset leads to smarter equals better, and attention to substance and quality.

Until now...

Until now, the U.S. Government has considered its *power to tax* to be its greatest asset:

> *The U.S. Government's most important financial resource, its ability to tax and regulate commerce, cannot be quantified and is not reflected [in the Financial Report].* 2001 USFR, p. 9

The Government's most significant asset is its power to tax, which is not valued in an accounting sense. 2002 USFR, p.6

It is important to note that the balance sheet excludes the Government's sovereign powers to tax, regulate commerce, and set monetary policy....Because of its sovereign power to tax and borrow, and the country's wide economic base, the Government has unique access to financial resources through generating tax revenues and issuing Federal debt securities. This provides the Government with the ability to meet present obligations and those that are anticipated from future operations and are not reflected in net position. 2005 USFR, p. 34

It is important to note that the balance sheet does not include the financial impact of the Government's sovereign powers to tax, regulate commerce, and set monetary policy. 2006 USFR, p.16

By 2006, the statement has been softened and stated more obliquely, but it carries the same thought—the power to tax is the most significant asset. The statement about the "greatest asset is the power to tax" is not a partisan statement; it is a boilerplate assumption that is expressed in all of the financial reports issued by Presidents Clinton and Bush II through 2006. (And remember, there were no consolidated and comprehensive financial reports prior to 1997.)

When power is the prized asset, the size of the pie is the key

If government's most important financial resource is its power to tax, then government can look to the size of the economy to measure its appropriate and potential share. All you have to do is look to see how big the whole pie is, the Gross Domestic Product (GDP), and you can gauge how big a slice government can safely take.

The 2006 statement goes further to state that because government can tax and create money out of thin air, the future is in good stead. Government is assured a slice of the pie because it has the power to take it or create it. Keep the size of the pie growing and you can keep government's slice growing to match. There is no need to consider spending smart...just ask, "Is the economy growing bigger?" "Can our spending be sustained?"

And, that is just what we do; when we talk about government spending, most of the attention is on size—the size of spending, the size of government and the size of the economic pie out of which government takes its slice.

Pie size and sound bites

The financial report of the U.S. Government gets very little airtime and tends to be presented in sound bites. Therefore, the crucial summary reports need to give us the best and most important information. The first and foremost current financial report and Table #1 of each budget present the federal spending and the federal overspending *as a percentage of the Gross Domestic Product (GDP)*, as if that is the most critical number that we should be watching. Making the relationship between government *over*-spending and the GDP the most important piece of information promotes the assumption that as long as we can keep growing that economy, government can keep grabbing its share, so everything is all right.

Following government's lead, public conversations are about the size of the pie and government's slice

Type in "big government" on Google and you'll get 212 million entries. Type in "small government" and you'll get 297 million. Now try "smart government" and it drops to 63 million (9/2007). The same applies to the economy. Look for articles and listen for discussion about growing a bigger economy and you will be overwhelmed. Every night on the news we are told whether the economy is getting bigger, represented by the increase in the GDP. Getting bigger is supposed to be good. You will have a hard time finding any discussions about creating a *smarter* economy.

People who think the power to tax is the greatest asset of government, are asking, "Is this level of overspending sustainable?" "Is the economy going to be big enough so that we will be able to get the needed principle and interest and annual operating money out of future taxpayers?" "What percent of the GDP is government spending?" "Is Government's share of the GDP within historical bounds?"

Here are some examples...

However, Bush administration officials noted that the 2003 deficit represented just 3.5 percent of the country's total economic output...The administration prefers to link the deficit to total economic output as a better measure of the country's ability to carry the debt burden. CBS New, 10/20/03

Economists say the fairest way to measure deficits over time is to compare them with the size of the economy, the gross domestic product. The projected deficit this year, 4.2% of GDP, is not the biggest in recent history, but it is close to some of the largest in the Reagan and first Bush administrations. USA Today, 1/26/04

... the 2005 deficit of $319 billion, when expressed as a percent of Gross Domestic Product, was lower than the deficits in 16 of the last 25 years. 2005 USFR, Message from Secretary of the Treasury

(Please note that these statements refer to the *cash-based consolidated budget* deficit, not to an accrual-based real total spending projection or to the accrual-based total spending stated in the financial reports. Remember "deficit" is another way to say overspending.)

In addition to the disadvantages of thinking bigger instead of smarter, our current measure of success, the GDP, is, at best, a minimally useful measurement of our total economic activity. It leaves out the underground economy, productive but unpaid work, and all illegal activity. Costly crisis management is valued over cheaper prevention when growing the GDP is the measure of success. My local paper carried a happy story in the business section about the "booming cancer therapy" business. Wahoo! Love that increasing incidence of cancers that requires expensive therapy–it sends the GDP soaring!

Comparing a cash-based budget deficit to the GDP, instead of comparing the true annual cost stated in the accrual-based financial report is of questionable use.

Yet, the first few tables in the President's Budget, do just that.

The accrual-based overspending in 2005 was $760 billion!

Have you or a loved one had your GDP growth enhancing cancer yet? Odds are, you will have your turn.

The size of the economy does matter—but it is secondary to smarter and better. The size of the economy and projections for the future can be used to substantiate forecasts of potential income for government. However, making the size of the economy and the size of government the primary focus, takes our attention away from creating a smarter economy and smarter government in which the burden of taxation rests lightly on the citizenry. Focusing on growing bigger also takes our focus away from prudent management of long-term obligations. After all, if the economy is going to grow bigger, then government's income is going to grow bigger. So, why worry about that borrowing and using pension and insurance income for operations today. Tomorrow there will be a bigger pie to slice and dice.

Fundamental flaws in thinking

It does not matter how much power you have to tax if the people who pay taxes have little income with which to pay them. The power to tax does not matter if the tax burden is forcing your workforce to choose between food, healthcare and taxes. A sick and sleepless workforce is less productive.

It does not matter how powerful your pump is, if the well is dry. The size of the GDP/economy is not a clear reflection of the ability of citizens to support their government or support a high quality of life for all Americans. There can be a lot of dollars moving around in the GDP and it can all belong to a tiny few, be nontaxable corporate spending, nontaxable capital gains, nontaxable illegal or underground economic activity.

In a dictatorship, the power to tax may be an asset. However, in a functioning democracy, the power to tax is simply a tool; it is not an asset. In a great democracy, we will pay attention to how smart our economy is growing, instead of how big.

Different perspective—different discussion

It is important to shift our thinking about assets–which is currently enshrined in the way that we keep accounts and report on our financial situation–because how you think about government assets frames our entire discussion about taxation, spending, the importance of growing our economy, and what constitutes good government. The focus on government power as an asset—power to make people do things whether they want to or not, by the will of the majority or the will of those with the most money to buy agreement in Washington—leads to tangled tug-of-wars over who has the most power behind their fixed and resolute positions. Who wins and who loses is the fodder for discussion, rather than addressing the issues. Discussion and debate is about winning your position or paying off your supporters, not about finding solutions that work best.

Smart government does not have to be an oxymoron. With the right systems in place, government can aggregate our highest wisdom and we can take our democracy from mediocre to great. Smart government will always trump big or small government. Smart spending will beat small spending or big spending every time.

Government's greatest asset equals citizen's ability to pay

Change your thinking: The ability of U.S. citizens to pay is the asset, not the ability of the government to tax. The ability of citizens to pay is dependent on the quality of our lives. Quality of life depends on the abundance and sustainability, cleanliness and healthiness of our living environment. Our earning ability and productivity are dependent on the educational and experiential richness of our culture and the power of our economy. The power of our economy depends on a strong infrastructure of natural, human, manufactured, social and financial resources.

When citizens' abilities to contribute to the common good are the assets, investment in the future is the key.

When you think that the ability of citizens to pay is the greatest asset of government, you will be asking, "Are we spending wisely and investing in the future so that citizens are better able to pay taxes *and* government costs can be reduced? How big we are growing the economy becomes of secondary concern. Different questions get different answers, some more useful than others. We will have a much more useful and productive discussion about how the government is doing when we make this simple change in our thinking. While the ability of citizens to pay cannot be fully valued in an accounting sense, we know the value of education and health and we have measured the costs of disease, disability, poverty, grief, and other stressors. We know how important our infrastructure is to business and consequently to our citizens' productivity and their consequent ability to pay taxes.

When we are ready to pay attention to the ability of Americans to contribute taxes, we will develop systems to book all of our assets, including the intangibles that constitute our ability to contribute to the common good. (See Chapter 10)

When you hear politicians and reporters talk about the government's budget deficit as a percent of the GDP, call them. Ask them to *first* report on how wisely they spent the taxes that were collected: What did they achieve for the common good? Ask them to report on the values and priorities demonstrated by their spending. How successful were their spending choices in building up our national assets—human assets, natural assets, manufactured assets and financial assets? How do they know that they have been successful? What are their standards of measure?

Developmental mindset—we learn and mature

Why do we think size is power and bigger is better? This thinking is set in our reflex brain and is a stage of cognitive development. As Richard Conniff notes in his delightful book, *The Natural History of the Rich*

(2002), we are programmed on our most basic animal level to pay attention to size, hence puffery and peacock tails abound. And, because our most basic nature will always subconsciously pay attention to size, size does bestow some real power. However, we can grow our ability to think beyond this basic aspect of our nature into a higher stage of human development, even though the inclination to perceive bigger as better will remain with us.

There is a classic test that is given to young children to measure cognitive development. Two identical glasses are filled with two different colors of liquid and presented to a child who is asked which glass has more liquid. At an early age, a child can recognize that the glasses have the same amount because they look the same.

In the experiment, the liquid from one of the glasses is poured into a taller, skinnier glass in which it rises to a higher apparent level. The child is asked again which glass has more liquid. At about three years of age, most children will point to the taller, *bigger looking* glass. Even if you pour the same water back and forth between the two different glasses, a young child cannot hold on to the idea of the same amount of water, and will continue to tell you that the glass that looks bigger, has more water. Focusing on the appearance of size represents a developmentally early perception of value.

Somewhere between four and six years of age, children's brains develop and they can hold onto the idea of constancy and relative size. Children will then watch you pour in the same amount of water, and despite the difference in appearance in the different glasses, they will know that the amount of water is the same.

Our reflex brain may always look at big size and think better. We must train and practice and deliberately call on our higher thinking capacities to see beyond bigger to smarter, deeper and more complex expressions of value. Let's demonstrate our ability to move up to a higher level of value measurement when looking at our financial situation. We currently view our economy and financial situation from the developmental perspective of the three-year-old: if it looks bigger, it must be better. And this creates the window through which we view our financial reports; we look to see if the economic pie is growing bigger so that government's slice of the pie can continue to grow, too.

While growing bigger is natural, it is wise to remember that ceasing to grow bigger and growing smarter is also natural—as is dying. Childish awe of the BIG and faith in infinite growth may lead to an early financial demise.

Growing up from thinking bigger to thinking better

When we shift our assumption from government's greatest asset is its power and ability to tax, to government's greatest asset is the ability of citizens to contribute to the common good, we will be looking for smart spending instead of big or little spending. We will look at the financial report of the U.S. Government and use it to assess how we can achieve a smarter and better government and a smarter and better nation.

When we change our assumptions,
> ⇨ we change our thinking, which will
> ⇨ change the quality of our discussions, and
> ⇨ improve the quality of our decision-making, leading to
> ⇨ better outcomes.

Change our assumption from government's greatest asset is its power to tax, to

Government's greatest asset is the ability of its citizens to contribute to the common good.

Change our public policy discussions from, "Are we growing a bigger economy?," to

"Are we growing a smarter economy?"

Chapter Eight

☞**KINK IN THE FLOW OF INFORMATION:**
Cash-based budget - *Accrual-based* Financial Report ☜

⇨ **TAKE OUT KINK #2 :**

Be consistent or PAY ATTENTION !

My mother subscribed to several health newsletters and we had recently been reading about signs of heart problems in women. The signs are different and sometimes less obvious than in men. One sign is a sudden change in vision.

We have a sofa in the living room where we read and nap. My mother woke from an afternoon nap one day, put on glasses she had set aside for her nap, and went back about her business. She noticed that while she could see perfectly well at a distance, her reading vision was seriously impaired.

We worried and talked and finally called the emergency nurse for her health provider. The nurse suggested that we head for the emergency room. It was after office hours—isn't it always, when you have an emergency!

We waited for hours and finally the doctor did a thorough review, checking for mental sharpness and checking her vision and vital signs for heart or brain trouble.

The doctor said that she could not find any problem and suggested that Mother call her eye doctor the next day.

By now it was after 11:00 p.m. We went home and began to get ready for bed. Mother got out her dental floss and as she looked at herself in the mirror, she noticed that her glasses looked odd. The frames were brown wire instead of red wire. She puzzled for a moment before realizing that she had picked up my reading glasses instead of hers when she got up from her nap. Relief made us laugh until we were crying.

There is a lesson here: Mother and I both failed to notice that she was wearing the wrong glasses. The nurses and doctor failed to ask if she were sure she was wearing the right glasses. Many service desk personnel in the electronics field have learned this lesson; when people call in to say something is not working, they are trained to ask first if the appliance is plugged in. Sometimes the fix is blindingly simple.

Sometimes the fix is blindingly simple!

When it comes to understanding the financial situation of our nation and our government, the first thing we have to do is make sure we have the right glasses on our collective nose. We can have all the best information in the world in plain sight, but if no one *puts on the lenses required to see it*, it will make no difference in our decision-making.

How we see it now

The 2006 U.S. Government Financial Report describes a deficit of $248 billion. The same report also describes a net operating cost of $450 billion. Both of these figures refer to costs that we did not have revenues to cover. If we want to keep our glasses on and our eyes on the ball, which ball should we be watching? There is a big difference in the size of those balls.

When it comes to overseeing the financial situation and financial choices of our government, we are wearing the wrong glasses and watching the wrong ball nearly all the time. How often did you see the $450 billion net operating cost figure in 2006? Every single headline that I could find reported on the $248 billion budget deficit. The difference between $450 billion and $248 billion is $202 billion in very real costs—hiding in plain sight, and off the discussion table. In 2005 the difference was a whopping $441 billion.

We currently have two major ways of looking at the U.S. Government's financial situation and actions:

2005
Cash-based budget deficit (overspending): **$319 billion**

Accrual-based financial report overspending: **$760 billion**

Difference: **$441 billion**

1. Cash-based Budget and Budget Report

The Budget is cash-based and therefore leaves out all the past and future commitments. The $248 billion 2006 deficit is from the cash-based budget report. The Budget is intended to project what will be coming in and to plan how it will go out in an up-coming year. The Budget Report comes out at the end of the year to report on how actual spending matched the cash-based budget. Neither a cash-based budget, nor a cash-based budget report is intended to provide a long-term or fully comprehensive view because it leaves out all the spending commitments from the past and for the future. Cash-based budgets and budget reports are manager's tools for looking at a discrete block of money for a one-year block of time.   Cash-based multi-year projections add some depth, but do not offer the full picture that multi-year accrual projections could provide.

2. Accrual-based Financial Report

The Financial Report is accrual-based and therefore includes past and future commitments.   Accrual-based information shifts the focus of attention away from money-in-money-out reporting to long-term outcome or results reporting. That is a critical shift for any business, agency, organization or government that wants to survive into the future. Since 1997, we have had an accrual-based consolidated financial report for the U.S. Government–a step in the right direction.

The negative $450 billion net (2006) is from the consolidated, accrual-based financial report. When you count what we committed to spend in 2006, we spent $202 billion more than the cash-based budget shows. Here is the income, expense and net difference between the 2006 consolidated cash-based budget for managers and the accrual-based financial report for long-term leadership:

US Government 2006 Consolidated Totals

Cash-based		Accrual-based	
BUDGET		**FINANCIAL REPORT**	
Income	2,406,700,000,000	Income*	2,678,200,000,000
Expense	2,654,400,000,000	Expense	3,127,700,000,000
NET $	**- 247**,700,000,000	**NET** $	**- 449**,500,000,000

*Includes an $11 billion oops-there's-extra-income, called, "unreconciled transactions."

And, the difference is: **$202**,000,000,000 – that's $202 **billion**!

The $202 billion difference between the budget and financial report consists of obligations we incur in this year, but which will be paid for in the future. These obligations include federal employee retirement benefits, veterans' compensation, deterioration (depreciation) of our assets, and liabilities incurred for environmental cleanup costs.

The cost of care for veterans and the cost of government employee pensions and post-retirement health care *in the future* is part of the cost of *today's* government; these are real costs that we incur. The retirement and veterans' benefits are long-term commitments. The projected future cost may change as interest rates, life expectancies and other factors go up and down. For this reason, these liabilities for future costs are re-visited and adjustments are made to the books each year to accommodate revised assumptions. These revisions constitute updates to our best estimates of real future expenses and the change in a liability must be booked as either new income or new expense. Prudent leadership pays attention.

The cash-based budget ignores clean-up responsibilities until we pay to do the work, and ignores depreciation until we pay for repairs or replacements. The budget report pretends that these real costs for today's operations do not exist. The financial report puts these costs on the books—as it should. Doesn't this sound like a more grown-up approach to responsibility?

Public discussion now

We currently center our thinking, discussing, debating, dialogue and decision-making on the cash-based budget. This is true of our leadership, true of our media, true of nearly all our public discussions. In the U.S. Government, our executive team is focused primarily on managing year-to-year operations with very little leadership attention going to the comprehensive and long-view of a true executive—either in Congress or in the executive branch. How can we tell? We can tell because all they talk about is the budget. Talking cash-based budget is management talk. Talking accrual-based financial report is oversight executive talk.

Have you ever heard a president give an address on the financial report numbers instead of the budget? Has your lawmaker addressed his/her constituents on the state of the United States Government's finances (not just the budget deficit)? Did your local paper run a summary of the U.S. Government Financial Report when it was issued in December?

Our President and Congress are still thinking, talking and deciding from the mindset of cash-in, cash-out small-time project managers, with their eyes on the cash-based budget.

> *The focus of the budget of the United States is by agency...Budgets are prepared, defended and monitored by agency.* 2005 USFR, p. 31

Until now, the President has tied his vision to the budget rather than to the financial report—so it is the vision of a manager, not the vision of a leader.

> *Receipts and outlays in the President's budget are measured primarily on a cash basis and differ from the basis of accounting measures used in the financial report.* 2004 FR, p. 56

Congress reviews, revises and approves the cash-based budget and makes cash-based appropriations. So, Congress is also functioning in the managerial role.

The newspaper headlines and the public discussion never get past the first consolidated summary in the cash-based budget reports, so citizen-taxpayers are misled. Think of the headlines about the deficit, which is just another way to say overspending covered by new debt:

> *President Bush today will propose a 2007 federal budget...Bush's plan assumes a budget deficit of about $423 billion this year.* USA Today, 2/9/06

> *Federal budget deficit sparks worries. Higher borrowing costs could slow economic activity...The government's budget deficit last year was $319 billion. While smaller than the record $413 billion in 2004, it still was the third highest ever.* MSNBC, January 15, 2000

> *Record '05 Deficit Forecast; War Costs to Raise Total to $427 Billion.* Washington Post, January 26, 2005

Type deficit into a search engine and see if you can find *any* report that gives the accrual-based financial report net, instead of the cash-based budget deficit. Look to see if any of the reports on the budget deficit note that this is a cash-based deficit and that it does not include all the spending commitments made for the year.

The President, Congress and the media all pay attention to the budget reports and their resulting numbers, so it is reasonable to assume that the President, Congress and the press all see themselves in the role of managers.

With our collective focus on the cash-based budget, we are playing a dangerous game of out-of-sight-out-of-mind. We pretend that these costs that we incur today and must pay tomorrow do not require our full and immediate consideration. There is simply no way to have productive dialogue, debate, deliberation and decisions when $200-400 billion is out of the picture and off the discussion table.

The 2006 USFR Executive Summary includes this heading:

Two Sets of Books? - - Absolutely Not - - Comparing the Financial Report to the Budget Deficit.

This section goes on to say,

> *The Financial Report has as its base ALL the transactions that form the budget results. Adjustments to convert costs and revenues from the cash basis to the accrual basis are shown in the Statement of Reconciliations of Net Operating Cost and Unified Budget Deficit in this report. The amounts itemized on this statement are intended to represent the difference between the two bases for reporting. There is no magic, no sleight of hand; just cost accruals to adjust for the time of the cash outlay versus the portion of non cash-based attributable to the current period.*

"Absolutely Not." "No magic, no sleight of hand." This is disingenuous. In order to produce a cash-based report, you have to have accounts that reflect a cash-based perspective. In order to produce an accrual-based report, you have to have accounts that reflect an accrual-based perspective. One, two. As they themselves note, they have "*two* bases for reporting." Yes, they are related and the relationship is documented and reported. However, an accrual-based financial report and a cash-based budget report *do* represent two different accounting and reporting systems.

Bold-faced falsehoods are not helpful. Saying black is white loudly and often will not make it true.

A choice: see at the highest power

We have a choice—a more difficult option that would be most effective long term and a quick-and-simple option: 1. We can switch to full accrual accounting, budgeting and reporting; or, 2. We can keep doing what we are doing, but give appropriate attention to the accrual-based financial report.

Remove a huge kink:

Use ONE system of accounting for both budgeting and reporting.

Option #1 – All accrual-based

We can follow the leadership of astute business (and several countries that are far ahead of us...Australia, New Zealand, the UK) and shift to full accrual accounting, budgeting and reporting. This offers many advantages. Foremost, it takes out the enormous kink in the financial information pipes right at the very beginning of the flow of information, which is created by using two different accounting formats. Equally important, accrual budgeting supports more mature, long-term, full-picture thinking. Leadership can step into a more prudent and responsible role and act for long-term success, avoiding many of the dangers of short-term thinking.

All-accrual: remove a big kink in the flow of information

Reconciling is hard and confusing work. It takes hundreds of pages of notes to explain and reconcile the differences between the present financial report and the budget numbers. Every single explanation of why numbers do not match increases the potential for misunderstanding.

Many people who need to know, drop out before they understand all the information they need in order to make good decisions.

All accrual: remove the potential for error

In 2006, in order to reconcile the budget deficit result of $248 billion to the financial report net operating cost of $450 billion, Treasury had to enter a net $.8 billion "All other reconciling items" (formerly called, "net amount of all other differences") to force the statements into balance. This is an improvement, and an improving trend. (2005: $4.8 billion, 2004: $-3.4 billion, 2003: $23.2 billion.) The four year average is $8 billion per year. This is roughly the equivalent of finding your checkbook off $8 for every $3,000 in monthly income.

Is this an acceptable standard for the world's biggest government? Do you suppose that big banks and businesses are writing off $8 billion in accounting errors for every $3,000 billion in transactions? It seems unlikely. Is there any good reason why our government is functioning at this low standard? I can't help thinking of those duffle bags of cash the government was handing out in Iraq with little or no paperwork (and the medal given to the man responsible) and think that we can surely do better.[25]

Using a consistent accrual-based accounting method throughout the budgeting and reporting process would go a long way toward eliminating the potential for error. We will go a long way toward simplicity, clarity and honesty when we use the same type of accounting for all steps of budgeting, spending and reporting. The process of oversight and accountability will be measurably stronger.

All accrual: support mature, long-term, full-picture thinking

You only get the long-term full picture with accrual accounts. Cash accounts only work for a day-to-day/ year-to-year perspective. We have been supporting a public decision-making system that thrives on the pathos and bathos of crisis management funding—what some special interest needs NOW! Cash-based, short-term thinking systemizes and institutionalizes get-me-through-the-next-election thinking, and that does not serve the best interests of the country.

We can choose to grow our system up; we can choose to institutionalize more mature thinking. Switching to an all accrual-based financial accounting, budgeting and reporting system would be a first step.

All accrual : make long-term planning easier

When we want to make multi-year commitments to major infrastructure investments using a cash-based, agency focused annual budget, it requires confusing loop-de-loops of convoluted accounting and reporting. Switching to an accrual-based budget that matches the financial reports could eliminate this confusion, too.

With an accrual-based budget, we could see at a glance what commitments have been made for the future and we could make plans for the best ways to shoulder these future burdens.

All accrual: galvanize effective, responsible and prudent leadership

In the government of the United States of America, who is minding the store for future prosperity?

In a democracy, citizens function as the board of directors; we have ultimate oversight and bottom line responsibility. We elect a president and Congress to share the responsibilities of chief executives and operational leadership; we call upon our elected leadership to work for the greater long-term good, and to appoint effective people to manage the day-to-day, year-to-year operations of government well. Unfortunately, up until now, few have answered the call to long-term oversight and leadership; most of our elected officials are mired in the short-term interests of a cash-based budget process, therefore no one is in the executive leadership and oversight role. We, the citizen board of directors, are out of the loop because only a tiny few read and understand the 170-page financial report. Besides a few chirping canaries, no one is paying attention in a broadly noted and systemic way to the big picture, the long view, the comprehensive whole, the relationship of the parts to each other and the larger systems. The financial report is issued largely without comment in the press or public dialogue.

Perhaps it is a matter of maturing, and as a nation, we are just not quite there, yet. This means that we have an opportunity to learn and mature today and tomorrow. Energy and expert guidance will follow our intention to improve.

All-accrual: avoid the dangers in a cash-based mindset

Cash-based budgeting encourages government agencies to take the short-view. They are focused on spending the cash-in-hand, rather than focused on outcomes and on achieving the long-term mission. Agencies and programs protect the size of their annual allotment, by spending every cent before the year is up to demonstrate their need. The system does not encourage agency heads to plan for the long-term. We systemize immature and irresponsible spending with cash-based budgeting.

Since cash budgeting focuses on this year's cash income and expense, there is a temptation to think in terms of *how big a payment can I cover* with my current income, with little thought to total cost, to the future or to net worth. This immature, irresponsible and imprudent fiscal management culture exists in the public and private sector and has been seriously escalating in recent years. Our leadership models behavior, and that behavior echoes in the general public. The last six years have been a travesty for both public and private fiscal responsibility.

Following a five-year pattern, in 2006 the government Operating Fund spent $1.6 trillion, 39% more that we gave it to spend for operations, and government debt soared to over $10 trillion to support the overspending. Private sector numbers for 2005 show that Americans spent $41.6 billion more than we earned. To support private overspending both individuals and businesses sold off assets to foreign nationals and the nation's personal savings rate sank to -.5% for the first time since 1933. In the private sector, debt increased in part by refinancing mort-

From 2002-2006, the Bush II administration spent, on average, 158% of its operating income.

gages to take out equity. In 2005, 80% of refinanced mortgages took out a total of $243 billion in cash to spend.[26] In many U.S. housing markets, 20-70% of houses have been purchased with interest only loans that allow people to buy more house for a lower monthly payment—for the first few years.[27] People have been encouraged to think only in terms of their current income and how big a house payment it will allow them to make.

Saint Peter,
don't ya call us,
'cause we can't go,
we owe our soul
to...

People who succumb without due thought for the future are going to be hammered by predictably rising interest rates, predictably higher heating and transportation costs, and the switch to paying interest *and* principle, which will hit them three to five years after they took out the mortgage. Many will not be able to stretch their budget to cover the additional costs. The Continuously-rising Housing Price Fairy may come for some of these people and save their bacon—but not for all of them. This outcome is predictable, making a national economic meltdown not only possible but likely.

National leadership models behavior which echoes throughout the nation; when WE-our government focus on cash-based budgeting, and spend everything that we think we can get away with each year, we may also be hammered by rising energy, transportation, health care and interest costs. This outcome is also predictable, and increases the possibility of an abrupt collapse of our financial system. We are counting on a Faith-based, Sound-dollar, Increasing-GDP Fairy to come and keep us afloat. It may happen, but in our increasingly global economy, it is a high-risk bet.

Option #2
Pay attention to the financial report!
We can keep on the same path we are on, improving the accrual-based financial reports and their integration with a cash-based budget, and simply, **PAY ATTENTION TO THE FINANCIAL REPORT!** This is a simple thing to do without shaking up our entire system of budgeting.

Shifting our focus to see the U.S. Government Financial Report *first and foremost* is the foundation of good oversight and leadership. The tools are at hand to perform annual managerial duties, *and* to maintain long-term oversight and leadership. If we want a great democracy—a government of the people, by the people and for the people—then the people have to pay attention to the financial report of the United States Government, because that is where the information for the chief executive officer and the board of directors is found.

Chief executives and boards of directors must pay attention to the financial report or their business will flounder. A cash-based budget and an accrual-based financial report can both be important documents as long as one keeps in mind that the budget only looks closely at what is coming up immediately and a financial report puts it in context. The accrual-based financial report must be out front and center for citizens and lawmakers to make good decisions for long-term prosperity.

A cash-based budget is important; it is simply not enough. With attention on the financial report, every citizen in the United States can step into the role of the board of directors and our president and Congress can step into the role of executive management. We can all step beyond the role of project managers, "Oh goody, here's some money, let's spend it." We can step up and pay attention to the long-term overview which is only available in the financial report.

And, next...

Mature thinking is critical to great democracy

To get to best decisions, we need everyone on board with an understanding of the full fiscal situation. We need a way to keep it all simple, clear and comprehensive so that we can focus on achieving our goals, instead of just dividing up a pie, or deciding who gets to dip into a big candy jar. We need to grow our financial savvy if we want to start making decisions that look to the future. Cash-based budgeting is the product of an adolescent financial mind, I-am-invulnerable to future catastrophe, I live in the NOW—fight, feast, fornicate, and flee! We have the capacity to grow up into full accrual accounting, budgeting and reporting; we can be prudent stewards and make long-term plans.

We could still produce cash-based agency budgets and reports for each government department, but smart agency leadership would also be required to see their realm of government in relation to the whole, to the past and to the future—they would all be required to pay attention to an accrual-based budget and financial report. The disadvantage of moving to full accrual accounting and budgeting is short-term. People will need some training to begin thinking in accrual-based budget terms, but we are paying our leadership to be smart on our behalf. Let's hold them to the highest standards.

The process of switching over is a major undertaking for the Office of Management and Budget—not so much because no one knows how to do it, more because it is always difficult to alter deep channels in a big bureaucracy. However, in the United States of America, we are rich in resources. We have the expertise and we have the money, and if we want we can elect leadership that will make credible, honest, simple, clear, comprehensive financial accounting, budgeting and reporting a high priority. When we want it, we can do it. There will be up front costs to get from OK to great —but it will be a small amount in relation to the total money that is moved around now. The long-term savings from taking this huge kink out of our information pipes will be well worth it.

The shift begins NOW with YOU.

So, first and foremost we need to shift our attention to the accrual-based U.S. Government Financial Report. We can take this action now. Right this minute you are participating in this shift.

Think accrual-based financial report.

Clear reporting will lead to a widespread understanding of our financial situation and to prudent fiscal management and constructive action. Ask your media outlets at least to put the cash-based budget in perspective by including the accrual-based financial report's respective numbers.

Then let us begin a dialogue and deliberation about shifting to fully accrual-based accounting, budgeting and accounting.

BEST:
All accrual budget, accounting and reporting,
because it will:

- Remove kinks in the flow of information.

- Remove the potential for error.

- Support mature, long-term, full-picture thinking.

- Make long-term planning easier.

- Galvanize effective, responsible and prudent leadership.

- Avoid the dangers of a cash-based, spend-all-you-can-get-away-with mindset.

- Take our democracy from good to great.

and/or, at least BETTER:

PAY ATTENTION TO THE FINANCIAL REPORT!

Chapter Nine

⌔KINK IN THE FLOW OF INFORMATION:
A front & center consolidated budget & financial report ⇨

⇨ **TAKE OUT KINK #3:**

Separate reports
for separate funds

There is an old African proverb that a bundle of sticks cannot be broken—togetherness is strength. However, the benefits of togetherness do not extend to financial reporting. In this case, togetherness is a fortress against easy understanding—a plug in the pipes of free and flowing information. "Consolidated reports," also called "unified reports," confuse rather than clarify the financial situation for everyone outside the realm of the accounting wizards. This is easy to remedy.

Chapter 8 explained how $202 billion in 2006 spending, equal to roughly 13% of the total available Operating Fund income, drops off the table when we focus on the cash-based budget reports instead of the accrual-based financial report; the obligations that *we incur now*, but that we will *pay later* are swept off the table. We address only the budget deficit, which leaves out $202 billion, instead of the net operating cost in the financial report, which includes all of these real costs. Policy decisions are made based on these severely compromised discussions.

It get's worse. Even more drops out of sight and under the table when the consolidated or "unified" reports are the center of attention, instead of the separate fund accounts. Using *consolidated* statements, whether they be cash-based or accrual, drops hundreds of billions of dollars in overspending off the table and out of sight; any expenses paid or owed another government department vanish from consideration. Real costs are hidden from sight and oversight. Prudent, responsible, mature discussions are impossible under these conditions.

An expense to one agency that is income to another government agency is netted out and disappears from view.

> *Net cost for governmentwide reporting purposes...is net of intra-governmental eliminations. For this reason, individual agency net cost amounts will not agree with the agency's financial statements.* 2005 USFR, p. 31

Income	+ 1
Expense	- 1
Total	0

Again, financial statements that do not agree are a major kink in the information pipes. If I am getting my information about an agency's finances from the agency reports and you are getting your information from the net costs in the consolidated financial report, net of "earned revenue" (see Chapter 11) and net of intragovernmental transfers, we are going to have a difficult time discussing policy impact because the numbers are different. We are talking apples and oranges, and that only leads to confusion and poor decision-making.

Look what is concealed from easy viewing in 2006:

2006

The accountants see multiple funds...

These are the numbers from the proposed draft format in section one. They add the "earned revenue" to the expenses and to the income for a more accurate picture of our total income and total expenses, and they include an estimated allocation of the $344 billion in interagency transactions (expense to Operating Fund and income to restricted funds).

OPERATING FUND	RESTRICTED FUNDS
Income 1,611,000,000,000	Income 1,514,000,000,000
Expense 2,233,000,000,000	Expense 1,342,000,000,000
NET $ **- 622**,000,000,000	NET $ **172**,000,000,000

☹   ☺

The public is presented with a consolidation...

CONSOLIDATED FINANCIAL REPORT
Income   2,667,200,000,000
Expense   3,127,700,000,000
NET $ **- 449**,500,000,000

☹

The difference in the reported deficit is $172 billion

By consolidating our financial report, we lose sight of $172 billion in Operating Fund net spending, The deficit in the ballyhooed budget is $247 billion. Add the $202 billion in accrual (commitments to future spending) and you get the $449.5 billion consolidated financial report deficit shown above. Add the $172 billion that the Operating Fund is borrowing from the restricted funds, which only shows up when you look at separate reports for separate funds, and you have the real Operating Fund deficit of $622 billion.

Understanding the purpose of fund accounting and understanding the basic operating fund and restricted funds is critical to understanding the federal financial situation. It is important that we know what the "consolidated" budget and financial report are consolidating into one number. And, it is important to understand what is lost in this consolidation. When we are ready to make good decisions, we will bring everything back onto the table so that we have a simple, clear and honest statement of our financial situation. That is the only way we will get to good decisions.

Here is the information that we need to see easily, and see first:

Operating Fund	Restricted Funds Summary
Total assets	Total assets
Total debts	Total debts
Net worth	**Net worth**
Gross income	Gross income
Gross expense	Gross expense
Net	**Net**
Change in assets	Change in assets
Change in debts	Change in debts
Net change	**Net change**
in net worth	**in net worth**

And, here is the information that our **financial** managers need:

Consolidated Fund Report

Total assets
Total debts
Net worth

Gross income
Gross expense
Net

Change in assets
Change in debts
Net change
in net worth

THANK YOU to hardworking government accountants on the Treasury and GAO staffs!

The 2006 Financial Report of the U.S. Government made a significant improvement when it broke down the Operating Fund and the restricted funds (as of 2006, called "Non-earmarked," and "Earmarked") in the Statements of Operations and Changes in Net Position. It is now possible to see the net income and expenses for the Operating Fund and the restricted funds separately. The next step will be to do the same for the Statements of Net Cost. It is not yet possible to discern how much of each department's costs are actually the costs of restricted funds that they manage. We have to guess at the cost of programs funded by the Operating Fund and the cost of programs funded by restricted funds.

More out of sight, out of mind

Finding the true cost of government is like peeling an onion; every layer is another veil of confusion. Add the accrual spending back in and we're one step closer to the truth. Report on the funds separately and we have a clearer picture of the total deficit/overspending. Report on the funds separately and we also have a clearer picture of the full cost of government and how we fund it. Here's what we are overlooking by presenting consolidated reports for our primary attention:

Any intragovernmental transfers, payments from one fund or department to another, are dropped from the consolidated summaries. In 2006, $529 billion in payments from the Operating Fund to the restricted funds vanished from the front and center attention grabbing reports.

$529 Billion Out of sight. Out of mind.

When an agency that is funded from the Operating Fund pays a restricted fund, this is recorded in the Operating Fund's expense column and in the restricted fund's income column. The cost of payroll taxes for each government agency's staff is the biggest cost that vanishes from view in the consolidated budget report and financial statements. Netting out income and expense between government agencies and restricted funds for a consolidated total is accurate from an accounting perspective. The separate account data is there in the details, but managers and decision-makers have lost critical information about the full cost of programs and the income available, because that information is no longer present in any of the summary tables. Currently the Executive Summary of the U.S. Government Financial Report includes no mention of the netting out of intragovernmental expenses/income and that the reported expenses and incomes in the summaries are all nets. It is a simple matter to change the report to address this deficiency.

Good management requires looking at the funds separately in a simple summary. Good lawmaking, good taxing and spending and good government require looking at the funds separately.

Here are some of the biggest numbers that drop out of sight through consolidating budget and financial reports. (And, remember, these are in addition to the $200-440 billion that drops out of sight when you look at the cash-based budget instead of the accrual-based financial report):

In 2006, on the consolidated financial report balance sheet, $172 billion in new restricted funds' *assets* and $172 billion in new Operating Fund *debt* were lost to mindful consideration.

ASSETS & DEBTS—Out of sight, out of mind

For many years Social Security and many of the other restricted funds have taken in substantially more money than they need to spend in a given year (or in some cases, than they are allowed to spend by Congress, regardless of what the need may be). The extra money by law is funneled into the Operating Fund, and the restricted funds get IOU Treasury Securities.

In 2006 the major restricted funds took in a net of $172 billion over their spending needs for the year. This $172 billion went into the Operating Fund and was spent on general operations—out-the-door-gone forever spending. An IOU for $172 billion went into the asset column of the restricted funds' balance sheet.

When the restricted funds loan their extra income to the Operating Fund, the loan shows up on the balance sheets of both—as a debt of the Operating fund, and as an asset of the restricted funds. When the funds are all combined, into a consolidated total, the assets and debts between funds cancel each other out, and the information is lost in the consolidated summary. We lose a full understanding of the change in the assets and the debts for each of these funds.

INCOME & EXPENSES—Out of sight, out of mind

Interest payments and receipts

When the Operating Fund borrows from the restricted funds by taking their annual surpluses, it gives Treasury Securities to the Restricted Funds–IOUs with a set interest rate. Then the Operating Fund must pay the restricted funds interest every year on the money that was borrowed. In 2006, interest due of $185 billion was booked as an expense to the Operating Fund and income to the restricted funds. When the funds are consolidated, the income and expense cancel out and these transactions disappear from view and from consideration. Our understanding of the full cost of government's overspending, borrowing and debt service is thus severely compromised.

Because of continuous overspending, the interest to the restricted funds does not actually get paid in the year that it is owed. It is added to the debts of the Operating Fund and the assets of the restricted funds. This is all recorded, and then dropped from view by the consolidated financial report. This interest expense booked as an expense and then owed to the restricted funds is a significant expense, representing 12% of the money collected for the Operating Fund in 2006. A previous commitment to spend twelve percent of your income is an important consideration, and decision-making suffers when it is dropped off the table by the consolidated financial report.

This disappearing act occurs in both the consolidated cash-based budget and the consolidated financial report. They both net out the Operating Fund interest expense that is owed to the restricted funds.

Payroll taxes for government employees

Every government agency and department must pay payroll taxes for its employees (except Congress which has its own pension system). These tax payments are real costs to the agencies and income for the Social Security and Medicare Trust Funds (restricted funds). In the consolidated reports, the income and expense net out in the intragovernmental transfers, disappearing from view. This represents a substantial loss to our understanding of the cost of government.

For example, when the Department of Defense pays FICA to the Social Security and Medicare Trust Funds for its employer share, this is a DoD expense and restricted fund income. In the consolidated report, the income (+) to one agency is expense (-) to another. The income and expense net out in the consolidated report, so that this departmental expense and restricted fund income disappears, distorting the picture of our costs and the income that we have to cover them. FICA-7.65% of the total Department of Defense payroll is a considerable chunk of change. The current format financial report says that the DoD spent $704 billion in 2005 and $658 billion in 2006, this sum *did not include the payroll tax costs owed to the restricted funds.* Take 2.3 million DoD

Another $185 billion in restricted funds' interest income and $185 billion in Operating Fund interest expense were lost to mindful consideration in the consolidated financial statements.

employees, multiply by an average pay of, say, $30,000, then multiply by an employers 7.65% for FICA, and you are talking big money.

Here's what the 2006 Budget says about intragovernmental transactions:

> *[there are]...two kinds of intragovernmental transactions— agencies' payments as employers into Federal employee retirement trust funds and interest received by trust funds—are classified as undistributed offsetting receipts. They appear...as special deductions in computing total budget authority and outlays for the Government rather than as offsets at the agency level. This special treatment is necessary because the amounts are large and* **would distort measures of the agency's activities if they were attributed to the agency.** p. 415 (emphasis is mine)

By "distort measures of the agency's activities" they appear to mean, give a true picture. Why not have the full long-term cost of today's employee pool on each agency's books? And likewise, what would be distorted by crediting the restricted funds' annual interest receipts as income?

The 2006 Financial Report, for the first time makes it easy to find out this total of intragovernmental transfers. There is a line item in the Statements of Operations and Changes in Net Position (p. 38), called, "Intragovernmental transfers." Thank you for this improvement! In 2006, intragovernmental transfers totalled $344.3 billion (in addition to the $185 billion in interest owed, which got its own line). The information is in the current financial report, but most discussions never get past the front summaries, so this information vanishes from mindful consideration.

Nets and Totals—out of sight, out of mind

Interest expense of $185 billion plus $344 billion in additional intragovernmental transfers (mostly payroll expenses) equals $529 billion in expenses to the Operating Fund and income to the restricted funds that is disappearing from view through consolidation. The total income available to the Operating Fund in 2006 was $1,611 billion. The out-of-

Another $344 billion in Operating Fund general *expense,* and $344 billion in restricted funds' *income* is lost to mindful consideration in the consolidated financial statements.

sight $529 billion represents 33%. There is simply no way that discussion can be truly productive when the budget nets and totals that get all the attention are missing such enormous sums. Some people may have read the fine print, but many, many others are making their arguments on unreliable data—and that simply is untenable in a great democracy.

Productive public discourse

Separate reports for separate funds will open the door to useful discussions about our government operations and our government commitments. It is important to get to these discussions as quickly as possible, because there are problems looming on the horizon. For example, any productive discussion about Social Security has to separate the Social Security Trust Fund account from the Operating Fund. Similarly, any good discussion about altering (and hopefully streamlining) the tax code requires a foundation of true understanding of our financial situation.

Separate reports for separate funds clear up the muddle of information in many ways. What is truly mandatory spending and what is discretionary becomes clear. "Excess" restricted fund monies can be clearly seen, which will promote a more useful dialogue about long-term stability in the restricted funds. And, with the burden of income, profit and payroll taxes clearly defined, we can finally have a productive discussion about fair and effective taxation.

Simple and clear: "mandatory" and "discretionary"

When Congress is reviewing taxing and spending, it would be very useful to know quickly and easily the sum that is already committed by previous laws. What spending is already mandatory and what spending is discretionary?

Congress does produce charts and tables of mandatory and discretionary spending and uses these designations to determine whether their decisions count towards spending limits. However, there are many kinks around this issue that confuse the definitions of mandatory and discretionary, and so confuse the public discourse. Reporting separately on the Operating Fund and the restricted funds would make the distinction between mandatory and discretionary simple and clear.

Mandatory

Mandatory spending means that we have no choice in the matter. Commitments have already been made. When the Operating Fund and restricted funds are consolidated, calling restricted fund spending mandatory and calling some operating fund spending mandatory is confusing, and confuses the issues that determine policy.

Mandatory spending from the restricted funds. Restricted funds by their nature have *mandates* for spending. Restricted funds covenant to collect in a certain way for limited, special purpose spending. If we collect money for a specific purpose, we are obligated morally and ethically to use if for that purpose—even when the law allows room to fudge.

Whenever Congress creates a separate fund that will collect its own revenue according to specific rules, for a specific purpose, this is a restricted fund and should be labeled and bundled with the restricted funds. All the money collected for the restricted funds is collected for specific purposes. As long as the purposes and needs exist, the spending of these funds should be mandatory to meet the need at the highest possible level. When a fund collects by special tax more than is needed, or more than it is authorized to spend, then it is time to look at whether its authorization needs to be increased, its tax income decreased, or the excess funds prudently set aside for a rainy day.

However, we do not yet operate at this level of integrity and maturity. Some of the restricted funds' spending is considered "mandatory," like Social Security and Medicare/Medicaid. (Although we get around this by borrowing and using the excess funds for operations.)

The Highway Trust Fund is one example of a restricted fund whose spending is not yet considered mandatory spending. We collect specific fuel and transportation taxes and then throw the revenues into the general pot, and decide how much of the collected restricted fund revenues we will actually spend on the dedicated purpose each year.

The Securities and Exchange Commission (SEC) fund is a particularly egregious example of a breach of covenant with taxpayers. The SEC collects fees on every stock transaction to pay for its oversight work. Prior to 2001, this fund collected about $1.3 *billion* each year. Congress refused to allow the SEC to use this full income on oversight and monitoring, keeping the SEC budget to about $300 million and grabbing the remaining $1.1 billion for the Operating Fund (Enron, et.al. was the result of inadequately funded and executed oversight). In 2001 Congress, with almost no fan fare passed a law reducing the fees to match the level of the SEC spending at the time–a big time bonus for big investors (who were the ones paying the most in fees because they are the ones who benefit most by a market with integrity).[28] Then, after the Enron debacle, Congress increased the SEC budget without increasing the funding mechanism, shifting the burden of market oversight from players to the taxpaying public. In the private sector this breach of trust could be illegal.

When we say we are going to tax for a specific purpose, is there a good reason why spending the money for the intended purpose should be optional instead of mandatory? Is there a good reason why we blithely overlook our failure to keep our covenants with ourselves and with our children and grandchildren?

Mandatory spending from the Operating Fund. The Operating Fund has mandatory obligations for previous contractual commitments that *cannot* be altered by new laws. We have made ongoing commitments to spend a substantial portion of our Operating Fund income. It would be helpful to prudent taxing and spending to have these commitments distinct and clear. It would be easier to make distinctions when the Operating Fund and restricted funds are separate.

In 2006, $406.8 billion in interest payments came off the top of the Operating Fund, which had an income total of $1,611 billion.

We now have a previous commitment to pay 26% of our Operating Fund income just for interest on our debts.

And, our debts are increasing dramatically.

Interest payments are a primary example of mandatory contractual spending from the Operating Fund. In 2006, 26% of all operating fund income went off the top to pay interest on government debt.

The Operating Fund also has "mandatory obligations" that *can* be altered by new laws (e.g. to support the restricted funds when their income is insufficient to meet their responsibilities). Whenever Congress passes a law that *requires* spending out of the Operating Fund, this is mandatory spending from the Operating Fund. Laws set certain thresholds for eligibility for restricted fund expenditures. If you meet the eligibility requirements set by law, then you must be paid. In a given year, the number of people who meet these thresholds determines the amount of spending that is mandated. Sometimes the restricted fund's income is not enough to cover the mandated spending. Then the difference must be made up by the Operating Fund. This is considered mandatory spending in the Operating Fund.

Many laws mandate spending from specific agencies that are funded through the Operating Fund, not by special collections. For example, food stamps are paid for from the Department of Agriculture's budget. The amount that must be paid is determined by how many people qualify according to the laws in place. The new Medicare Part D Drug Benefit is a program that will require mandatory spending from the Operating Fund, since no supplemental taxes were set up to cover the cost of the program. The Supplemental Medical Insurance Trust Fund (SMI, Medicare Part B) is an example of a restricted fund that is chronically under-funded by its designated funding mechanisms, meaning it must be subsidized by mandatory spending from the Operating Fund.

Mandatory spending without any specific fund collection should be distinct and clear. When we have separate accounts for separate funds, it will be. Simple and clear and effective choice-making is lost in the shuffle of the current consolidated format.

Discretionary

Discretionary means we get to choose how to spend this money each year. By definition, there is no discretionary spending in the restricted funds. The only discretionary spending in the Operating Fund is what is left over after interest payments and other spending mandated by laws have been allocated from the Operating Fund. Congress can choose each year how to spend these funds. It would be nice to know how much truly discretionary spending exists in our Operating Fund.

Eliminate confusion about mandatory and discretionary spending

The failure of the financial reports to separate operating funds from restricted funds creates a lot of confusion; it makes it difficult for decision makers to make good decisions and makes it difficult for citizens to hold decision-makers accountable for the choices that they make. The simplest and clearest and most useful way to present government spending is to FIRST present separate budgets and separate financial reports for the Federal Operating Fund and for the restricted funds, and then identify what is mandatory within the Operating Fund. With separate reports for separate funds, mandatory and discretionary will have clear meaning, leading to better decision-making.

Simple and clear: integrity and "excess funds"

Some of the restricted funds are able to collect more in taxes than they need (e.g. Social Security), and some restricted funds collect much less than they need and the shortfall comes from the Operating Fund (e.g. Medicare).

When a restricted fund has extra income and this "excess income" is transferred into the general Operating Fund, (and an I.O.U. from the Operating Fund put on the books of the restricted fund), why not designate this amount as mandatory investment for the future of the particular restricted fund? Acting with integrity dictates that we use money we collect for one purpose for that purpose—keeping the covenants we make when we establish the tax. It is the grown up thing to do.

For the last 20 years, the largest restricted fund, The Old Age and Survivors Insurance Trust Fund, generally known as "Social Security," has taken in more money than it needed to pay out. The high rate of revenue was set deliberately, ostensibly to build up a reserve for the predictable strain on the fund when baby boomers come of age. However there is a plausible argument that President Lyndon Johnson (Democrat) and his Congress (Democratic) made this change to camouflage the continuing and escalating cost of the Vietnam War.

By law, we have confused the matter of the restricted funds' annual excess income. On the one hand, we have declared that surplus restricted funds are "Trust Funds," a reminder that we have special covenants with ourselves for their collection and spending. Then by law, we require that the excess funds be put into the Operating Fund and that IOU Treasury Securities be put on the restricted fund's books. Every administration has had the opportunity to present a budget that sets the restricted funds aside and invests them for the future. If President Bush II wants to privatize some of Social Security, he could say, "I will honor the covenant we make when we tax for Social Security; I will not spend the money raised for Social Security for any other purpose. I will take all of the annual surplus in the restricted funds and invest it for the future stable funding of these funds' obligations." And, a wise president would ask, "How can we invest so that we increase our greatest asset, the ability of taxpayers to contribute to the common good?" Imagine a special capital fund investing in the research and development of solutions for a healthy, wealthy, wise and prosperous citizenry.

People acknowledge that the funds transferred from the Social Security Trust Fund into the Operating Fund turn the restricted funds into 'pay-as-you-go' systems. **If this is truly acceptable and what we intend, then why not do so honestly?** Either eliminate the Social Security Trust Fund altogether, collect taxes for it at the same time and in the same way that taxes are collected for the Operating Fund, and pay-as-we-go for Social Security out of the Operating Fund. In the same way that we pay as we go for food stamps for the needy, we could pay for Social Security for the needy.

Imagine a Social Venture fund making investments in tools that increase natural and human capital, with the restricted funds profiting as shareholders of successful enterprises.

The equivalent of 1% of our GDP invested in innovation for a sustainable future could meet best case scenarios for rolling back our impact on global warming, *and* stimulate productivity in our economy.

Or, treat the Social Security Trust Fund like a TRUST/ restricted fund. Continue to collect taxes under appropriate fairness principles, then spend and invest them for their covenanted purpose. And, if there is a surplus collected, invest it for future income production. If the Operating Fund is going to borrow the surplus, then report on it separately so everyone knows what is going on. We have it in us to recognize and practice honest reporting. Are there values that we hold dearer than honesty and integrity in our government that dictate keeping the reporting as it is?

Intentional integrity and honesty: structure the financing to match the reality.

Simple and clear: the burden of overspending and debt

When we consolidate the Operating Fund and the restricted funds for the Big Summaries that capture everyone's attention, we hide the true annual cost of operations. This deceit is a disservice to America; we get poor decisions because decision makers—citizens, representatives and leadership—are starting with misleading numbers. We will have more useful discussions and make better decisions when everyone is clear about the fundamentals: assets, debts, net worth; income, expense, net for the Operating Fund and separately for the restricted funds.

When we misrepresent the size of our operating deficit by pretending that restricted funds are part of income, and that future and past commitments do not count, we block the possibility of honest and productive discussion on the problems facing our nation. We also make light of the debt service that now eats up a whopping 26% of our Operating Fund. This interest commitment is set to skyrocket thanks to the ballooning debt created by the fiscal policies and the immature problem-solving skills of the Bush II administration, and the near guarantee of increasing interest rates.

In the six years from September 2000 to September 2006, the National Debt increased by $1.3 billion PER DAY, from $5,674 billion to $8,507 billion.

In September 2000, the federal debt was $5,674,178,209,336. At the end of September 2006 it had risen to $8,506,973,899,215. In just six years this Republican administration increased the debt by $2,832 billion. This is a six-year increase of 50%. In March 2006, to accommodate their spending, the Republican controlled Congress, on a party line vote, increased the debt ceiling–the maximum amount Congress is

By the end of his eight years in office, Bush II will have **doubled** U.S. debt.

One man, responsible for more than half of $10 **t**rillion in debt, and the Republican Party supporting him every step of the way.

Amazing.

allowed to borrow– once again to an extraordinary $9 trillion.   When Reagan came into office this debt represented 33% of the total GDP. Today it represents 64%. (The debt is mounting at such a rapid rate, it is hard to keep this up-to-date through the book production process.)

This astounding increase in debt from overspending is camouflaged by consolidating the Operating Fund and restricted funds and by focusing on budget numbers instead of accrual-based financial report numbers.

Simple and clear: stable funding for Social Security

The Operating Fund's *tax-based* income in 2006 was only $1,526 billion (not counting the "earned revenue" from marketplace sales and services). The Operating Fund borrowed another $172 billion from the restricted funds—an amount equal to 11% of its available funds. Many people do not understand that the Operating Fund is borrowing 11% more than it takes in every year just from the restricted funds to help cover annual overspending for general operations.

Republicans are pushing to privatize Social Security. President Bush II and the Republicans are promoting private savings accounts as a solution to stabilize Social Security funding; they are advocating shifting some of the restricted fund tax income of this social insurance program into private retirement savings accounts—changing the purpose of the Old Age and Survivors Insurance Trust Fund from insurance to retirement savings.

We can only have a useful dialogue and clear discussion about this possibility when we are honest about the insurance fund's financial situation, its mingling with the Operating Fund, and its covenanted purpose. Clear, honest financial reports will support the most productive discussion of all the complex issues relating to Social Security Insurance and private retirement savings.

We can only have a useful discussion about shifting Social Security (Old Age and Survivors Insurance) from an insurance program to private retirement savings accounts, when it is clear to everyone that reducing the social security tax income will impact both the trust fund's ability to pay out benefits, *and* the ability of the government to meet its general operating obligations. Under the current administration's spending policies, if we privatize Social Security so that it no longer collects a surplus available for the Operating Fund to borrow, the Operating Fund would have to borrow significantly more money from the public—another bonus for wealthy investors and foreign governments–or cut government spending on its operations dramatically.   This becomes clear if we present the financial reports in this improved format—separate reports for separate funds. Only clarity will lead to good decisions.

Simple and clear: the tax burden

We pay income taxes designated for general operations and payroll taxes designated for the Social Security and Medicare Trust Funds. The $172 billion in restricted fund revenues, that is hijacked by the Operating Fund to subsidize operating expenses, represents 12% of the total revenues of the restricted funds.

Since this transfer is hidden in the consolidated reports, consolidated reporting leads many people to misunderstand the tax burden; they fail to understand that even people who make too little to pay income taxes, which are designated for the Operating Fund, still pay payroll taxes into the restricted funds—7.65% of every paycheck. Even if I'm only making $10,000 each year, I am paying $765 into the Social Insurance Trust Funds (or twice that, if I am self-employed). And, even for the person only making $10,000 per year, 12% of their *payroll trust fund taxes* are going into the Operating Fund to cover operating costs—a breach of covenant, however legal it may be.

We are asking the people who make less than $94,200 per year to pay a share of the operating budget that steps beyond the fairness principles and taxing covenants that we have established.   Twelve percent of the 7.65% that they contribute from their paycheck for FICA (SS, Medicare & Medicaid) is used for the general operating fund. Whereas, the person who makes $1,000,000 and paid 7.65% on only the first $94,200 (as is required), paid $7,206 into the restricted funds, or .7% of their income.

And, 12% of that .7% went from the restricted funds into the operating budget—a very tiny amount. Confounding the separate fund accounts confuses all arguments about who carries the burden of taxation and by how much.

Everyone will understand better and we can *begin* useful discussion about how to correct problems when we are straightforward and honest in our reporting and provide separate reports for separate funds.

Simple and clear: looking at function priorities

We need a clear and simple way to look at our mission priorities and goals and determine whether we are collecting revenue and spending it effectively. This will be easier to do when it is clear what we are collecting for a specific purpose (restricted funding) and what we are setting aside from our Operating Fund.

Simple, clear: cornerstones of great democracy

In a democracy, WE, as government, take responsibility for collecting and spending our citizens' money. If government cannot be honest and trustworthy, our democracy is in serious trouble. Honesty and trustworthiness require that the operating account and the restricted fund accounts be held, governed and reported on as separate and distinct entities. Throwing them into the same pot for primary reporting is a breach of trust, invites fraud, malfeasance, misappropriation, manipulation of the numbers, and leads to pointless, baseless discussions of non-issues. The consolidated budget report is a shell game when presented to citizens as the primary set of summary numbers for reporting on the United States Government.

We will begin to make good management decisions when we look carefully at the funds separately—preferably in an accrual-based full cost format. Separate accounts are simple, clear, honest and useful. Separate accounts honor the covenants we create with future taxpayers when we set up schedules of collection for specific purposes. Separate accounts make it possible to identify the crux of problems. A unified or consolidated budget and financial report, however valuable they are to finance professionals as a critical component of sound accounting practice, are at best, misleading when used as the One Big Summary—and at the worst, they are dishonest, and deceitful.

The time has come for simple, clear and honest financial reports

It is well within our ability to keep it simple, keep it clear and keep it honest in the reports to the President, to Congress and to the American people. The consolidated reports can be available to the accountants and financial managers who need to see that all the numbers combine and balance and tell the truth that accountants need. *AND*, we can have a comprehensive summary for citizens and lawmakers with separate reports for separate funds, so that when our lawmakers sit down to tax and spend wisely, prudently and responsibly, they know what they are doing. And, WE know what they are doing. We can improve our practice of democracy by improving the quality of financial reporting.

It is a simple matter to take all of the funds that collect their own money for their specific purpose, out of the Operating Fund. When the Operating Fund contributes to these funds it will show up as a simple and clear line item expense in the Operating Fund report. When the restricted funds have more in revenue than they need to spend in a given year and the Operating Fund takes and uses these funds either by way of a direct grab (e.g. SEC) or as a loan (e.g. Social Security), it will show up in the Operating Fund account as either income from a distinct source or a loan. Separate accounts for separate funds will tell us whether the money collected for one intended purpose is being used for another, and tell us whether or not the fund is self-supporting. Separate reports will show clearly where money comes from, where it goes, and whether government is keeping the covenants it created when it made the laws to collect money for a specific purpose—all critical information for good decision-making.

In the 2006 consolidated financial report format summary $529 billion in very real expenses dropped out of sight ($185 interest and $344 billion in "intragovernmental transfers"–mostly government payroll costs). To be very clear, this is in addition to the $202 billion that disappeared from view between the cash-based budget and the accrual-based financial report. This additional dropout is a result of consolidating the reporting, instead of producing separate reports for separate funds. It is no secret that we are doing this. This is not a big discovery or new revelation to people who study the financial report.

It is time to say, we are ready to change. We require simple, clear and honest reporting on the U.S. Government's financial situation. We trust that when people have good information, they will make better decisions, and better decisions are good for each of us, good for America and good for the planet. We are ready to face every single dollar of our taxing, spending, assets and debts. Currently we systematically treat the money that drops out of sight as if it does not exist—severely compromising the quality of dialogue, debate and decisions. Separate accounts for separate funds are a key to clarity. Separate reports are common sense and common practice in the private sector. Demand clear and honest reports on the separate funds. This is a simple and easy to accomplish improvement with a dramatic impact. We are ready to move from good to great and demonstrate how government accounting to its citizens in a great democracy can be simple, clear, honest and comprehensible.

Our public discourse will be most productive when we have separate reports for separate funds.
Currently, information that drops out of sight and out of mind in the consolidated reports:

2006 Statements of Net Position (net worth):

- **$172 billion in restricted funds' assets**

- **$172 billion in Operating Fund debt**

2006 Statements of Net Cost (income, expense, net):

- **$185 billion in restricted funds' interest income**

- **$185 billion in Operating Fund interest expense**

- **$344 billion in restricted funds' income from all other intragovernmental transfers**

- **$344 billion in all other expenses incurred by operations and owed to the Restricted funds.**

The total of $529 billion in expenses that disappears from sight when the Operating Fund and restricted funds are consolidated represents 30% of the total Operating Fund income.

It is impossible to hold a responsible discussion and to make prudent financial plans when it is necessary to dig deep for full information on the cost of government. Sadly, few do this digging and consequently few understand the full cost of government.

This is easy to fix by providing separate reports for separate funds.

Glenn McCoy ©2005 Belleville News-Democrat.

Chapter Ten

☞**KINK IN THE FLOW OF INFORMATION:**
Many assets and debts are OFF the books ☜

⇨ **TAKE OUT KINK #4:**

Book all the assets and all the debts

When we are ready to begin making good decisions for our future, we must know, "Where are we now?" The balance sheet of a financial report provides this snapshot of our financial situation. When the balance sheet is incomplete, our decision-making is compromised and we make poor and inadequate choices. Until now, the balance sheet of the U.S. Government's Financial Report has neither included all our government's assets nor all our liabilities.

Good news: this change is partly underway. Some assets that have previously been excluded from the books are in the pipeline to appear where they belong. It requires a yes, please, continue with all due speed. Get it done fully and comprehensively as expeditiously as is possible with the assignment of adequate funding and staffing. Bad news: even with the changes underway, there will still be a lot left out.

The government has made small moves towards a more accurate balance sheet.
A change in Federal accounting standards, effective in fiscal year 2003, resulted in a net book value of $325.1 billion in military equipment at the Department of Defense being presented on the balance sheet for the first time.
2004 USFR, p. 9.

That is a step in the right direction. The military spends big money on equipment and that equipment should be booked as an asset. Good thinking in 2003. Notice that $325.1 billion in Defense equipment represents about half the total property, plant and equipment listed in the assets below. This Defense equipment was put on the books in 2003.

ALL Assets

The only assets on the books are some basic hard assets. The 2006 Financial Report lists these assets (p.41):

2006 *accrual*-based, *consolidated* financial report

ASSETS, In billions

	2005	2006
Cash and other monetary assets	85.8	97.9
Accounts and taxes receivable	66.1	68.8
Loans receivable	221.8	220.8
Inventories and related property	272.0	281.3
General property, plant, and equipment	670.2	688.5
Securities and investments	75.3	83.8
Other assets	56.7	55.4
TOTAL ASSETS	**1,447.9**	**1,496.5**
INCREASE in assets		**+ 58.6**

And, for the first time, this balance sheet includes under "Assets" the lines, "Stewardship property, plant, and equipment," and "Stewardship Land." No value is given, but this is a move in the right direction–at least noting that these assets exist and have not been given any value and put on the books.

Remember that we lose information by consolidating the Operating Fund and restricted funds. As you look at the consolidated tables of assets and debts, keep in mind that what is *on the books* as an asset to the restricted funds, and as a debt to the Operating Fund is net out of sight in the *consolidated* report summaries reproduced on the previous page. The restricted fund assets that are debts to the Operating Fund in 2006, and net out of the consolidated report, are worth:

$ 3,554,757,900,000
  3,554,757   million
  3,555   billion
  3.6   trillion

Our restricted funds have double the assets that appear in the consolidated financial report. This is confusing to many people.

In addition to what is booked, but dropped from sight in the consolidated report, up until now, most of our government assets have not been booked at all.

> *Assets included on the balance sheets are resources of the Government that remain available to meet future needs. The most significant assets that are reported on the balance sheets are property, plant, and equipment, inventories, and loans receivable. There are, however, **other significant resources available to the Government that extend beyond the assets presented in these financial statements. Those resources include stewardship assets, including natural resources** (see Stewardship Information section), and the Government's sovereign powers to tax, regulate commerce, and set monetary policy.* 2005 USFR, p.33 (bold added)

Aside from the goofiness of including the powers to tax, regulate commerce and set monetary policy in a paragraph about assets (see Chapter 7), leaving out stewardship assets and natural resource assets is a huge oversight.

What assets are still off the books?

There are three main kinds of assets that deliberately do not appear on our balance sheet: 1) General assets that should be booked, but are not; 2) "Stewardship assets," which at least get a substantial section in the report, even though they are not on the books, and not given a monetary value–and in 2006 got a line to at least note their existence on the Statement of Net Position; and, 3) Natural, manufactured, human and intangible assets, which do not appear in the financial report at all.

General assets

What proportion of our military hardware assets have been depleted by the Bush II Occupation of Iraq?

Who knows?

How can we plan prudently for our future security without this information?

Our government has only recently moved to establish standards and to require that assets be booked. The 2003 Department of Defense addition of $325.1 billion in assets to their balance sheet is an example of this effort. (Although given a budget of at least that much annually for decades, it seems highly unlikely that this sum represents the total value of our investment in military plant, hardware and equipment.)

WE, through our federal tax dollars, spend billions every year on national infrastructure (highways, bridges, air terminals, bikeways, rapid transit, educational facilities, etc.). When these assets are not booked and depreciated, we lose track of their value, their need for ongoing maintenance, and the need to replace aging infrastructure.

Inattention leads to bridges that collapse, bumpy roads that cause accidents and a general failure to continuously maintain the value of our infrastructure investments, which are the foundation of a healthy economy.

Stewardship assets

The government differentiates between assets that are booked as assets and reported on the balance sheet and what it calls "stewardship assets," which are not reported on the balance sheet. Stewardship assets include land, and cultural and historical assets.

> *Stewardship land refers to federally-owned land that is set aside for the use and enjoyment of present and future generations and land on which military bases are located. Except for military bases, this land is not used or held for use in general Government operations. Stewardship land is land that the Government does not expect to use to meet its obligations, unlike the assets listed in the Balance sheets. Stewardship land is measured in nonfinancial units such as acres of land and lakes, miles of parkways, and miles of wild and scenic rivers. Examples of stewardship land include national parks, national forests, wilderness areas, and land used to enhance ecosystems to encourage animal and plant species and to conserve nature.* 2002 USFR, p.59

The list of stewardship assets that are left off the books includes most federally owned land used by the Department of Defense, national parks and forests, historical and cultural buildings, and objects of cultural and historical significance.

While it may not be the government's intent to use these stewardship assets for ready cash, it has been known to do so. The Bush II administration is aggressively pursuing a policy of "right-sizing" our stewardship assets, and booking the revenue from sales under "earned revenue," "user fees," or other miscellany. The 2006 Budget includes a line item in Table 6, "Southern Nevada land sales," projecting an income of nearly $5.8 billion between 2006 and 2015 from Nevada land sales. In February 2006, the Bush II administration put forward a plan to sell off over 300,000 acres of our national forests. Have we had public discussions about choosing to sell these assets? These lands are not booked as assets. This sell-off of our commonwealth land to pay operating costs does not show up in the main summary tables of either the budget or the financial report because they are not booked as assets.

How and when did we have a national dialogue about using our heritage lands to cover operating costs?

One current practice in government is to obscure the sale of assets by calling the sale a misnomer, "User Charges."

> *The term [user charges] encompasses proceeds from the sale or use of government goods and services, including the sale of natural resources (such as timber, oil, and minerals) and proceeds from asset sales (such as property, plant, and equipment). User charges are not necessarily earmarked for the activity they finance and may be credited to the general fund of the Treasury.*

> *The term "user charge" does not refer to a separate budget category for collections. User charges are classified in the budget as receipts, offsetting receipts, or offsetting collections according to the principles explained above.* ('principles' perhaps refers to a referenced OMB Circular A-25, "User Charges", July 8, 1993) p. 415

As you can see from the government's own analysis, the term "user charges" is used sometimes to camouflage the sale of our collective assets, our commonwealth. If these assets were on the books as assets, where they belong, then when they are sold, they would be booked as the sale of an asset, which is the case. This dishonest diminishment of our national heritage without due process seems to be deliberately perfidious.

Natural assets

The value of our natural resources—water, mineral reserves, sustainable forests—is not on the books as assets or as "stewardship assets." These assets only appear in footnotes when they are being sold off under "lease" terms or compromised by environmental degradation that has reached a level that triggers "toxic waste cleanup."

While it is easy to see that what is above and on the ground represents an asset, what is taken from the ground is also an asset that is being permanently diminished. Leases to extract minerals from public lands also belong as sales of public assets on the balance sheet. After all, the removal of mineral assets is permanent, not a loan or lease arrangement.

The "development of mineral resources on public lands" means the sale of those assets; this sale is a permanent, irretrievable loss on our balance sheet.

In 1995 a Republican Congress passed a bill, and a Democratic President signed it, that gave oil companies the right to extract oil and gas from the Gulf of Mexico up until 2011 without paying *any* royalties.[29] At the time oil prices averaged $18 per barrel and more exploration and extraction was deemed important. Royalty exemption was intended to encourage more extraction and it succeeded. The law required that royalties would kick in at $34.71 per barrel for oil. However, the law exempted any oil drilling commenced in 1998 and 1999, which accounts for about two thirds of the natural gas and millions of barrels of oil now being extracted. In 2006-2007 oil has been floating from $60-98 per barrel. While the oil companies have raked in the highest profit margins and highest profits that the world has *ever* seen on the resources, in part "extracted" from our commonwealth territory, they are obligated by contract to pay nothing at all back into the common good for these extractions. Oil resources are part of our commonwealth. Let's pay attention and book these assets on our balance sheet so that we keep track of what we are giving away.

We currently do not charge a fair market value to businesses that exploit any of the finite natural resources that we steward. For example, our shared water is sold so cheaply, that you will see farmlands spraying water into the air on hot days and wasting enormous amounts of water to evaporation. Businesses in Arizona mist their shoppers in the hot summer. We are depleting our aquifers faster than they can refill and there is nothing on the balance sheet to show either our loss or what we have left for our children. Our shared life-sustaining fresh water heritage is literally going down the drain or evaporating and few are paying attention.

What if these cool and happy shoppers are cutting 50 years off the life of the aquifer that future generations must count on to grow their food, eat and survive? Are we so hedonistic and irresponsible that we would not care? I don't think so. Farmers may argue that more conservative systems of watering are costly to implement. But what if it is cheaper in the long run to pay this cost now, so that our children have fresh water available to grow their food, instead of paying the cost of desalinization down the road? Perhaps this is a farm subsidy worth our tax dollars—an investment in life-sustaining water conservation for our grandchildren.

The extraction of oil, mineral and water resources oftentimes imposes irrevocable (at least for many generations to come) harm to the natural ecosystems for short-term gain. If we are truly a "pro-life" nation, then mature, responsible, ethical and moral imperatives dictate that we steward the natural ecosystems like our lives depend upon them–which they do. We can only judge the cost-benefit trade off when we acknowledge and record the value of the natural ecosystems. It is difficult to steward what is hidden from mindful consideration.

Let's get all of our natural resources on the books. There could be enormous value in sitting down and actually noting the full value of all of our shared natural assets. A thoughtful process of assigning value would require that we take into account all the existing values—the value of the minerals and water under the ground, the value of waterways as sources of power, transportation and as critical habitat for our life-sustaining biosystem, the value of the trees and plants—not just as commodities, but as life-sustaining critical components of our biosystem, the value of our wetlands as habitat and as buffer against hurricanes. As the Hurricane Katrina devastation in New Orleans demonstrated, there is a very real economic value to having barrier wetlands. Healthy ecosystems have economic value. It is prudent to assess that value and monitor its preservation *before* we lose it, rather than after it is gone and remediation is astronomically expensive–or impossible.

When we leave the monetary value of our natural and heritage assets off the books, the cost of their maintenance, the level of their degradation or preservation is out of sight and out of mind. They can be lost to our children and we will not know what happened because the loss/sale will be buried in obscure parts of government reports.

Let's have this discussion about the assets that need to be booked so that our financial report can be accurate.

Manufactured and human assets

Our national infrastructure of good transportation, communication, educational and health systems is the foundation of our wealth and it has been paid for with many of our tax dollars. This infrastructure has a dollar value. It depreciates and we need to know whether we are keeping this infrastructure sound. Booking the value gives us a place to monitor and record our stewardship of these assets. Currently, we have no effective way of attending to this responsibility.

It would be very useful to have a clear summary of federal infrastructure that includes: the type of infrastructure; description; location; investment by federal government, by states and total; dates of investment; depreciation to date; and the current values. It would be most useful to have this as a searchable data base that can be cross referenced with data on the quantitative burden on the infrastructure and the maintenance and repairs needed to keep the infrastructure in excellent condition.

The failure of the bridge in Minnesota in August 2007 and the $315 million "Bridge to Nowhere" for Gravina Island Alaska (population 13,125)[30] highlight our failure to make grown-up decisions about our infrastructure. We can do better, and better information is the first step.

Intangible assets

Once we have all the tangibles on the balance sheet, we might consider including intangibles. Many businesses today include a value for intangibles on their books. For example, many companies put a dollar value on their brand name, because a well-known brand that has positive associations is worth money in the bank. What is true for individual businesses is true for our nation as a whole: goodwill and a favorable brand is critical to our strategic and financial future.

A positive brand is critical to our national security and to our power and influence on the world stage. Without the respect of the rest of the world, we lose our ability to lead and to influence others; we cease to hold the initiative and become reactors to the actions of others.

A positive brand is critical to the health of our economy. Our faith-based monetary system leaves us vulnerable to the goodwill of other nations; we need them to continue to support our dollars as a world reserve currency. We also need the world to continue to choose brand America for economic exchanges.

Imagine if we put a value on brand America—the positive opinion, goodwill and respect of people around the world. Imagine that the respect and goodwill towards America are on our books and that we have been paying attention to the very real and serious hit they have taken under the Bush II administration—dropping well below 50% even among our allies.

When we see global surveys showing a six-year drop in world opinion about the United States from high 70s down into the 10s and 20th per-centiles, we must ask how much brand deterioration is costing America in strategic influence, security, real dollars and the lives of our service men and women who must face the hostility and aggressive bravado that a diminished presence invites. The Bush II administration's egregious (and surely criminally negligent) bungling of both the Iraqi Occupation and the Katrina disaster may mark a turning point in the U.S. role on the global stage. The Bush II administration's response effectively pulled the curtain back on the "great and terrible Oz." We will have to grow up and get real about being the best, instead of counting on rhetoric and soundbites to convince others of our value, if we want to regain our position of high standing in the world.

What economic and security price will we pay for losing the prestige of brand America? You can bet that any business intending to survive would be paying attention if their brand had taken such a big hit in such a short time. America should be paying attention, too. Perhaps, putting this value on the books would help us attend to good stewardship of brand America, and incline us to hold those who do it grievous damage accountable.

The non-partisan International Institute for Strategic Studies reports that America's loss of prestige in the past six year's has created a significant loss of global power, and it is

one of the most important security developments of 2007.

iiss.org

System thinking and value

American prosperity is sustained by a complex system of interrelationships between our financial, social, human and natural capital resources. Our measures of health and success must reflect the whole system if we are to sustain and enhance our well-being. When our natural assets, which serve as critical habitat and critical components of the complex ecosystems that sustain life, are left off the books, we are leaving out information that is critical. We need to know whether these assets are being well stewarded, and we will only pay attention when we give them a value and track that value. That is the way our minds work.

We need the information about all of our assets on our books so that we know what they are worth and so that we track whether we are squandering them or truly conserving them for the generations to come. Our assets are the foundation of our prosperity and our collective prosperity determines our ability to contribute to the common good by paying our individual fair share of taxes. We will begin to track the critical links between these natural, cultural and heritage assets and the ability of taxpayers to pay, when we put them on the books.

ALL debts and liabilities

Just as our books include only a small portion of our assets, so, too, with our liabilities. Referring to liabilities, the 2004 Financial Statement says,

> *Other responsibilities exist that cannot or have not yet been quantified, so this list is incomplete.* 2004 USFR, p. 11

The section of the 2004 Financial Statements that explains liabilities and net position, says,

> *Because of its sovereign power to tax and borrow, and the country's wide economic base, the Government has unique access to financial resources through generating tax revenues and issuing Federal debt securities. This provides the Government with the*

ability to meet present obligations and those that are anticipated from future operations and are not reflected in net position. (p. 58)

This is saying that the government can always tax, borrow and create money out of thin air, so, "What? Me? Worry?" When savings and loan banks go belly up due to criminals and poor oversight, we just make a little new money, tax or borrow to cover the malfeasance. It all works out. Or, at least it looks that way since we are leaving about half of our debts and half of our expenses off the summary tables.

First a few words about the debts that are on and off the balance sheet from our Comptroller General, David M. Walker, speaking in 2006:

> *The federal government's gross debt (debt held by the public and intragovernmental debt holdings) in the consolidated financial statements was about $8 trillion as of September 2005. This number **excludes** such items as the gap between the present value of future promised and funded Social Security and Medicare benefits, veterans' health care, and a range of other liabilities (e.g., federal employee and veteran benefits payable), commitments, and contingencies that the federal government has pledged to support. Including these items, the federal government's fiscal exposures now total more than $46 trillion, up from about $20 trillion in 2000. This translates into a burden of about $156,000 per American or approximately $375,000 per full-time worker, up from $72,000 and $165,000 respectively, in 2000. These amounts do not include future costs resulting from Hurricane Katrina or the conflicts in Iraq and Afghanistan.*

> *Continuing on this **unsustainable** path will gradually erode, if not suddenly damage, our economy, our standard of living, and ultimately our national security.*

2005 USFR, p. 28 (emphasis is mine)

UPDATE: By 2006, this burden was up to $170,000 per American or approximately $440,000 per household.

This represents a one year increase of 9%.

Are we paying attention, yet?

Earlier we noted the 50% increase in federal debt over the past six years to a 2006 total of over $10 trillion. According to Comptroller Walker's analysis, our total debt burden has more than doubled in 6 years. ($165,000 in 2000, $440,000 in 2006, per household or full-time worker). In 2005, the national mean wage was $37,440—roughly 1/10th of a full-time worker's debt burden. The median worker would have to pay $7,500 per year—20% of their gross wages—for 50 years *just to pay off current debt*. And, that does *not include future interest* or *future increases in the debt level*, which are certain if we continue on this unsustainable path.

We are paying an average interest rate of 4.7% ($221 billion in 2006) on $4,867.5 billion in debt to the public. Add another $185 billion of interest on the $3,071 billion in debt owed to the restricted funds. If the average interest rate holds steady (and, it is more likely to go up), this administration has *already* obligated every one of us to pay about *$500 per year just on interest on this administration's debt*—a total additional $97 billion each and every year into the future on interest only—and we have two more years to go. In other words, the Bush II Republican administration has committed us, *so far,* to shifting another 10% of the Operating Fund away from government services to pay debt service to 'his political base of have-mores.'[32] The Bush II administration has reduced the money available for all government operating expenses substantially, while cutting a few billion dollars per year for health, human service programs and student loan programs so that they could say they care about the deficit (overspending).

It is no wonder that ordinary citizens feel they do not get their tax dollar's worth in government services when 26% of the service is debt service (14% to the general public and 12% to the restricted funds). Spending 26% of the operating fund on interest is a boon to the investors and bankers, but a boohoo for the taxpayer.

Bankers and investors also have a clear conflict of interest that needs to be openly addressed when discussing the issue of federal deficit spending. When bankers and investors, who own and control all our major media

According to the Treasury Department, from 1776-2000, the first 224 years of U.S. history, 42 U.S. presidents borrowed a combined $1.01 trillion from foreign governments and financial institutions, but in the past four years (2001-2004) alone, the Bush administration borrowed $1.05 trillion.[31]

outlets, make light of the size of the deficit, we have cause to weigh their opinions very carefully.

Shouldn't we be paying attention to our mounting debt and interest commitments? That is a rhetorical question. Of course we should be paying attention. These numbers need to be in the financial report, in sight, under consideration.

How we report now

Here are the federal government liabilities that are presented for our consideration (p.41):

2006 accrual-based, consolidated financial report

LIABILITIES *on the books*, In billions

	2005	2006
Accounts payable	67.9	58.4
Federal debt securities held by the public and accrued interest	4,624.2	4867.5
*Federal employee and veteran benefits payable	4,491.8	4,679.0
Environmental and disposal liabilities	259.8	305.2
*Benefits due and payable	117.0	129.3
*Insurance program liabilities	93.2	72.8
Loan guarantee liabilities	47.7	66.4
Other liabilities	213.2	234.3
TOTAL LIABILITIES	**9,914.8**	**10,412.9**

5% INCREASE in liabilities   **- $ 498.1 billion**

☹

And, the *consolidated* net worth for 2006

Assets	1,496.5
Debts	10,412.9
Net worth	**- 8,916.4**

And the change from 2005	
Increase in assets	48.6
Increase in debts	498.1
Net change in net worth	**- $ 449.5**

*When reporting separately for the Operating Fund and the restricted funds, the liabilities noted with the asterisk probably belong to the restricted funds.

The bottom line of the consolidated, accrual-based 2006 Financial Report is that in 2006, we gave the government $1,532 billion in taxes for the Operating Fund, plus $1,094 billion for the restricted funds, paid an additional $226 billion to purchase goods and services from the government. The government spent all this money and then spent *another $450 billion* to support their policy choices and administrative style. In one year, we increased our debt by one third of one full year's government Operating Fund income. IF we were spending *within* our income, your taxes would have to go up 30% today to cover our spending (or someone's taxes would).

What is missing?

Remember once again that while the debt that the Operating Fund owes the restricted funds is on the books, it does not show up in the consolidated financial report because it is owed between government funds and is netted out.

In the 2006 report, in addition to the missing $ 3,555 billion in restricted fund assets/ Operating Fund debts, which are on the books but do not appear in the consolidated report, some of our biggest debts and liabilities are currently not included in the financial report at all, except as supplemental information in the attachments.

Long-term federal and veteran benefits payable

As you can see on page 184, the government includes the Federal employee and veteran's benefits payable on the balance sheet. These are only the benefits due and payable to people currently collecting benefits; it does not include the future benefits that we are incurring for present employees who will begin collecting later. We will have a clearer picture of the cost of government when the future benefits, incurred today, are included in this year's financial statement.

The "Notes to the Financial Statements" includes an explanation of the assumptions that are made to justify the numbers that are on the books. The booked costs for veterans and government employee benefits are the product of tables that predict how long people will live and what their medical care will cost. Factors change, so the liabilities go up and down each year as these factors are updated.

Social Insurance Liabilities

The 2006 Financial Report made another significant improvement. The Executive Summary, on the first page, now includes our liabilities for Social Insurance, while noting that they are "off-balance sheet." This is an improvement over burying the information in supplemental "Stewardship Reports."

However, these sums are still not on the balance sheet where they belong, and where they will get the attention that they deserve. For social insurance programs, the balance sheet only includes the liabilities for social insurance benefits that are *due and payable as of the reporting date.* This means that all the future obligations for these programs are not in plain sight where they belong.

Here is the rationale:

> *The magnitude and complexity of social insurance programs, coupled with the extreme sensitivity of projections relating to the many assumptions of the programs, produce a wide range of possible results. The Stewardship Responsibilities section describes the social insurance programs, reports long-range estimates that can be used to assess the financial condition of the programs, and explains some of the factors that impact the various programs. Using this information, readers can apply their own judgment as to the condition and sustainability of the individual programs.*
> 2005 US FR, p. 34.

"Readers can apply their own judgement."??? Is that good enough for a great democracy? I am absolutely clueless about actuarial projections—how they are made, what all needs to be considered. My own judgment is inadequate. How about you? Are you a good judge of actuarial projections?

My tax dollars are paying for professionals—let them give their best estimates. Put a best professional guess on the books, and put the rationale in the supplementary material—just like we do for the current government employee pensions and veterans benefits payable. If the guess is off, or we learn something new that changes our assessment of future liabilities, then make an adjustment to the books and explain it. But, at least the liabilities, which are enormous, are there to be clearly seen. In the Restricted Fund Summary in Part I, all known liabilities have been included.

Other liabilities not on the books

The list of "significant entities" that are excluded from the financial statements altogether, but that create substantial taxpayer liabilities, includes:

- Army and Air Force Exchange Service
- Board of Governors of the Federal Reserve System
- Farm Credit system
- Federal Home Loan Banks
- Federal Home Loan Mortgage Corporation (Freddie Mac)
- Federal National Mortgage Association (Fannie Mae)
- Federal Reserve Banks
- Federal Retirement Thrift Investment Board
- Marine Corps Exchange
- Navy Exchange Service Command
- Resolution Funding Corporation
- Thrift Savings Fund
- U.S.A. Education Inc. (Sallie Mae)

A number of these entities are "government sponsored" and privately owned. The profits are distributed privately while the public carries the ultimate risk—privatized profit-publicized risk. In every one of these entities, the U.S. Government carries a liability. Here are some of the market projections for some of these liabilities:

The government is currently on the line for the following:[32]

Potential liabilities NOT included in the Financial Report:	
Insurer of last resort for banks (FDIC)	3,400,000,000,000
Crop failure subsidies to private insurance	41,000,000,000
Flood insurance	643,000,000,000
Pension Benefit Guaranty Corp guarantees	1,500,000,000,000
Guarantees for terrorism insurance payouts	100,000,000,000
Estimated total	**$ 5,684**,000,000,000

So, our consolidated books show $10,413 billion in liabilities. This number nets out the $3,446 billion in Operating Fund liabilities owed the restricted funds, and leaves out $44,147 billion in the Social Insurance liabilities of the restricted funds themselves, AND, at least another $5,000 billion in liabilities that we the people shoulder for privately held, profit-making institutions. That means that the liabilities on the books represent a tiny fraction of our full liabilities, and that's no way to be prudent, responsible or smart.

We can only make good decisions when we have all our liabilities and all our assets on the table in plain sight. That means putting them on the books where they belong.

OFF THE BOOKS

Missing Assets:

- General assets–property, plant and equipment that is not booked
- Heritage and cultural assets
- Natural capital assets, including land, forests, minerals, oil, natural gas and water resources
- Manufactured capital assets, including transportation, security and health care systems funded federally
- Human and social assets, including the federally funded educational support systems
- Intangible assets–Brand America–goodwill, positive image, respect

Assets on the books: $ 1.5 billion
All assets: Who knows?!

Missing Debts and Liabilities

- Long-term liabilities for federal employees and veterans
- Social Insurance Trust Fund Liabilities
- Liabilities for insuring pensions, banks, mortgage lenders, etc.

Liabilities on the books: $ 9,107 billion
All liabilities: (approximately) $ 65,000 billion

What you do not know *can* hurt you.

When the full burden of 2006 debts and liabilities is taken into account, it translates into a current burden of about $170,000 per man, woman and child in America, or approximately $440,000 per American Household. 2006 USFR, Statement of the Comptroller General

When you know, you can take constructive action.

We will only BEGIN to make good decisions when we have ALL our liabilities and ALL our assets on the table in plain sight. That means putting them on the books where they belong.

Chapter Eleven

☞KINK IN THE FLOW OF INFORMATION:
Booking income: sometimes as income, sometimes as an expense ☞

⇨TAKE OUT KINK #5:

If it's income,
call it income

Nothing is ever as simple as we would like it to be. Any time that we sit down to create a system to account for life's complexity, there will be square pegs that will just not fit into our round holes. In our government's accounting practice, there are a few critical pegs that have a big impact on the way we look at our government accounts. It's worth taking a moment to look at the pegs and at the holes we design to fit.

Imagine again our factory with the water heating in a boiler and then piped in to service machines. Imagine if we put in a little spigot right at the beginning of the flow that just discharged water into the yard. That is approximately what we currently do with an accounting rule that turns income into credits against expenses. This is confusing and drops valuable information off the table.

In 2006, $226 billion in income and spending dropped out of sight because of an accounting choice to call certain income "earned revenue" or "offsetting receipts" and to put it on the expense side of the ledger (as a credit against expenses). Consider that the total consolidated income (without this $226 billion) was $2,440 billion. Removing another $226 billion (9%) from consideration is a substantial kink in the flow of information .

When is income, income?

How should we record different kinds of income?

Accounting offers choices about where to record new money coming in; it can be recorded as income or it can be recorded as a credit against expenses. Both methods are acceptable accounting practice.

Money "comes in" to government in two general ways: 1) by political choice, which includes taxes and fees and any demand for payment created by law; and 2) by choices made in the marketplace – purchases freely made for government services. These distinctions are made and applied inconsistently to the way each kind of income is recorded.

The Analytical Perspectives of the 2006 Budget defines "offsetting collections," the income that is recorded on the expense side of the ledger:

> *Offsetting governmental transactions–collections from the public that are governmental in nature (e.g., tax receipts, regulatory fees, compulsory user charges, custom duties, license fees) but **required by law to be misclassified** as offsetting.* (p. 414, emphasis added)

The Treasury Department in its FY 2006 Performance and Accountability Report says,

> *To the extent practical or reasonable to do so, earned revenue is deducted from the gross costs of the programs to determine their net cost. There are no precise guidelines to determine the degree to which earned revenue can reasonably be attributed to programs. The attribution of earned revenues requires the exercise of managerial judgement.* (p.145)

Whether to record income as income or as a credit against expenses is an important choice that can change summary financial statements significantly—and in the U.S. Government Financial Reports, it does just that.

Let's say that you are an agency in charge of preserving your local park. The city gives you a budget of $500,000 each year to keep the landscape beautiful, the playground equipment safe, and the restrooms clean. Your agency income account will show your income of $500,000 from the city, and your expense accounts will show the amounts that you pay for maintenance—broken down into whatever categories make sense to you.

You have a choice in accounting

With the city's permission, you begin charging a fee to use the toilets, to help offset the cost of the cleaning crew and the supplies.

Do you create a new income account called, "Toilet Use Fees," or do you just put a credit on the "Toilet cleaning" expense account and call it "offsetting revenue"? It is OK by accounting standards to do it either way.

We must ask some questions: What do we need to know to make good decisions? How will the information be most useful to us? What are the questions that we want the reports to answer? What accounting practice will give us the most useful information?

Here are two options for the city park's financial report:

A. If it comes IN, It is INCOME		B. Kinky Information flow	
INCOME		INCOME	
City	$ 500,000	City	$ 500,000
Toilet use fees	$ 20,000		
TOTAL INCOME	**$ 520,000**	**TOTAL INCOME**	**$ 500,000**
EXPENSE		EXPENSE	
Clean toilets	$ 100,000	Clean toilets	$ 100,000
		Toilet use fees	- $ 20,000
TOTAL EXPENSE	**$ 100,000**	**TOTAL EXPENSE**	**$ 80,000**

You can see that your choice gives you a different picture when you go to your summary report, although the net is the same:

Total income	$ 520,000	Total Income	$ 500,000
Total expense	$ 100,000	Total expense	$ 80,000
NET	**$ 420,000**	**NET**	**$ 420,000**

As far as accounting goes, you have the same information and the same end result, so your accountant will be happy with the information either way. As a professional paid manager, you may read the full detailed report, understand the whole picture, and understand that one "total" income is gross and one "total" income is net.

But if you choose the kinky pipe financial report format, when you report to the citizens in the city paying the bills, they will ***misunderstand the full cost of your operations,*** and they will ***misunderstand how your operations are financed.*** Twenty thousand dollars that citizens are paying in use fees have dropped out of the picture, and so have twenty thousand dollars in expenses.

Big kink in the US Government financial report pipes

The United States Government has decided to use the kinky pipe format in some instances and not in others. There are "earned income/user fees/premiums" that are net out on the expense side of the accounts and their are "user fees" that are included as income—inconsistencies that create more kinks in the information flow and confuse us all about the full cost of government and where the revenue comes from to pay for it.

In the Financial Report, you will see a line item under income called "Miscellaneous earned revenue." This consists of

"earned revenues received from the public with virtually no associated cost. This category includes revenues generated by the Federal Communications Commission from the sale of spectrum licenses...rents and royalties on the Outer Continental Shelf Lands resulting from the leasing and development of mineral resources on public lands..." 2005 USFR, p.32

In 2006, this "earned revenue" on the *income* side of the ledger amounted to $17.1 billion.

Then, if you look at the expenses for government on page 37 of the official government financial report, you will find that another $226 billion is earned in the market place, called "earned revenue" and booked *as a credit against expenses—never appearing on the income side of the ledger.*

Here is the reason the government chooses to net out the bulk of the earned income on the expense side of the ledger:

*The purpose of this treatment is to produce budget totals for receipts, outlays and budget authority in terms of the amount of resources allocated governmentally through **collective political choice,** rather than **through the market.*** Analytical Perspectives, 2006 Budget, p. 301 (emphasis added)

The important distinction to the framers of the current report format is the distinction between money collected from the public through collective political choice (taxation) and money collected for specific fee-based services (like postage stamps, patent fees, park fees, insurance premiums, etc.) that are purchased in the marketplace.

However, surely if it counts as political choice to charge a fee for communication spectrum and for the development and exploitation of natural resources on public land, then it is political choice to charge people to use the national parks. Our current distinction is neither clear nor useful.

It may be more useful to create a bigger picture frame in the summary reports that makes the full amount of money taken in by government simple and clear, and the full cost of government programs simple and clear. How and for what can be line item descriptors. (See the proposed format in Part I).

Further, the above justification assumes a consistency in the government's definitions of user charges and offsetting receipts. They are not consistent.

> *The remaining user charges, an estimated $203.9 billion in 2006, are classified as offsetting collections and receipts on the spending side of the budget. Some of these are collected by the Federal Government by the exercise of its sovereign powers and **conceptually would appear on the receipts side of the budget, but are required by law to be classified on the spending side as offsetting collections** or receipts.* 2006 Budget Analytical Perspectives, p. 303 (emphasis added)

Inconsistency with the treatment of "offsetting receipts" is a major cause of the discrepancies between Treasury's agency accounts and the agencies' own accounts. In 2003, this unreconciled difference was $140 billion. In 2004 it was $69 billion. By 2006 this "Other–unmatched transactions and balances," was down to $11 billion. A significant improvement, but still a whopping amount of money. (Although to keep it in perspective, it is only .3% of the combined revenues of the funds–not so outrageous.)

By 2004, Treasury was able to reconcile some of 2003's $140 billion, but as of September 30, 2004, $75 billion still remained unreconciled for 2003 and then whatever remains drops off the reporting radar into oblivion. That 2004 discrepancy was more than the entire budget of all but two operating fund agencies in 2003. The unreconciled "other" in 2006 is more than the individual budgets of roughly half the 24 major operating fund agencies. The 2006 unreconciled other was more than the same amount that Congress was patting itself on the back for cutting from Medicare and student loans in 2005 in order to reduce their over-spending (a $40 billion cut spread over 5 years).[33]

So the confusion created by recording some income as an expense credit resulted in amounts equivalent to more than most agencies have in their total budgets. And that is just the money going who knows where because of screw-ups or poor accounting systems. In addition to the money lost in the system, the system deliberately leaves hundreds of billions off the table. The combined total is staggering.

This chapter is about booking all income as income, so for convenience, the following table uses the current official consolidated financial report income and expense numbers (which net out all the exchanges between the Operating Fund and restricted funds). The 2006 total consolidated income was $2,441 billion. The earned revenue total was $226 billion, bringing the full *consolidated* income up to $2,667. Using the earned revenue number from the GAO, here is our choice:

A. **If it comes IN, It is INCOME**	B. **Current kinky Information flow**
Consolidated INCOME	*Consolidated* INCOME
Taxes and other $ **2,423**,700,000,000	Taxes and other $ **2,423**,700,000,000
	Some earned revenue **17**,100,000,000
All earned revenue **243**,500,000,000	
TOTAL INCOME $ **2,667,200,000,000**	**TOTAL INCOME** $ **2,440,800,000,000**
Consolidated EXPENSE*	*Consolidated EXPENSE**
Gross costs $ 3,127,700,000,000	Net costs $ **3,127**,700,000,000
	Earned revenue - **226**,400,000,000
TOTAL EXPENSE $ **3,127,700,000,000**	**TOTAL EXPENSE** $ **2,901,300,000,000**
Reconciliation adjustment $ + 11,000,000,000	Reconciliation adjustment $ + 11,000,000,000
Consolidated NET $ - 449,500,000,000	*Consolidated NET* $ - 449,500,000,000

*Remember, this is not the whole picture of expenses because it nets out all the intradepartmental expenses–$344 billion in 2006 (e.g. the cost of FICA for government employees), and the $185 billion in interest paid the restricted funds.

And, here is a summary, which is just about all anyone looks at and uses for dialogue and debate:

A. If it comes IN, It is INCOME		B. Kinky Information flow	
INCOME	$ 2,667,200,000,000	INCOME	$ 2,440,800,000,000
EXPENSE	3,127,700,000,000	EXPENSE	2,901,300,000,000
NET	$ - 449,500,000,000	NET	$ - 449,500,000,000

As you can see, the net number is the same either way you keep the accounts. The accountants are happy, whichever choice we make.

By choosing the kinky pipe financial report format, most people in the United States *misunderstand the full cost of our government operations,* and *misunderstand how operations are funded.* Two hundred and twenty six billion dollars that we are paying directly to the government in user fees for services have dropped out of the picture, and so have $226 billion dollars in very real expenses.

Within the past five years, the total amount of earned revenue increased dramatically (adjusted for the decline in the value of the dollar), representing a change in policy about how we pay for government:[34]

2002	$ 175,400,000,000	
2003	$ 172,300,000,000	- 2%
2004	$ 176,300,000,000	up 2%
2005	$ 231,500,000,000	up 31%
2006	$ 226,400,000,000	- 2%

These totals only include the "earned revenue" listed on the expense side. When you include the "earned revenue" listed on the income side, the increase has been steadier (up 12%, 14%, 16%, 15%, and even into 2006). The total real increase in the five years from 2001-2005 (adjusted for the devaluation of the dollar) was 27%.

Either we are shifting more toward a pay-as-you-need-it and if-you-can-afford-it government, or our government is increasingly in the marketplace selling general goods and services. It is hard to know which it is, when these sums are out of sight, out of mind. This is a significant trend toward more fee-based government. Is that what we want?

Do we want a commonwealth where those who have more can afford more of the services that government currently provides? How do we decide what marketplace services are best provided by government? What government services should be available to all without charge and the cost shared? What services do we want available to those who can afford them? Police? Fire? Road access? Libraries? Education? Health care? National defense? What is the impact on the quality of our democracy and the quality of governance as the balance slides toward more fee-based government services, especially in an economy where the top 1% of Americans now own over 40% of all private assets? These are important issues of governance and it is difficult to pay attention and even more difficult to discuss the issues when the financial impact of our choices is out of sight and out of mind.

If it is income and we book it as income, then we can quickly see in the summary of all income, that $244 billion comes in via marketing and selling government services. ($226 billion is on the expense side and $18 billion on the income side in the 2006 report.) This income can be easily seen in relation to the income that comes in via "collective political choice," a.k.a taxes. This is important information that is lost in the current accounting and reporting practices.

The top one percent of households have 44.1% of all privately held stock, 58.0% of financial securities, and 57.3% of business equity.

The top 10% have 85% to 90% of stock, bonds, trust funds, and business equity, and over 75% of non-home real estate.[35]

When is an expense an expense?

Just as we currently have income on the expense side of the ledger, we also have spending on the income side.

A quirk or a kink?

Just as earned income is booked in the expense column, there are expenses that are booked in the income column. The primary example would be income tax refunds, which are simply subtracted from income.

For example, corporate profit tax receipts in 2005 were actually $230.4 billion. But, the government gave enough refunds, or made enough changes to taxes receivable to reduce the reported net corporate income tax to $183.8 billion. In 2006 the total corporate receipts were $380.4 billion and we refunded $30.5 billion, leaving a reported net corporate profit tax income in 2006 of $350 billion.

In this case, where the income was temporary, collected in error and returned, it makes sense to keep the refund checks on the income side of the ledger, and use the *net* corporate profit tax receipt number, which represents the real tax income. However, what does it say about our tax system, that we take in $230 billion in taxes and give back $47 billion? Or take in $380 billion and give back $31 billion? Our legitimate tax base was $184 (2005) and $350 (2006) billion, then we took in another 8-25% and gave it back, just in corporate profit tax revenues. How kinky is that? Taxation is a discussion for another time, but we get information for our discussion from the accounts, so we want the account reports to be as clear and as useful as possible.

Big kink—spending that is not on the ledger at all

When Congress passes a law that exempts certain people from paying a general tax, this is called a "tax expenditure." But it is not booked on the income or the expense side of the ledger. It is foregone revenue that simply vanishes from the table.

The reduction of income that results from preferential provisions in the tax code has been growing substantially. The GAO reported in September 2005 that the number of tax expenditure revenue losses has more than doubled since 1974, and the sum of tax-expenditure revenue loss estimates tripled in real terms to nearly $730 billion by 2004.

When you keep in mind that the total revenue available to the Operating Fund in 2004 was less than $1,400 billion, failing to keep half again as much as your total budget hidden from mindful consideration is a prescription for poor decision-making. There is really no way to compare the values behind income and expense and to set clear priorities. Poor decision-making hurts us all.

Mortgage interest deduction/ tax expenditure is not a home "owners" deduction. The bank owns most of your home until you pay off your loan.

Once you fully own your home, there is no tax deduction to your benefit.

Mortgage interest deduction is an interest-payer deduction that benefits borrowers and banks–and helps get people into homes that they can call their own.

It would be enormously helpful to see a breakdown of "tax expenditures" in the second tier summaries of income sources and expense categories. For example, when we give a tax break to home "owners" for mortgage interest, we are saying that we value, and we are willing to subtract money from our income to support home ownership based on borrowing. The bigger your interest payment, the bigger your deduction. In 2005 the estimated total cost of this homeowners interest deduction was $62 billion–a loss equivalent to 8.4% of the individual income tax revenue. Compare this to the money that we allocate to other purposes on page 23. What value does this borrowers' interest deduction (tax expenditure) represent? How does the value that we place on borrowing to buy a home compare to the value that we place on other priorities like healthcare, education and a safe environment? The tax expenditure to reward borrowing to buy a home, "ownership" on credit, is enormous and clearly a very high priority expenditure. Is this priority congruent with our national values?

Smart spending requires that we ask these questions of every tax expenditure. It is currently impossible to do so when the tax expenditures are marginalized or hidden in the reporting process.

What is in the net?

Dropping out the intragovernmental costs and income
What is the most useful thing to do with the exchanges between government departments? When it is an exchange between the Operating Fund and a restricted fund, it seems clear that these transactions simply need to be recorded and the separate reports for separate funds presented in the summary report. This will keep the true cost and income for each fund clear.

But what do we do with the information when Operating Fund departments and agencies buy, sell and trade with each other? For example, if the Environmental Protection Agency (EPA) pays the Federal Emergency Management Agency (FEMA) for some information gathering, it would be an expense to EPA and income to FEMA. It will net out, even in a separate report for the Operating Fund. Is this OK?

Right now, this information all drops out in the summary financial reports.

> *Net cost for Governmentwide reporting purposes ...is net of intragovernmental eliminations. For this reason, individual agency net cost amounts will not agree with the agency's financial statements.* 2005 USFR, p. 31

Fundamentally, again, financial statements that do not agree are a big kink in the flow of information—and a huge headache.

There is really no way to tell how much business the departments do with one another, or how or why. This would be useful information, especially when one wants to look at the functions of government and the size of the income and expenditures that fuel it. The income and expenses that net out are exchanges of real money. When reported they show a different picture of agency costs.

The income and expenses of most government department are different by 5-10% because the intragovernmental transfers disappear from view, this is an enormous sum of real agencies' costs or revenues dropping out of sight and off the discussion table.

When people talk about the full cost of government or even the total cost of government as a piece of the GDP, a big chunk is left out.

We can only have truly useful discussions about issues and begin to make good decisions when all the relevant information is on the table. It should be relatively easy to identify in summaries of each department's accounts the amount of income and expense that they have from transactions with other government agencies and with the restricted funds. And, it would be useful to decision-makers to see this information in reports.

What can we do?

If it comes in, book it as income.
Let's include all earned revenue on the income side of the ledger. If that means including it twice in the governmentwide summaries—once on the income side and once on the expense side, then so be it.

It is simple enough to include separate categories under "Income" to distinguish income from political choice, income from market choice and income from other government departments.

If it is an expense, book it as an expense.
Likewise it is simple enough to include separate categories under "Expense" to distinguish between direct expenses to the public, expenses to restricted funds or other government departments, and expenses that are the result of preferential tax exemptions.

Tax exemptions, AKA "tax expenditures," are both foregone income and another form of spending. They belong in our financial report.

We CAN keep the reporting of ALL revenues and costs of government clear AND comprehensive.

Chapter Twelve

☞**KINKS IN THE FLOW OF INFORMATION:**
"On" and "Off" Budget
Missing information in the financial report
Predictable spending ignored
Spending hidden in the footnotes ☜

⇨ **TAKE OUT KINKS #6:**

Tell All
Tell the truth, the whole truth
and nothing but the truth

Good decision-making depends upon good information; we cannot possibly make the best decisions when we do not have all the information, or when some of the information that we have is false or misleading.

Telling the truth is a moral value. We claim that it is an American value. We can choose to practice truth-telling and walk the talk of our values. Practicing truth-telling honors our country by drawing on our courage and drawing out the best that we have to offer. Leaving out critical information and confused reporting are a disservice to good decision-making, and disrespect our nation.

Babies cover their eyes and think you cannot see them. Our inner adult knows that refusing to look at bad news does not make it go away. We have the ability to do better than we are doing. Making sure we tell the truth in financial reporting means that whatever the definition of income and expense we set, the budget, the interim financial reports and the financial report must then include *all* income and *all* expenses in the summaries. Anything less is dishonest.

Tell all in the budget

All: everything is "on-budget"

First, get rid of the distinction between "on-budget" and "off-budget." A budget is a planning document. The President is responsible for planning for *every aspect* of the administration of the federal government, so the financial plan that is presented to Congress for approval should include every aspect of government in a simple and comprehensible format. Nothing should be "off-budget."

"On-budget" currently refers to all government spending except the Social Security Trust Fund and the Post Office. So, "on-budget" includes all of the operating fund agencies (except the Postal Service) *and* all of the restricted funds (except the Social Security Trust Fund.) No logic there.

"Off-budget" currently refers to the Social Security Trust Fund spending and the Post Office. Congress has decided that the Post Office and Social Security function somewhat independently and Congress will keep their hands off—the rest is "on-budget" and open season for spending choice. This confuses the concepts of mandatory and discretionary spending.

There is considerable cause for leaving the Social Security Trust Fund out of the Operating Budget, because its revenues are dedicated to a specific purpose, and this rationale applies to all of the restricted funds.

The Post Office collects and spends money, but it is not an official restricted fund. There are other agencies that also collect money from the public for services that offset their expenses. Fees at National Parks are one example. In 2004, 2005 and 2006, the Post Office took in more money than it spent. It is a profitable department, but that is not necessarily a good reason to keep it off budget. Other departments cough up revenues into the general fund, too.

However, the Post Office is run essentially as an independent entity that neither contributes to, nor draws from the Operating Fund. A good argument can be made for putting the Post Office in a separate category of "Independent Agencies" that neither take from, nor put back into the Operating Fund. This group of agencies includes the Tennessee Valley Authority, Federal Deposit Insurance Corporation and Export-Import Bank. This group of agencies still belongs in the budget and the financial reports, it is simply clearer to group these agencies separately. This is what I have done in the suggested financial report format in Part I.

Currently, "off-budget" is used to mean that Congress and the President have no immediate authority to decide how the funds of the Post Office and the Social Security Insurance Fund spend their money. It would be clearer to put a line in the budget and distinguish it by color, by bold type, or asterisk and footnote, to designate that it requires a new law to change the spending for a particular agency or fund. It is not helpful to have important pieces of government spending off the table.

The "on-budget" and "off-budget" distinction is a big kink in the information flow that requires countless pages to clarify. It takes pages and pages to differentiate and explain totals that refer to "on-budget" and totals that refer to "off-budget" and their relationship to the financial report, which includes it all. Whatever legitimate reasons existed for this distinction, they are long gone or could be addressed in simpler, clearer ways. It is time to take our financial reporting and planning up a notch and eliminate this distinction. Eliminate this kink and put everything "on-budget."

All: past, present and future

Currently the budget process leaves out past and future commitments because it is cash-based, instead of accrual-based. It's worth another mention here, because every bit of spending should be in the President's planning document, the budget, and all reports, so that a simple, clear and honest overview is possible and comprehensible. In 2005 past and future commitments added another $441 billion to a $319 billion consolidated budget deficit. In 2006 past and future commitments added another $202 billion, bringing the budget deficit of $248 billion to $450 billion in the financial report. More than half (58%) of our real, accrual-based, deficit spending commitment is too much to leave off the table in a cash-based budget process.

All: ten year projections

Whether we choose to continue to use a cash-based budget or switch to accrual budgeting, some attempt to project over the long-term is critical to good decision-making. The Clinton era 10-year projections have been abandoned in favor of 5-year projections. Whatever the reason for avoiding long-term projections, prudent planning requires them. Let's demand 10-year projections at least once every four years. Perhaps the second budget of an administration could include 10 year projections for a start.

All: include the supplemental spending

Congress currently allows the President's Budget to leave out substantial expected planned spending. Everyone gripes, but Congress seems to lack the courage or the common sense to simply say, "This is unacceptable." Higher quality standards can and should be met. With an election on the horizon, in the summer of 2006, Congress mustered a little courage and amended a defense funding bill to require that the White House include future war spending in the regular Pentagon budget, instead of relying on supplemental appropriations.

President Bush II submitted his 2008 Budget to Congress in February 2007. For the first time his budget included funds for the Afghan and Iraqi occupations. However, the presentation of a $124 billion supplemental appropriation in March 2007–the largest emergency supplemental spending request *ever* submitted by a president for *any* purpose– and then, a new record-breaking request for $196 billion in emergency, supplemental funding for the Iraqi Occupation and Afghan retrenchment in October 2007–suggests that the White House continues to avoid its responsibilities for prudent planning, and like battered wives, Congress is still unable to put a stop to this law-breaking, criminally irresponsible abuse. The new Democratic leadership has an opportunity to take the lead, and demand excellence. Set high expectations and hold your lawmaker accountable in November 2008.

The first four years of the Iraq war and occupation were all funded by supplemental "emergency" spending. In contrast the Vietnam War used one supplementary spending bill and the rest was included in the budget.

President Bush II's Budgets do not include any projections for general emergency spending. Zero. Nada. Nothing has yet appeared in the budgets for emergencies. While emergencies are not specifically predictable, prudent management will include a contingency line item to cover the inevitable emergencies.

The Vietnam War used one

1

supplemental spending bill.

Here's the recent "emergency" supplemental spending history and projection from the 2008 budget, Table 2:[36]

2001 -	$ 20 billion
2002 -	44 billion
2003 -	91 billion
2004 -	117 billion
2005 -	143 billion
2006 -	153 billion
2007 -	124 billion as of April
Budget 2008 -	0 billion

Over these years, the operating fund has run from roughly $1,200-1,600 billion and about $200-400 billion had to come off the top to pay interest on our debt, leaving $1,000-1,200 billion for national operations. Any additional spending has been done by borrowing.

Emergency supplemental spending has been running at **more than 10% of the total money available** to the Operating Fund on average over the past six years. In 2001, at the beginning of the Bush II administration, emergency supplemental spending was 2%, which seems like a moderate and reasonable amount of whoa-what-a-surprise-spending. In 2006, supplemental emergency spending under the Bush II administration and Republican controlled Congress had increased to nearly 14% of the total available income in the Operating Fund. In 2006 our Operating Fund had only $986 billion left over after subtracting earned income that paid directly for services ($88 billion), after paying interest

In 2001 Emergency spending was 2%.

In 2006 emergency spending was up to 6% of total cash-based consolidated budget outlay, and nearly

14%

of available Operating Fund income.

on past debt, ($407 billion), and after setting aside $130 billion to meet our moral obligations to our veterans.

When the President leaves out $153 billion in **reasonably projected spending (calling it "emergency"**—14% of all our available cash on hand in the operating fund, we are much less likely to make good decisions. This high proportion of emergency spending indicates a failure to plan and a failure to spend on prevention strategies that can protect against expensive crisis management. Any percentage is too much to shuffle under the rug or wink-wink pretend it will not be needed. Good, smart and prudent projections require that supplemental spending be included in the budget and in the interim financial reports.

There are several reasons why emergency supplemental spending has grown, and they all reflect poorly on the integrity and maturity of this administration, and both the Republican, and now Democratically controlled Congress. They boil down to self-centered greed and a willingness to be dishonest–to grab what you can for your own.

In 2002, under Republican leadership, many fiscal disciplines that the Budget Enforcement Act (1990) made law, were allowed to expire. This has meant that emergency supplemental spending bills have become a way for our lawmakers to evade annual budget limits and fiscal responsibility controls while increasing spending. The emergency spending bill process includes only perfunctory review. Items can be included that would not normally pass through the full budgeting process. Emergency supplemental spending is not counted in the "formal deficit and debt projections," allowing the President and lawmakers to tout lower deficit projections and fiscal discipline, knowing the bad news will follow later and few will pay attention. No one has the information that they need. We end up with poor spending choices and an imprudent, repeating pattern of supplemental emergency spending.

Some may justify the absence of projections for emergency spending as a tool to keep one-time spending from becoming part of the on-going budget by "keeping it out of the budget base." That is nonsense. There is a specific column for supplemental spending that makes it clear that these expenditures are not part of the "base" budget. We can put all the projected spending in the budget and make smarter long-term decisions. I'd like to see a requirement that every budget going forward include an "emergency" spending set aside that is equivalent to the previous 5 years running average, and a requirement that the use of these funds be strictly limited to genuinely unforeseen emergencies. How about you?

NON SEQUITUR cartoon ©2006 Wiley Miller.
Reprinted with permission of Universal Press Syndicate. All rights reserved.

Tell all in the financial reports

Interim reports—NO big bucks in the footnotes

If you have appropriated the money or expect to appropriate the money, it must be included in the budget and in the interim financial reports. While common sense, we seem to need a law to make this happen or new representation willing to demand excellence. Congress appears to need our support to develop some backbone on financial reporting. The failure to include all expenses is an ongoing practice, not just in planning budgets, but also in the interim financial reports to Congress from the President. In President Bush II's 2003 interim budget report, after Table #10, here is what he put in notes, rather than in the tables:

> *The total excludes $ 79 billion that was provided in a Supplemental Act for the Iraq War and $10 billion that was provided in the Omnibus Appropriations Act as a Defense war reserve.*

It doesn't say so, but the report also excluded the cost of the occupation of Iraq running at more than $5 billion per month at the time. This expense could have been predicted to continue from May (when the report was issued) through the end of the fiscal year in September. Honest, responsible and prudent leadership would have included another $25 billion minimum in the interim reports.

In the first year of the occupation of Iraq, Presidential appointee, Coalition Provisional Authority Director Paul Bremer successfully followed a 101-page plan developed by the Bush Administration.[37] Annex D of this plan was a schedule of executive actions that required at least 270 days of occupation to complete. Bremer was given a plan requiring nearly a full year of occupation. He followed this plan. Some costs could be predicted. Prudent fiscal management would have included a conservative estimate of say, $140 billion for this planned Iraqi occupation and related security cost increases in the interim budget report.

The Bush II administration has repeatedly said that they have not known how much to put in the projections for Iraq because they have not known whether the situation would go well or go badly. That is an unacceptable excuse from national leadership. They get paid to make a best estimate so that prudent and responsible financial stewardship plans can be made. If they are unable to make a prudent estimate, then they need to step down and step aside, so that capable people can step in and give us the projections that we need, the excellence and good oversight that America deserves. (Not to mention people with the ability to see that selling off another country's assets to crony corporations, and protecting private contractors from the legal consequences of misbehavior, before allowing the country's citizens to vote in their own government, is a sure fire way to stimulate a dangerous revolt.)

Adding easily missed footnotes about spending commitments deep into the text is unacceptable. All discussion is ungrounded when summary numbers are significantly inaccurate. Congress! Fasten on your cojones and just say, "No!" Send the budget back to the President until it is complete.

The failure to budget for the occupation of Iraq reflected the larger failure to make coherent and transparent plans for the occupation. If Congress had demanded fiscal planning, the lack of coherent plans could have been addressed and discussed publicly. The errors of judgement in the planned occupation might have become apparent, when they could have been corrected in a timely manner. The blithe trust in the Republican-controlled Congress that the President knew best and did not need to answer questions comes from a Congress choosing to function at a stage of human development they should have long-since outgrown—the stage when our inner child clings to believing that daddy knows best and that loyalty to people and ideology is more important than loyalty to principle.

Congress failed to demand prudent planning and stewardship; without this crucial check and balance, we were stuck with an administration that invaded a country with seriously inadequate and counterproductive plans for the aftermath. Planning (or the lack thereof) for the occupation of Iraq is an issue outside the realm of this book, but with a total cost heading past $1.1 TRILLION,[38] it will have an enormous impact on prudent and responsible fiscal management of U.S. resources for at least a generation to come. Our great grandchildren will be slicing a huge chunk off the top of their Operating Fund just to pay interest on our debts for this war of choice and folly.

Whatever their party affiliation, Congress's job is to tax, spend and **maintain oversight of the budget**. It is their job to demand the highest standards of reporting from the administration. Congress needs to send the interim financial reports back to the President until they accurately reflect ALL anticipated spending, plus a reasonable cushion for emergencies. They are not doing their job when they accept financial reports that leave out spending that represents 10-15% of the total money available for the operating fund. Supplemental spending belongs in the budget and in the interim financial reports. It is simple prudence and responsible fiscal management. Demand excellence when you vote. Demand zero tolerance for out-of-sight predictable costs. No more billion-dollar footnotes.

Tell all: reports for all branches & twigs

Currently, the full financial reports for the legislative and judiciary branches are not included in the financial reports of the U.S. Government. These two branches of government are not required by law to submit their financial statements for oversight.

> *Information from the judicial branch is limited to budgetary activity because its entities are not required by law to submit and do not submit comprehensive financial statement information to the Treasury. Even though the legislative branch is not required by law to submit comprehensive financial statement information to the Treasury, parts of it do so voluntarily while the information for other parts is limited to budgetary activity.* USFR 2005, p. 4

Separation and balance of power is a legitimate reason why the legislative and judicial branches of government are not required to submit their financial statements to the Treasury department (which falls under the administrative branch of government).

However, how about a full and audited financial statement for the American people, that can be attached to the financial statement for the rest of government? I would like to know what the legislative and judicial branches of government do with my tax dollars. How about you? In a democracy, citizens are responsible for the government in total, and we cannot live up to these responsibilities when we have no information about the financial behavior of either the legislative branch which we elect, or the judicial branch.

Tell all to the taxpayers: reports for entities that are either subsidized by US or for whom WE have agreed to accept significant risk

There are many agencies that have special relationships with the U.S. Government, privately owned, but publicly backed. WE the people have agreed to bear ultimate fiscal responsibility for the actions of these entities, yet it can be extremely difficult to get full disclosure financial reports for these entities. Full disclosure should be similar to that required of nonprofits. WE need to be fully informed when our dollars are on the line.

We can achieve the highest standards of accountability and excellence in government. It can be done. But clearly, we must stand up and demand it. It is a mistake to assume that Congress and the President will choose common sense solutions in a timely manner on their own. Citizens must push them in the right direction, or push them out of office.

Tell the truth, the whole truth, and nothing but the truth:

It is all "On-budget."

Include commitments to past, present and future spending; use an accrual-based budget.

Plan and budget for emergencies. They happen.

No hiding big expenses in the footnotes.

Provide citizens with easily accessible financial reports for the legislative and judicial branches of government, and all entities that create financial responsibility and risk for taxpayers.

Chapter Thirteen

✏ **KINK IN THE FLOW OF INFORMATION:**
Spending in relation to the GDP is of primary importance ✏

⇨   **TAKE OUT KINK #7:**

A stand-alone report
comes first

Imagine that you issue your business's financial report to your board of directors and the first summary lists the business's net loss as a percent of the local economy. Your board of directors would scratch their heads, and wonder what relevant point you were trying to make. It is likely that your business will do better in a good economy. More people with jobs will mean more people spending. But, they may not be spending in your business. A good economy does not equal a healthy business; this is not a cause and effect relationship. The economic well being of the *community* will not tell you how well your *business* is doing; you have a business to run and to evaluate on its own. Your business's net operating loss or deficit might only be 6% of the entire community economy, which does not sound too bad. It is also irrelevant to oversight of your business. That deficit may mean that the business is spending nearly double what it has to spend. And that is a problem that needs immediate attention if your business is going to survive and thrive.

Government is no different than business in this regard; it has a stand-alone job to do and must be evaluated *first* on how it is doing at its job with the money we allocate to it.

How we report now

The first, foremost table in both the budget and the financial report gives the overspending (deficit) as a percentage of the Gross Domestic Product (GDP). Comparing government overspending to the GDP only makes sense if our primary focus is the ability of government to take as big a slice as it needs or wants from the bigger pie. Once we shift our thinking about government's assets from the power to tax to the ability of tax-payers to pay, this change in reporting follows naturally. Once we are focused on accomplishing our mission ("a more perfect union"), we will be continuously improving the ability of taxpayers to contribute to the common good and continuously reducing the need for remediation and crisis management. Then, we will want to see how well government is doing with the money it is assigned to accomplish this mission.

After we have taken a hard look at the stand-alone report, *then* we can have a good discussion about what is a fair and reasonable proportion of government *spending* to the total GDP. And, we can evaluate the effectiveness of specific spending. Then we will be ready to make our projections and do our budget planning for the upcoming years.

In planning for the future, the size of the economy may be a useful tool to help project the amount of tax income that the government can expect under existing laws; the size of the economy may give some indication of potential tax revenues. The more business activity, the greater the possibility of greater profits and hence greater corporate profit tax—though no guarantee. More consumer activity means there is a greater possibility that more people will be employed, and hence, greater individual income tax. The size of the economy and economic growth is important to an understanding of the potential economic situation, so it is a useful planning tool for the coming year. It is simply not the most important consideration when looking at the size of our overspending or when determining how and when to hold our elected government accountable.

While there may be good planning reasons for looking at how well the overall economy is doing, there are no good reasons for focusing as much attention as we do on the cash-based income, expense and budget deficit as a percent of GDP. But, the #1 table in the 2008 Budget of the United States Government (and every budget before), Table S-1 Budget Totals, reports:

Cash-based consolidated 2008 budget totals: (in billions)

	2006 ACTUAL	2007 PROJECTIONS	2008 PROJECTIONS
Budget totals:			
Receipts	2,407	2,540	2,662
Outlays	2,655	2,784	2,902
Deficit in $ billions	- 248	- 244	- 239
Gross domestic Product (GDP)	13,061	13,761	14,515
Budget Totals as a Percent of GDP:			
Receipts	18.4%	18.5%	18.3%
Outlays	20.3%	20.2%	20.0%
Deficit	**- 1.9%**	**- 1.8%**	**- 1.6%**

Whatever percent of the total GDP our cash-based budget totals and deficit represent may be of interest to advanced economics game board whizzes. But it simply does not give the average lawmaker and citizen the information that they need to know how well government is doing with the tax dollars we contribute.

If anyone is looking to these totals to get a sense of what proportion of national spending is a product of government action, then using the cash-based budget receipts and outlays is leading them astray. In 2006 these cash-based consolidated budget numbers left out $202 billion in commitments to pay in the future. And, they left out another $226 billion in spending via the marketplace ("earned revenue"). Using the numbers from the accrual-based financial report, here is a more accurate look at the percent of GDP:

Accrual-based *consolidated* 2006 financial report totals:

Using **net costs:**

		Plus all the "earned revenue" and offsetting expenses:	
Receipts	2,441	Receipts	2,667
Outlays	2,901	Outlays	3,128
Deficit	- 450	Deficit	- 450
GDP	13,061	GDP	13,061

Totals as a Percent of GDP:

Receipts	18.7%	Receipts	20.4%
Outlays	22.2%	Outlays	23.9%
Deficit	**3.4%**	**Deficit**	**3.4%**

Accrual-based, consolidated, net, government outlays represent

24%
of GDP.

And...

Remember that these consolidated numbers, while more accurate than the cash-based budget, still net out the entire cost of services between government departments and funds–$185 billion in interest owed to the restricted funds and $344 billion in intragovernmental transfers (mostly payroll costs). These are real costs, but if it is income to one department/fund and an expense to another, it has disappeared from these numbers above. So, the comparisons of total government spending to GDP, even using accrual numbers with all the "earned revenue," are still not an accurate reflection of the total cost of government.

In 2006, the Operating Fund spent $622 billion more than it had in revenue. This is 4.8% of GDP. So decision-makers are looking at a 2006 ratio of deficit to GDP of 1.9%, while the actual ratio of Operating Fund overspending to GDP is nearly 5%–more than double. This is a recipe for inaccurate impact assessment and consequently poor decision-making.

The ratios of budget receipts, outlays and deficit to GDP are mostly irrelevant in a productive discussion about smart government spending. They have very little meaning, and function as game board numbers that are followed for their ups and downs, rather than for any intrinsically valuable information that they provide.

When the government's *first* tables in the financial reports give the government deficit as a percent of the GDP, it leads to national discussion focusing on whether or not the economy will be big enough to sustain the weight of the federal spending and debt (see Chapter 7). This is misguided. The size of the economy does not tell us how well the government is doing with the money we allot to it for the jobs of government—and that is the first and most important question.

So, what ratios do we need to see?

The 2006 cash-based budget deficit was 1.9% of GDP.

The 2006 accrual-based operating fund *overspending* was 4.8% of GDP.

–a significant discrepancy!

Net spending in relation to income

How well is this government doing with the dollars that we give it?

Remember your class treasurer's report. If we had $1,000, and we spent $1,200, then we spent $200 or 20% more than we had. Our spending was 120% of our income. This is the ratio we need to see to put our overspending in context. We need the ratio of our government overspending to the total amount of income that we had available.

greatdemocracy.org

For example in 2006, the Operating Fund had an income of $1,611 billion from taxation and from "earned revenue." Government spent $2,233 billion on operating costs. We borrowed $622 billion to make up the difference.

For every dollar that you put into the Operating Fund, the government spent it and then borrowed another 39 cents—which will increase the amount of interest that the OperatingFund pays next year, and the year after, and the year after, on into the future.

In 2006, for every $1.00 that you contributed to government operations, the Republican-controlled Congress spent $1.39.

The official report notes that the consolidated deficit is only 1.9% of the GDP. Whoopi-doo. That information is of marginal usefulness in assessing whether or not the government is spending tax dollars wisely. We can focus on smart spending by FIRST asking how government is doing with the money that we give it, and report so that the answer is simple and clear.

What happened last year?

You will have to speak up if you want the new Congress to do better.

2006 Financial Report: separate reports for funds
Accrual-based

OPERATING FUND		**TRUST FUNDS**	
Income	1,611	Income	1,514
Expense	2,233	Expense	1,342
Net	**- 622**		**172**
Net/ Income	1.4 / 1		.89/1
⇨ **As a percentage**	**139%**		**89%**

The ratio of this year's net worth to last year's net worth

What impact did last year have on our net worth?

If you have a family or a business to manage, and last year's activity has made a change in your net worth, you will want to know, how significant is the change? We want to know the same for government. Ratios tell us the significance of change.

In government we are dealing with mighty big numbers, so we could increase our debt by 2,000 or 2,000,000 or 2,000,000,000 and most people's eyes glaze over. The size of the impact does not register. An enormous number might be relatively small in proportion to the whole. We need a percent of change number to put the change in net worth in context.

To evaluate the performance of our elected government, we need to know how the change in our net worth relates to the net worth we had at the beginning of the year. Did our overall net worth go up or down, by a little or by a lot? We can help our comprehension along, by including the percentage change in our net worth. Here is an example of what it could look like, using the numbers from the consolidated, accrual-based financial reports:

Where were we at the beginning of the year?

	OPERATING FUND	RESTRICTED FUNDS
2005 Net Worth	-8,935	not enough info

Where are we now?

	OPERATING FUND	RESTRICTED FUNDS
2006 Net worth	- 9,336	- 43,728

How much did our net worth change in one year?

	OPERATING FUND	RESTRICTED FUNDS
Net change in worth	- 622	+ 172
	- 7 %	+ .4%

☹   ☺

This improvement in reporting will provide more useful information and turn the government financial reports into better management tools.

A stand-alone report comes first

FIRST we must know how government is doing with the tax dollars and tasks that we give it now. What is our current financial situation? How is this elected government changing our financial situation?

THEN we can have some useful discussions about the size of government, which to most people, either means the amount of money we pay in taxes or the kind of tasks we assign to government. These will be productive discussions only when we have the information we need about how well government is doing with the dollars that we give it, readily available and commonly understood.

Make the following changes in the budget and financial report summaries:

SPENDING TO INCOME RATIO
Show net spending in relation to income so we know how we did last year. (Put the tables about the ratio of overspending (deficit) to the GDP in the back of the reference appendix–or the round file according to your preference.)

PERCENT CHANGE IN NET WORTH
Show each end-of-year net worth in relation to the previous year's net worth, so that we know the impact of last year's operations.

In the interim, before we succeed in making the above changes, when you look at the current summaries that compare our overspending to the total GDP, keep in mind, that currently when anyone uses the consolidated, cash-based *budget deficit* to report a ratio of deficit to overall economy, the numbers that they are using have dropped out:

- **Any expenses that we have *incurred* during the year, that will be paid in another year.**

- **All transfers and exchanges between funds, including all interest owed between government funds, and any other payments made or owed between government departments or agencies.**

- **All earned income and all the expenses that they offset.**

So, the current budget deficit is not a particularly useful number for government oversight, and it is of very little, if any, value in relation to the total GDP.

Chapter Fourteen

⌂**KINK IN THE FLOW OF INFORMATION:**
Inconsistencies in format and terminology ⌂

⇨ **TAKE OUT KINK #8:**

Use consistent terms

The hobgoblin of little minds?

Ralph Waldo Emerson said, "A foolish consistency is the hobgoblin of little minds." He was making a point and did not go on to say what is equally true—a wise consistency is the helpmeet to big minds. We will do better when we use consistent accounting methods, accounts and terms.

There are eight major steps in the taxing and spending process, from the planning budget through Congress, Treasury, the individual agencies, back to Treasury and out the end as a financial report. These steps currently use different forms of accounting, different sets of accounts, and use and confuse some financial vocabulary. There are so many inconsistencies in the federal financial system, that all we can do is cite a few examples to illustrate the principle that inconsistencies hamper understanding and effective decision-making.

Account categories

The Department of the Treasury serves as the banker for all the government departments. Congress passes a law that puts money into each department's account. The departments write checks on their account at treasury and keep their own accounts of their spending.

In 2003, the Comptroller General found $140 billion in differences between the total net outlays reported in selected federal agencies' audited Statements of Budgetary Resources and Treasury's central accounting records. While there is an ongoing effort to develop a new government-wide financial reporting system, to help fix this problem, in 2004 the difference was still $69 billion. In 2006, there is an entry of $11 billion that is "Unmatched transactions and balances." Eleven billion is a huge improvement, but still a consequential difference. Correcting this may create useful savings.

On November 4, 2005, media reported,
   *-- Senate Republicans voted Thursday to cut spending on federal entitlement programs for the first time in eight years... "Today, the Senate took an important step forward in cutting the deficit." Bush said...*CNN

   Senate passes bill to slash spending; Measure cuts $35 billion over five years, WASHINGTON (AP)

Bush II's great "important step," and "slash" cut in spending was $7 billion per year. The Republican controlled Congress hoped to win accolades for chopping this relatively paltry amount off healthcare, Medicare and student loan programs. Cleaning up the accounting between Treasury and the agencies could save some or all of the unreconciled $11 billion difference—more than their great 'cut' in spending.

Simply keeping excellent account of the money that departments have right now might save 10 times the amount that Congress is nibbling, not slashing, off the budget. We do not know how true this is because the accounts cannot be reconciled. But, in any event, the amount of irreconcilable difference is a very large amount of money.

Standardizing the names of accounts and the names of types of accounts in the Treasury Department (that acts as banker), in the budget process (planning, authorizing and appropriating by the President and Congress), and in the financial reports prepared by the GAO, would provide consistency, clarity and ultimately, accountability.

Good news in 2004

*During fiscal year 2004, Treasury **made progress in laying the foundation** to address certain long-standing material deficiencies in preparing the consolidated financial statements. Foremost is the ongoing development of a new system, the Government wide Financial Reporting System (GFRS), to collect agency financial statement information directly from federal agencies' audited financial statements rather than using federal agencies' Standard General Ledger data as Treasury had done in previous years to compile the consolidated financial statements.* 2004 USFR, p. 44, Statement of the Comptroller General (emphasis added).

Bad news in 2004

*The automated system, though, was not yet at the stage of development that it could be used to compile the consolidated financial statements from the information that was captured. Therefore, for fiscal year 2004, Treasury had to **rely primarily on Excel spreadsheets and extensive manual procedures** to prepare the consolidated financial statements...Treasury's process for compiling the consolidated financial statements did not ensure that the information in these statements was fully consistent with the underlying information in federal agencies' audited financial statements and other financial data.* 2004 USFR, p. 45 (emphasis added).

Excel spreadsheets in 2004!? Thankfully significant improvements have been made in the past two years. However, there is plenty of room to improve. We need to utter some encouraging words to speed the movement towards excellence. We must make it clear to our lawmakers that this is a critical issue that deserves adequate funding. Inconsistent reporting platforms, spreadsheets and extensive manual procedures are inconsistent with an American commitment to excellence.

Consistent Vocabulary

Names are used to mean different things throughout the budgeting and financial reporting process. Following are just a few. We can build a comprehensive list on the website, GreatDemocracy.org and discuss alternatives that are simpler, clearer and honest.

"Operating" and "operating"

Every fund in fund accounting has annual operations–income, expense and net. These numbers answer the question, "What happened last year in this fund's operations?" When you look at the income, expense and net in any account, fund account or summary account, you are looking at the operations for the year for a particular fund. This can be confusing when there are multiple funds.

When the U.S. Government consolidated financial report refers to a "net operating cost," they are not referring to the net operating cost (overspending/loss) of the Operating Fund, they are referring to the operating cost (overspending/loss) that appears when you bundle all of the funds together and net out any income and expense between the funds. They are referring to the *net operating cost (overspending/loss) of the consolidated funds.* This is confusing, and not particularly useful.

There are too many "operating costs." In 2006, the "net operating cost" of $450 billion reported in the consolidated, accrual-based financial report, is the net income and expense of the consolidated funds, it is not the actual net of the Operating Fund ($622 billion)—this is because to the consolidated report, "operations" includes the operations of the Operating Fund and the operations of the restricted funds. Yikes!

The official U.S. Government Financial report uses the term "operating cost" in a confusing manner. Since we have a "net operating cost" for the operating fund, it is confusing to call the net of the *consolidation* of the operating and restricted funds, the "net operating cost." It is not useful to have two "net operating costs" that are totally different numbers.

Accountants may be able to decipher this, but to the average person, it is confusing, and lawmakers' understanding of accounting is no better than the average citizen's. That means we have lawmakers making decisions without understanding the financial impact. This is easy to change by reporting on the actual Operating Fund separately from the restricted funds and by using the term "operating net" only to refer to the net income and expense in our Operating Fund. Call the consolidated net, the "consolidated net income or expense" instead of the "net operating cost."

Trust Fund - "Trust Fund" - Restricted Fund - "Earmarked"

When is a trust fund a "Trust Fund"?

There is a legal difference between a trust fund and a restricted fund account. In both cases, there is a legal commitment to use funds for a specific purpose. However, they are different with regard to the ownership of the trust assets: in a trust fund the assets are owned by someone other than the trustee; in a restricted fund the assets are owned by the trustee, but the trustee has a legal obligation to use the funds in a specific manner.

Trust Fund

In the private sector by legal definition, in a trust fund, one person(s) owns the money and another person(s) is the trustee for the money. The trustee is legally obligated to use prudent judgment and care to preserve the trust fund assets *for their owner.*

If grandparents set up an irrevocable trust fund for a grandchild, the funds actually belong to the child. The grandparents may be the trustees, and be responsible for managing the money on behalf of the child, but they no longer own the money in the fund.

Within our Government, the Indian Trust Fund is an example of a true legal trust fund. The monies in this fund belong to a specific subset of Americans, Native Americans. The U.S. Government is the Trustee of their accounts (and shamefully doing a very poor job of it). Some of the retirement accounts that the government holds are also true trust accounts. If you are a government employee and put your own money into your retirement account, this portion of your retirement account is legally considered a true trust fund. For example, the goverment Thrift Savings Plan Fund is a true trust fund. This fund includes a number of federal employee trust funds. Federal employees own the assets of these funds. For this reason they are excluded from the financial statements of the U.S. Government, as are the Indian Trust Funds. This is as it should be.

Restricted fund

With a restricted fund, the person(s) holding the money may also be the owner(s). In Grandma's travel account in Chapter 3, you may legally own the money that your grandmother gives you. However, you may also have a legal contractual obligation to her to use the money in a specific and restricted manner. This would be true for a school with operating, building and scholarship funds. The school owns all the money, but they have a legal obligation to reserve the restricted building and scholarship funds only for their designated purpose. This is a legally enforceable obligation. If a school spends their scholarship fund on football jerseys, the scholarship fund donor can take them to court. In a common restricted fund, the person giving the money for a restricted purpose has a legally enforceable right to assurance that the funds will be spent as they have designated. If I donate $1 million to my alma mater for a specific building and they do not build the building, I can get my money back.

"Trust Funds"

Nearly all of the government "Trust Funds" are restricted funds in that we the people own them and we the people have set them up as restricted use accounts. However, the government "Trust Funds" are considered unique in that the owner (we the people) and the Trustee (we the people) have the legal right to change the terms of the trust agreement. More accurately, one could call these funds, "conditionally restricted fund accounts." This is why most government documents put quotation marks around the "Trust Fund" designation. It is a subtle way of saying, "Not!"

Neither ownership nor restricted spending assurance go with the restricted funds that the government designates as "Trust Funds" or "restricted funds" or "earmarked funds," or an assortment of other titles. We the people collectively as the Government own the assets, and we the people (as represented in Congress) reserve the right to change the collecting and spending covenants.

For example, the Supreme Court has ruled that an individual has no legally enforceable right to any particular social security benefits.[39] We the people through our Congress can change the laws that determine the benefits. Workers contribute 7.615% of the first $92,400 (2006) of their paychecks, and their employers contribute another 7.615%. However, unlike the $1 million building fund donor, individual citizens do not have any legal recourse if we-the-government decide to use the funds collected for these specific purposes in a different way. An individual cannot sue him/herself.

It would be very helpful to use consistent and accurate nomenclature. We could use, "Trust Fund" only for true trust funds, which are rightfully not included in the U.S. Government financial report as the government does not own the assets—someone else does. The government only acts as trustee. We could use "conditionally restricted funds" for what are now called "Trust Funds." Or, we can stick with consistent, but not quite accurate, and call these funds "Trust Funds" since they are the only funds with that name in the financial report and the name will remind us that we have a covenant with future taxpayers to hold the funds in trust for specific purposes.

Whatever we decide, let's be consistent, clear and honest. I have used "restricted fund" in this book.

"Earmarked" and "Earmarked Fund"

The term earmarked comes from a form of branding cattle, sheep or pigs. Nothing like having pork on our mind, and a rustler mentality—grab what isn't already tied down when thinking about government spending. "Earmarked" has historically been used to refer to the specific spending appropriations in big bills. For example, little paragraphs that say, so much of this money appropriated to the Department of Transportation must be spent on a "bridge to nowhere"—"Alaska's Gravina Island (population less than 50) will soon be connected to the megalopolis of Ketchikan (pop. 8,000) by a bridge nearly as long as the Golden Gate and higher than the Brooklyn Bridge. Alaska residents can thank Rep. Don Young, who just brought home $941 million worth of bacon." That was an "earmark," and one of 6,500 in the Transportation Bill–and one that was later removed, it was so outrageous (then the funds were resnagged by the Alaska delegation).

"Earmarked Funds" has been a term used by FASAB (The Federal Accounting Standards Advisory Board) to refer to some restricted funds—funds that must use their revenues for specific, mandatory expenditures like the Social Security Trust fund. In 2006, someone decided to change the reference in the financial reports from "dedicated funds" or "trust funds" to "earmarked funds." This new nomenclature confuses the covenanted restricted funds with the pork barrel spending add-ons to appropriation bills. There is an enormous difference between a "Trust Fund" like Social Security and a pet project like a bridge to nowhere. FASAB, please correct this confusion and call the conditionally restricted funds, "restricted funds."

Millions, billions, trillions

Very few people are good at quickly understanding the difference in magnitude between 1 million, 1 billion and 1 trillion. Public dialogue could be improved if the news and media committed to using just one reference in any given article, and included some comparison to put the funds in context. If the article is about specific federal spending, then the total amount available should be included.

For example, in the first days after the tsunami disaster in Asia, the U.S. Government offered $15 *million* in immediate aid while we "assessed" the situation. By the fifth day, we raised this to $35 *million*. (Less than the $40 million cost for Bush II's second inauguration bash, occurring a few weeks later). At the same time, we were spending $5.8 *billion* or $5,800 *million* per month on a war in Iraq. Many people lose track of the proportions when we compare $5.8 billion to $35 million.

In 2003 we added $76,000 million ($76 billion) to the military budget for six months of war in Iraq and at the same time Congress added $300 million to the budget for humanitarian aid to Afghanistan. Talking about millions and billions in the same context makes it difficult to make comparisons. In the above two instances, we needed to look clearly at the numbers to understand why some people are calling us stingy about our aid, and screwy about our priorities.

A reasoned debate requires keeping the numbers clear; everyone lost out without the productive dialogue that could have followed if we had asked whether $300 million in aid could help Afghanistan very far along

91% of our aid to the Afghanis MUST BE used to pay U.S. companies for services.

The global average for foreign aid restricted to purchases from the "giving" country is 51%.[40]

What values does this practice reflect?

a path to a stable and prosperous democracy in the aftermath of 20 years of U.S. supported war that devastated the Afghan infrastructure.

In 2007 as Afghanistan turns into a narco-state controlled by warlords and stressed by a resurgent Taliban, the penny-wise pound-foolish Republican-controlled Congressional spending and policy choices for the past six years are bearing strange fruit. Would they have understood these choices more clearly if it was easier for them to comprehend the difference between $300 million in drinking water, food and medicine and $76,000 million ($76 billion) in bombs and bombadiers?

On and on...

The list of inconsistencies goes on and on. Let's use the website, GreatDemocracy.org to track them all down and work out some clarity and honesty. It can be done.

Be consistent, clear and honest.
It's the right thing to do.
It's the smartest way to make decisions.
Smart decisions are good for all.

The accounts of the U.S. Government are full of terms that are used in multiple ways. Confusion abounds. We will take great strides toward becoming a great democracy when we are able to be fully clear, honest and comprehensible in our financial reporting. Inconsistency and confusion only lead to poor results. Consistency will make it much easier for everyone to understand what is going on in the government's taxing, budgeting, prioritizing, spending and reporting. We must make it a priority and appropriate the funding to make it possible. Spending pennies to save billions, makes sense.

DAVID HORSEY ©2006 David Horsey.   All rights reserved.
Reprinted with permission of Tribune Media Services.

Chapter Fifteen

⇨   **IMPROVE THE INFORMATION FLOW** ⇨   ⇨   ⇨   ⇨

State the change in the Value of the dollar

How often have you heard, "A dollar just doesn't buy what it used to anymore"?

You spend dollars daily and astute shoppers notice the slowly increasing prices. You know when your paycheck simply won't stretch as far as it did the year before and you know that the value of the dollar has changed.

We pay a little less attention to the change in the value of the dollar when we are thinking about our long-term personal investments. We notice that they are now worth more. Our reflexive primitive mind is hard wired to see bigger value and feel good. Feeling good can stop the mind from further thought. For example, we often look at the value of our homes and see the increase from the dollars we paid to the value today and feel smug, before we factor in the drop in the value of the dollar— 12% over the past five years alone.

To maintain an honest appraisal of our financial health, it is useful to include the change in the value of the dollar as a primary component of a good summary of the nation's and the government's financial status. A reminder helps us keep our financial situation in context.

The United States chooses a monetary system that is designed to create slow and steady devaluation of the dollar. (This is generally reported as a steady inflation of the supply of money and the consequent inflation of prices.) By design, the money that we all have at the beginning of every year is worth less at the end of the year. How much less varies from year to year. By design, this monetary system benefits most those who are closest to the creation of the new money that floods into the system and disadvantages wage earners and people on fixed incomes. Those at the top have many resources to hedge the impact of the devalued dollar that those below do not have. Our monetary system inspires comparison to pyramid schemes that benefit those at the top at the expense of an inevitably limited supply of rubes below.

It is difficult to think of one number that is of greater significance to each and every citizen's finances and to our oversight of government. The value of our dollars matters because when the value of the dollar goes down it takes more dollars to buy the same amount of goods. If you had $100,000 in your savings on January 1, 2006, on December 31st you would be able to buy $97,000 worth of goods. If you had $100,000 at the beginning of 2002, by the end of 2006, you could only buy $88,000 worth of goods.

Keep this in mind when you look at the constantly rising cost of everything, including government services. If your government spending is not going up, it is not keeping up with the devaluation of the dollar and services must be cut. Government spending had to rise 12% from 2002 to 2006 just to maintain the *same* level of purchasing power.

This significant change in the value of your dollar happens before and beyond any changes in your wages, your income, your taxes or your expenses. It makes sense to pay attention to it. We only pay attention to the things that we measure and report.

The elected government's domestic and foreign policies have an impact on the value of the dollar and consequently on the financial situation of the U.S. Government. The value of the dollar both domestically and internationally is bound up in complex supply and demand relationships between global reserve currency holdings, the currency of choice for oil trading, and the goodwill of nations. The Bush II administration has done significant damage to the value of the dollar; its use of bullying, intimidation and violent force, in part to keep nations in the dollar fold has exacerbated trends away from a globally dominant dollar. Predictably, one cannot force goodwill, and you are paying daily for this administration's policy choices, with a seriously devalued dollar.[41]

Noticing the change in the value of the dollar is part of assessing the effectiveness of an administration's policies. When people are discussing the increase in government spending, ask if they are using numbers that have been adjusted for the declining value of the dollar. Be clear.

If you want to check out the domestic dollar value for any point in time, try the inflation calculator at http://data.bls.gov/cgi-bin/cpicalc.pl. To find the change in the value of the dollar in the international marketplace, go to the Treasury Department, http://federalre-serve.gov and look for the "Broad Index" under foreign exchange rates.

Add the change in the value of the dollar to the financial reports in a prominent place.

2006

1-yr change in the value of the dollar: down 3%

5-yr change in the value of the dollar: down 12%

TOLES ©2005 The Washington Post
Reprinted with permission of Universal Press syndicate. All rights reserved.

Chapter Sixteen

⇨ **IMPROVE THE INFORMATION FLOW** ⇨ ⇨ ⇨ ⇨

Add a cost of borrowing statement

At the beginning of every budget, bill and report, *prominently* state how overspending is covered and the projected cost of borrowing.

Interest is the fastest growing component of federal spending. Between 2005 and 2006 interest payments rose from $181 billion to $222 billion–a one year increase of 22%. Currently neither the President's Budget summary nor any bills make clear up-front mention of the income available for spending, the ratio of overspending to income, where the money for overspending will come from, and what it will cost to borrow. We can do better.

When you borrow money for a car or take out a mortgage, the lenders are required by law to let you know what the total cost of your loan will be before the loan contract is final. It is often double the cost of the house or car. You need this information to decide whether paying cash, leasing or purchasing on credit is your best option, or whether it is even a good idea to buy the car at all. Maybe mass transit is your best option. Sometimes you do not have any choice, but at least you know what the choice is going to cost short-term, and over the life of the loan.

Knowing the full cost helps you make smart choices. Knowing what our choices cost is equally important in government and it is a simple improvement to include the full cost of government spending in the budget, authorization and appropriation bills.

When our lawmakers make laws to spend tax money, they need to know how much money is available and how we are going to borrow the money we plan to spend, but do not have. The President can be required to make a simple statement of funding at the beginning of every budget. Congress can be required to make a simple summary statement at the beginning of any budget resolution, authorization or appropriation bill. The Treasury can be required to make a simple statement of funding at the beginning of every annual financial report.

In addition to the simple income and expense summary described in Chapter 2, every budget, every projection, every budget resolution, every appropriation bill can include on its first page a simple summary for the Operating Funds and a separate statement for the restricted funds:

NET INCOME & EXPENSE:

If the net is negative, if there is not enough income to pay expenses, and DEFICIT SPENDING is required, then:

Amount we are borrowing: _____
Projected interest rate: _____
Expected duration of the loan: _____
TOTAL cost of the spending: _____

If the net is positive, if there is more than enough income to pay expenses, and there is money left over to invest or spend elsewhere, then:

Amount we are investing: _____
Projected rate of return: _____
Expected duration of the investment: _____
TOTAL return on investment: _____

2008 Iraq-related *interest only* **- $25 billion.**

Compare to *cash-based* 2008 department budget requests:

Veterans Affairs- $40 billion
Homeland Security- $35 billion
Energy- $24 billion
Agriculture- $20 billion
Justice- $20 billion
Labor - $11 billion
Environmental Protection- $7 billion
Judicial Branch- $6 billion
Legislative Branch- $4.4 billion[42]

Your share:

$163.00[43]

Grumbles about how it is just not possible to predict interest rates, things change, blah-blah are unacceptable. We pay these people to make a best guess and my guess is that there are already people doing this work. It is simply a matter of bringing the information to the fore where citizens and lawmakers can see it. Attach appendices that explain the best guess rationale and high-low ranges. Include whatever caveats seem necessary. One option would be to use a floating average; take the average interest paid or earned by government for each of the past ten years and average these numbers to get a ten year floating average...or 3 year or 5 year or 20 year...whatever. Just pick one, explain the rationale and do it.

The need for clear information about total commitments and cost is another reason why switching to a full-accrual budget would be useful. Even with a summary and a statement of borrowing, the 2006 cash-based budget would have only reported on the need to borrow $248 billion to cover the cash-based budget deficit. It would not have reported on the need to borrow to cover the accrual-based $450 billion deficit. And, to take it to the next level of clarity and honesty, if we had begun to provide accrual-based separate budgets for separate funds, then we would have been looking at a need to borrow $622 billion for our 2006 Operating Fund expenditures (or sell off assets to fund operations).

The $622 billion deficit is the real deficit—the real, total amount that we borrowed for our operations. Pretending that $374 billion in additional debt that will need repayment and servicing does not exist is a serious problem. (What an understatement! Isn't it appalling that it needs to be said?)

The government makes decisions about incurring, then managing debt that cost taxpayers billions. Oversight is a critical component of smart spending and prudent allocation of resources. Reporting on debt management simply and clearly is critical to oversight. We will only have adequate oversight when the reporting is simple, clear, honest and **complete**.

We cannot have useful conversations about changing the size of government (bigger/smaller) without acknowledging the interest on the debt that is creamed off the top. In 2006 we paid $407 billion in interest from our Operating Fund—26% of all of the income we collected for the Operating Fund.   Imagine what running your house would be like if you took $26 out of every $100 that you take home and gave it to your banker—not to pay back debt, just to pay for debt service interest.

26% of all income collected for our Operating Fund is now spent on interest on our debts.

To demonstrate trends and political party values over the years, here's a history of our debt (as a percent of GDP–valuable for the direction of the lines, if not the actual numbers):

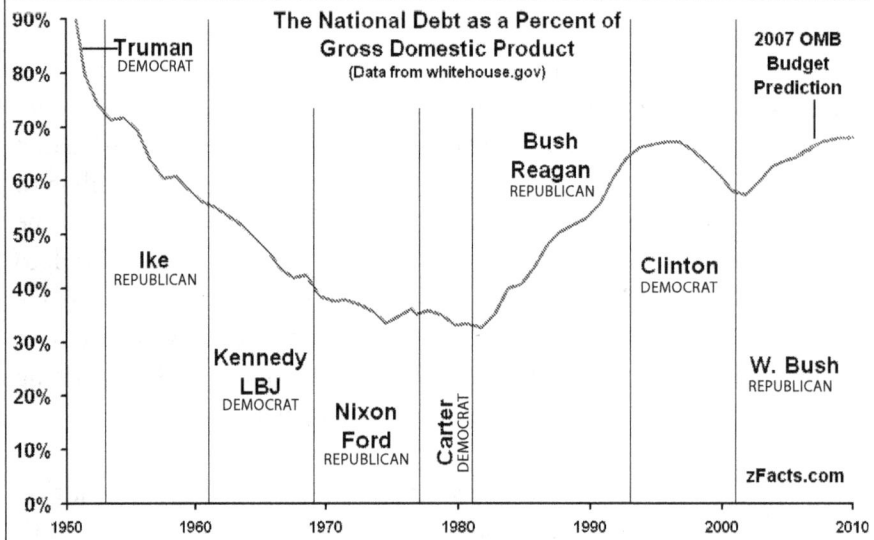

This graph presents a clear difference in the values about overspending and debt between Republican and Democratic administrations in the past thirty years. Prior to the Reagan administration, presidents of both parties worked to diminish our debts; the Reagan administration began a continuing Republican legacy of skyrocketing debt. The benefits, benefitting, burdens, burdened and implications are far reaching. It is useful to keep the financial records in mind when you vote so that your choice can match your values.

(If it seems partisan to keep harping on the choices of this Republican administration and Republican-controlled Congress, it is. The Republican party has a distinct fiscal attitude expressed by Vice President Cheney, "Reagan proved deficits don't matter." Republicans have been the party in control for the past six years, and their actions have been driven by party ideology. Their actions demonstrate clear patterns that reflect the party's values more accurately than their talking points. It is important to pay attention to the values reflected by *patterns of action* in both political parties because actions often differ from the values espoused. Walk and talk do not always match.

If you have a Republican Congressman, whatever they have been talking, they have been walking with the inadequate planning, incompetently managing, overspending, debt-incurring, oversight-resisting Bush II administration. And, you are going to be paying at least $500 every year into the future, out of your pockets for interest they have incurred on your behalf.)

When we overspend and need to borrow, some of our debt has been locked into 30-year bonds that are issued as "non-callable." This means that even if we have the money to pay them back, we cannot. We have to continue to pay interest for the full 30 years. President Reagan borrowed money at the ***highest rates in our country's history***—up to 14% interest. He locked in many of these loans as non-callable, so we will be paying an average of 11% interest on Reagan debt up until 2018.[44]

In 2003 we were still paying an average of 10.9% interest on $198 billion in debts incurred during President Ronald Reagan's term in office. Seventy-five percent ($147 billion) of this debt cannot be paid back until between 2011 and 2018. Just on government IOUs remaining from 1983-1988 during the Reagan era—at nearly 11% interest—we pay about $21.5 billion each and every year. That is ***more spending than half the departments in the U.S. Government have to spend each year***. In other words, that is one hell of a lot of interest from 20 years back.

We will be paying an average of 11% interest on Reagan administration debt up until 2018.

Many of these IOUs were 30-year bonds, at up to 14% interest, committing us to pay triple the borrowed amount in interest plus the principle, and loading it on the backs of future taxpayers—who would be you and me today. If you are paying income taxes today, roughly $2 out of every $100 you pay, is going to pay interest on the money borrowed just during President Reagan's tenure twenty years ago. Ouch! And you will have to keep paying most of this until 2018! No wonder bankers, investors and the ultra-rich, who own our media and control the national conversation, love Reagan. You too would be looking kindly on Reagan today, if you were earning tax-free interest of 11-14% on government bonds—with the bottom of this candy jar another 7 years out.

President Bush II took Reagan's legacy and ramped up to high octane debt escalation. He is creating the same legacy of transferring taxpayer dollars to wealthy investors and foreign governments. That is really the only way that you can manage huge deficits.   When President Bush II told an audience of extremely wealthy investors that they were his base,[46] he meant it; his policy of dramatically increasing the federal debt serves their interests best.   However, he can only continue to keep their investments safe as long as the world maintains its respect for the dollar, continues to use it as a global reserve currency, and as long as foreign governments are willing to continue to invest in our bonds. Given our current financial situation and the radical drop in global goodwill toward the U.S. over the past five years, we may face catastrophic financial restructuring. We simply do not have the resources to invade every single country that switches its reserve currency from dollars to euros or to a cooperative oil bourse (exchange). However, as long as the greatly diminished respect for the dollar does not lead to bankruptcy and the end of America as we know it, these big investors will profit handsomely. Their continuing support for Republican fiscal policy suggests that they are willing to take this risk. Are you?

Some of our debt is callable—the government can tell lenders that we are paying off the debt (calling it). This allows us to pay off high interest loans and switch to lower interest loans. Despite the lowest interest rates in history, the 2005-2006 U.S. Government Financial Reports stated that no debt was called in 2003, 2004, 2005 or 2006. The average interest rate paid by the government in 2006 was 4.7%.

During the Reagan administration, the U.S. moved from being the world's largest international creditor to the largest debtor nation, which we remain today.[45]

At the end of 2006, foreigners held $2,100 billion–44% of federal debt held by the public.[47]

This has a significant impact on our leverage in foreign policy.

Some people may say that we do not really pay 26% of the operating fund for interest—we pay only 14% to the public and the other 12% is in interest that is booked as owed to another government agency, therefore not of real concern (just "paper").   If President Bush II truly believes, as he has repeatedly stated in arguing for privatizing Social Security, that these Treasury Securities are worthless pieces of paper, he is a man of little faith and with a poor opinion of his country—and we hope that the world bond market is ignoring his opinion of our fiscal trustworthiness. [48]

Our primitive mind holds us hostage when we opt to see only what is before our eyes. Show a young child, from 6 months to 3 years of age, a bright ball. A normal child will begin to reach for it. Hide the ball under a towel. At six months most children will stop looking for the ball. If they cannot see it, it is simply not there for them. Their brain is not yet able to hold onto the memory of the ball. As the brain develops, the child will be able to remember that the ball is under the towel, even when it is out of sight, and they will lift the towel to find it.

As adults our minds have options. We can see through our child eyes or see through our adult eyes. Surely, we can do as well as a toddler and hold on to the fact that we are spending and borrowing to spend and the consequences are real, however hidden they may be by the towel thrown over simple, clear and honest reporting. We owe the restricted funds real money, whether or not we acknowledge it. When we exercise our integrity, a debt to our restricted funds, is as valid as a debt to the general public.

Let's call on our collective highest mind and insist that when we intend to place a burden on the future by borrowing, that we spell it out simply and clearly so that everyone understands our choice.

State the cost of borrowing; put a prominent summary of how spending will be funded at the beginning of:

- Every budget and every interim financial report issued by the White House Office of Management and Budget;

- Every budget resolution and spending authorization bill; and

- Every financial report,

To contribute to a better understanding of our financial situation and encourage more prudent and responsible decisions.

Chapter Seventeen

⇨ **IMPROVE THE INFORMATION FLOW** ⇨   ⇨   ⇨   ⇨

Summarize

When our lawmakers make decisions, they hold our lives in their hands. They are responsible for our nation's potential prosperity and likely survival. They need every available tool to assure that the decisions that they make are the best possible decisions.

Imagine a three foot high stack of papers-as high as your kitchen counter. This is the size of typical appropriation bills. Sometimes our Senators and Representatives get these bills only hours before they must vote on spending choices with life and death impact. There is very little doubt that the *intent* is to game a power-based system. This is early grade school playground decision-making. Surely we can do better.

The appropriation bills are monsters—hundreds and sometimes thousands of pages with little nuggets of spending hidden in obscure language tucked into long paragraphs. In addition to authorizing spending in each of the 23 major government departments, in 2006 the bills included 15,500 "earmarks," specific spending appropriations for individual projects totaling over $64 billion dollars (up from 3,000 worth $19 billion in 1996). The 2005 Transportation bill had 6,500 bacon bits, which can be contrasted with a bill in 1987 with 152 pork allocations that President Reagan vetoed because it had too much pork! The 2004 Omnibus Spending bill had over 8,000.[49]

Earmarks are pork barrel spending—you scratch my back; I'll scratch yours, who has the seniority and power to bring home the bacon decisions. The number and proportion of pork barrel spending to thoughtful, prioritized, value-based spending skyrocketed under the Bush II administration and the Republican-controlled Congress.

The Republican-controlled Congress developed a habit of presenting monster bills to our Representatives and Senators only hours before they had to vote and after allowing Conference Committee members to insert pork rinds into bills at the last minute–sometimes in the wee hours of the night before a vote. Congress had no opportunity to read the full bills through before voting. Often, few people outside the committees were even aware of important changes until after a bill's passage.

That's a poor excuse for decision-making and shameful.

With the change in control of Congress to the Democrats in 2006, some small steps have been taken to eliminate these middle of the night raids on taxpayer money. In March 2006 Congress passed a "reform" bill that requires that bills be presented to Congress *24 hours* before a vote. Is that a significant improvement? Just how fast can they read? Can *anyone* read a 3' stack overnight? Does your lawmaker think that reading a bill before voting on it is important? Is it important to you?

Also, earmarks will now at least have to be "owned" by a member of Congress and a data base is in the works to keep track and report publicly on the earmarking. Both Democrats and Republicans are making noises about reducing earmarks. Your encouragement could turn the noise into action.

There appears to be no systematic effort to base regular or earmark spending decisions on long-term state or national goals, or on state or national values, or on any consideration of what we can afford. Earmarks are purely greedy-grab-I-scratch-your-back-you-scratch-mine, with the highest booty going to the heads of the committees writing the bills. During the Republican Congress, Senator Ted Stevens (R-Alaska) headed the Appropriation Committee and brought home the highest

In 2000, $1 million was set aside for mobile computers for police cars in Wasilla, Alaska, population, 6,700. AP [50]

pork allotment to a state that has so much money it pays its state's residents instead of collecting state income taxes. With the Democratic take-over of Congress the pork has been very slightly reduced, but not enough to signal a new maturity in Congressional behavior. This I-grab-everything-I-can exemplifies the moral development of an untutored 2-year old. Trading favors unrelated to the issues on the table is a primitive and immature form of decision-making.

Pork spending may have a minimal role in smart negotiating and decision-making. However, good professional negotiators know how to focus on the issues and minimize off-issue concessions. Expect a high level of negotiation skills from your lawmakers. If we're going to spend smart, we must understand just how much room in the budget we are choosing to give pork and how this spending fits with our values, goals and priorities.

However, the giant bills that move through Congress do not yet include a simple, quick, easy to read, comprehensive summary. The current "summaries" are a couple of pages of generalities. For example the summary of the 2008 Defense Appropriation bill lists what the bill funds...the army, navy, et cetera...but it does not say for how much. That is not a helpful summary. Who can keep track of values and priorities with thousands of individual, specific spending allocations in a single bill, without a summary?

Here is a challenge to the President and our lawmakers: Do any of you read the entire three-foot stacks of papers that make up the spending bills? Did any of you understand all of the provisions in the spending bill? Would a simple summary make sense and improve your decision-making?

Congress seems to need our help to break out of the system that traps them into these poor and immature decision-making strategies. Good decision-making can begin with clear summaries at the beginning of all of the budgets, authorization and appropriation bills. Members of Congress should be happy to support a summary that makes understanding the bill quick and easy. The summary numbers can be adjusted when last minute changes are made deep within the spending bill. If last minute, middle-of-the-night additions are a move to avoid responsible democratic discussion about important issues, or to win-your-position anyway that you can, or to hand out billion dollar boondoggles to special interests willing to throw a few pennies into their campaign, then shame on Congress. We would do well to fire the people who think making this kind of decision is good for America, and vote some more responsible decision-makers into office. If you are voting for someone because of the pork they are able to bring back to your district, then you are part of the problem. Grow up and think past, "What's in it for me?," to "What is the right thing to do for our country?"

There is nothing revolutionary, outside our basic skill set, or over the top about having a summary of action when you are making life, death and prosperity decisions for the United States of America. A summary is a matter of common sense. I challenge our President and lawmakers to come up with one single, good reason why every budget, every bill and every financial report should not have a simple, clear and honest summary that includes the spending totals. Does anyone, in their highest mind, truly believe that you get the best decisions when the decision is complicated and confusing and billions of dollars in spending are tucked into obscure paragraphs?

America deserves our best decision-making. We owe our citizens, our children and the future an effort to make the best possible decisions. That means that we have to make a conscious effort to set up our decision-making so that we are engaging everyone's highest wisdom. We are cutting off our own nose to spite our face when our lawmakers engage in childish games obscuring information to win a position at any cost.

Let's insist that our decision-making process requires a clear, simple, honest summary of every decision—a standard, simple, useful tool. Our lawmakers have either been unable or unwilling to make it happen on their own. You, me, all of us must insist.

Add a summary at the beginning of every budget, bill and financial report so that we can make better decisions. We have to demand this summary; Congress has not been able to come up with one yet on their own. A one to five page summary for every single budget, bill and financial report can include:

INCOME
___

Total operating income for the year   _____

Less any amounts previously committed _____

Income remaining available for spending   _____

EXPENSE
___

Total spending in this bill (including tax expenditures)

(If borrowing to spend, then

      Total borrowed   _____

      Estimated interest   _____

      Duration of loan   _____

      Total cost of borrowing   _____

Spending by function:	1	2	3
Mandatory	___	___	___
Discretionary	___	___	___
"Earmarks"	___	___	___
Spending by managing department:			
Mandatory	___	___	___
Discretionary	___	___	___
"Earmarks"	___	___	___

Spending by State:
    Mandatory   _____ _____ ____
    Discretionary   _____ _____ ____
    "Earmarks"   _____ _____ ____
Spending by Industry
    Mandatory   _____ _____ ____
    Discretionary   _____ _____ ____
    "Earmarks"   _____ _____ ____

No matter how big the spending, there are only 24 government departments, 52 states and the Standard Industrial Code (SIC) can be used to identify the industries receiving special aid. A summary that is meaningful and that can be read and understood in 15 minutes or less can be done. Let's demand it.

Everyone loses when the truth is buried so that a political agenda can be pushed through. Even the pushers lose in the long run.

Include a summary at the beginning of every budget, bill and financial report, because it is:

– The smart thing to do.

– The right thing to do.

– The ethical thing to do.

*If you make yourself a sheep,
the wolves will eat you.*

--Benjamin Franklin

Where do we go from here?

Many people take a look at the financial report for the first time and feel despair. While there is good cause for despair, we can ***create cause for optimism***. The most effective action is grounded in a clear and honest appraisal of our current situation. We simply cannot get out of a hole, if we insist on keeping our head buried in the sand. The United States is not just about freedom, it is about responsibility. Be informed and take action.

Goldilocks and right-size government

Everyone wants government that is just right—not too big and not too small. Just right is a matter of achieving the mission in the most effective and economical way. Just right government is not a size issue; just right government is about how smart we are about collecting, spending and investing in the future.

Citizens on the right, the left and the center want government to be as efficient and effective with every tax dollar as is humanly possible. All citizens want our government to work at the highest levels of excellence and accountability. We can do it. Good financial information is the first step.

#1. Tell your lawmakers that clear and honest financial reports are important to you. Tell your lawmakers that you expect a high standard of excellence: the spending of every one of your tax dollars must pass an audit by 2008 or you will vote in someone who will make accurate accounting a priority. And follow up on your threat! This is a nation of 200,000,000 adults. You can find a candidate who matches your values in words and deeds, and who *acts to ensure* fiscal responsibility and accountability.

#2. Remember the simple nine numbers of the annual financial report, so that you have a context for all the information that comes your way during the year about government spending. When you hear talk about federal spending, keep in mind that after interest payments and after taking care of our veterans, we have less than $1,000 billion to spend on all other operations. A $190 billion supplemental war appropriation (October 2007) is 20% of that total in new *over*spending.

#3. If you have a little more time, go to GreatDemocracy.org and contribute to perfecting the improvements to the financial accounting and reporting. Once we have a clear statement of the improvements we require in order to have simple, clear and honest financial reports, then we can work to make them a reality.

#4. Spread the word. Purchase and distribute "coaster reports" (The Financial Report on a drink coaster) or the illustrated summary report, or sponsor their distribution. Our goal is to have a simple, clear and honest financial report summary in the hands of 90% of citizen-taxpayers by 2008. You can make it happen.

#5. Make a financial contribution to our work. GreatDemocracy.org is making a simple, clear and easily understandable financial report accessible to every citizen. Our next step is to get a bus on the road testing out strategies for making the financial reports clear–including a 3-D hands-on model of our financial situation. By 2008, we aim to have a replicable presentation that can be implemented at State Fairs every summer and other venues throughout the year. Your donation can help get us on the road.

We are each only as free as we are informed.

Otherwise we are easy marks for manipulators who likely do not have our best interest at heart.

If you read all the way through to this end, then thank you for honoring my effort. If I got everything right, it would be a miracle. Please let me know if I have made any errors and they will be promptly corrected–an advantage of print-on-demand publishing and a web nexis.

I hope I have inspired you with confidence that we can begin to take our democracy from mediocre to great by making some simple improvements to the way that we keep our accounts and report on our financial situation. If you like the direction we're heading with Great Democracy, your participation and support can put the gas in our tank and get us all moving on the road toward a more perfect union.

NOTES

PART ONE - The Financial Report

The United States Government Financial Report (USFR) is readily available online from the Treasury. In 2006 The Financial Report was also published privately as a paperback with a foreword by Representative Jim Cooper (D-TN), with a misleading cover band proclaiming, "THE OFFICIAL REPORT THE WHITE HOUSE DOES NOT WANT YOU TO READ." While Representative Cooper deserves a hats off thankyou for drawing some attention to the financial report, it is disingenuous to declare that it is the White House keeping this information from us. It is the current system–a media focused on a few simple numbers from a cash-based budget, a Congress unwilling or unable to pay attention to the financial report/fiscal situation, *and* a White House that probably does want to obscure its overspending any way that it can.

Here you can find all of the financial reports of the U.S. Government any time you want:
> http://fms.treas.gov/fr/index.html

More extensive financial information is presented in the budgets from the White House Office of Management and Budget (OMB), which include hundreds of pages on analytical and historical perspectives:
> http://www.whitehouse.gov/infocus/budget/2008/index.html

I spent almost six years working to first understand why the finances were so difficult to comprehend and then working to figure out how they could be more clearly presented to a broad audience. Over and over I have been sure that I have it all figured out, only to discover that I missed some important consideration. I am comfortable with my fallibility and have thick skin, so, please, let me know where I might still be off base. I am committed to eventually, with the help of others, arriving at a simple, clear and honest report that we can all understand and that gives us useful information for good decision-making. You can help.

The spreadsheets that I created to come up with the numbers in the draft format financial report in Part I are too big to print easily in this size book format. I am happy to e-mail you the spreadsheet files on request, if you would like to check and review these numbers. Please send your request to virginia@greatdemocracy.org.

Here's how I got my numbers:

1. VALUE OF THE DOLLAR
We are more accustomed to seeing these numbers as "inflation." However, devaluation of the dollar and inflation of prices/money supply are essentially two sides of the same coin. The value of the dollar numbers are from the Bureau of Labor Statistics (data.bls.gov/cgi-bin/cpicalc.pl) inflation calculator and were cross checked with Table 1.1.9. Implicit Price Deflators for Gross Domestic Product at the Bureau of Economic Analysis. (www.bls.gov and www.bea.gov). I also cross checked them with the "Broad Index at the Federal Reserve Bank (federalreserve.gov/RELEASES/h10/summary/indexb_m.txt).

2. BETA REPORT FORMAT: SEPARATE REPORTS FOR SEPARATE FUNDS

I wanted asset, debt, income, expense and change in assets and debts numbers for the Operating Fund and separately for the restricted funds. For the first time, the 2006 Financial Report, in the consolidated Statement of Operations and Changes in Net Position (basically, the income and expense statement) gave two columns: "Earmarked Funds," and "Non-Earmarked Funds"—new names for operating funds and restricted funds. This was hugely helpful and gave me the summary separation for income and for expenses. For the first time the "Intragovernmental transfers" (mostly payroll costs for government employees paid by the Operating Fund to the Social Insurance Trust Funds, $344 billion in 2006) were presented as a line item, so this sum was available for the first time—but not yet apportioned to the Operating Fund agencies and appropriate restricted funds. I had to come up with a way to guesstimate this apportionment, which is explained below.

The official report does not follow through with this summary separation on the Balance Sheets, so there is no readily available separation of assets and debts into those belonging to the Operating Fund and those belonging to the restricted funds (and those netting out because they are owed by one to the other). The 2006 summaries for the 16 major restricted funds includes a summary (p. 87) that I used in my calculations. Oddly, the same chart did not include a total column for 2005—a nuisance. My strategy for estimating these separate assets and debts is also explained below (page numbers are from the official 2006 Financial Report):

THE BALANCE SHEET-NET WORTH

The historical numbers in Part I, in all cases, have also been adjusted for the declining value of the dollar so that year to year comparisons of the totals are more accurate.

ASSETS

The 2006 USFR consolidated Balance Sheet (p.41) and the Balance Sheet summary for the restricted funds (p.87) are the basis for the 2006 numbers in Part I. The historical numbers are from the respective balance sheets in the 2002-2005 financial reports, and from the Note on "Dedicated Collections." I made assumptions about assigning the assets to either the Operating Fund or the restricted funds, that work for a ballpark understanding; they are not an accurate apportionment, since accurate apportionment is not yet available in the current reporting format.

ASSETS BELONGING TO THE OPERATING FUND

Property, plant and equipment (2006-$689 billion, p.41). I assumed that the bulk of the property, plant and equipment belongs either to the Department of Defense or other Operating Fund agencies that manage the restricted funds, and assigned 100% of this sum to the Operating Fund. There was no way to even guess how to divide it up accurately.

Historical 2002-2005. All years show 100% of "Property, plant and equipment belonging to the Operating Fund.

Inventories and related property (2006-$281 billion, p. 41). Ditto: I assigned 100% of this to the Operating Fund, and used 100% of the totals for 2002-2005 (again, adjusted for the devaluation of the dollar).

Loans receivable (2006-$221 billion, p. 41). While it is likely that some portion of the loans receivable belong to the restricted funds, I have again assigned 100% of these assets to the Operating Fund. Page 87 of the consolidated financial report, "Earmarked Funds" lists the assets of the restricted funds, and lists no loans receivable. These may be included with either the "other monetary assets," "other federal assets," or "non-federal assets," which I deal with under other categories. It should generally come out in the wash and give us a ballpark understanding. Historical numbers for 2002-2005 attributed 100% of the loans receivable to the Operating Fund and then adjusted these numbers for the devaluation of the dollar.

Cash & other monetary assets (2006-$98 billion, p. 41). The totals for restricted funds on page 87 (2006 USFR) lists a total of cash and other monetary assets belonging to the restricted funds of $24 billion. This restricted fund summary also lists a "balance with treasury" which means a cash balance of $87 billion. To get the $-13 billion number used in the financial report in Part I:

Cash & other monetary assets in the consolidated report, p. 41	98 billion
Less cash & other monetary assets attributed to the restricted funds, p. 87	- 24 billion
Less restricted funds' "fund balance with treasury," p. 87	- 87 billion
Operating Fund "Cash & other monetary assets"	$ - 13 billion

Historical 2002-2005. Essentially all of the cash and monetary assets in 2006 belong to the restricted funds by these calculations, so 0% of the cash and monetary assets in the consolidated reports for 2002-2005 has been allocated to the Operating Fund.

Accounts and taxes receivable (2006-$69 billion, p. 41). Note 3 of the 2006 USFR explains that in the consolidated report these "accounts receivable" include interest and "claims to cash or other assets from entities outside the Government." Taxes receivable consist "primarily of assessments, penalties, and related interest that were not paid or abated and which the taxpayers have agreed the amounts are owed or a court has determined the assessments are owed." Both accounts and taxes receivable totals given in the USFR are net of an allowance for uncollectible accounts. For the accounts receivable this uncollectible margin is $12.5 billion for 2006. The margin for uncollectible taxes is not given. Going with the $12.5 billion uncollectible, this means that the actual total of accounts receivable is at least $81 billion, and the annual write-off is 15%. How does this compare with good business practices? Is 15% a reasonable write-off? Since the sum being written off is $12.5 billion–nearly equal to the amount we give in foreign aid every year and considerably more than we spend to protect our environment upon which our lives and livelihood depend ($9 billion)–it seems likely that spending a little more to beef up our collection practices could pay off.

While it is likely that some of these taxes receivable belong to the restricted funds, it is likely that they are included in the "Cash & other monetary assets" listed for the restricted funds on page 87. I've already subtracted these from the "Cash & other monetary assets" total above, so all of the "Accounts and taxes receivable" in the consolidated report have been assigned to the Operating Fund in Part I. This is probably not strictly accurate, but again close enough.

Securities & investments and other assets (2006- $84 billion in "Securities and Investments" and $55 billion in "Other," p. 41–total $139 billion). According to page 87, the restricted funds have $87 billion in "Non-federal assets." So I took the total of $139 billion attributed to the consolidated funds and subtracted the $87 billion attributed to the restricted funds.

Consolidated securities and investments, p. 41	84 billion
Plus consolidated "Other assets," p. 41	+ 55 billion
Less restricted funds' "Non-federal assets," p. 87	- 97 billion
Operating Fund "Other assets"	$ 43 billion

Historical 2002-2005. The $43 billion in 2006 attributed to the Operating Fund represents 31% of the $139 billion total given in the consolidated financial report. So, to calculate a ballpark estimate of the "Other assets" (which includes securities and investments, only separated out in 2005), I have taken 31% of the "Other assets" plus the "Securities and Investments" for 2002-2005, and assigned this 31% to the Operating Fund and the balance to the restricted funds.

ASSETS BELONGING TO THE RESTRICTED FUNDS. The 2006 USFR, p. 87 gives a total for assets belong to the restricted funds of $3,865 billion. This is the figure used in Part I.

DEBTS
The consolidated debts/liabilities are listed on the United States Government Balance Sheets, p. 41, and those of the restricted funds are listed on page 87. Again, these were the basis for my separation of the Operating Fund debts and liabilities from those belonging to the restricted funds.

OPERATING FUND DEBTS & RESTRICTED FUND DEBTS
Federal debt securities held by the public (2006- $4,868 billion, p. 41). These are the result of Operating Fund overspending and have all been allocated to the Operating Fund.

Debts to the restricted funds (2006-$3,658 billion). The debts to the restricted funds net out in the consolidated report and do not appear on the consolidated Balance Sheet, p. 41. In the assets belonging to the restricted funds on page 87, "Investments in U.S. Treasury Securities" total $3,555 billion. Another $103 billion is listed on page 87 as "Other Federal assets." The total of these two is $3,658, and this is the total listed as a debt of the Operating Fund in Part one. It is balanced by its listing as an asset to the restricted funds in Part I, and it is net out in the consolidated report.

Environmental and disposal liabilities (2006- $305 billion). We have set up a restricted fund to cover the cost of environmental and disposal liabilities, the Hazardous Substance Superfund. This fund only shows $ .5 billion in liabilities, however, so I have to assume that the $305 billion in liabilities listed in the consolidated net all belongs to the Operating Fund. In 2006 and historically (2002-2005) 100% of environmental and disposal liabilities have been attributed to the Operating Fund.

(An aside: the Hazardous Substance Superfund appears to have program expenses of $1.4 billion in 2006. It collected $.3 billion from the public, $ .1 billion in investment revenue and another $1.2 billion from the Operating Fund to cover the balance of program costs and to leave a little left over to increase the assets on the balance sheet. Clearly, if this restricted fund was established to put the burden of cleanup on the industries creating and profiting from the pollution, that is not what is happening. The public is bearing the brunt of cleanup/risk/liability. The operating principle: privatize profit to keep the economy growing, place the burden of risk and liability on the public). The underlying assumption is: happy business equals happy people.

Loan guarantee liabilities (2006-$66 billion, p. 41). These have all been allocated to the Operating Fund, since I allocated all the "Loans receivable" to the Operating Fund.

Accounts payable (2006-$58 billion, p. 41). These have all been allocated to the Operating Fund.

Other liabilities. The consolidated net liabilities on page 41 of the 2006 USFR includes the following additional categories: Benefits due and payable ($129 billion), Insurance program liabilities ($73 billion), Federal employee and veteran benefits payable ($4,679 billion), and Other liabilities ($234 billion) for a remaining total of $5,115 billion.

The restricted fund liabilities reported on page 87 only includes the categories "Liabilities due and payable to beneficiaries" ($120 billion), "Other Federal liabilities" ($96 billion), and "Other non-federal liabilities" ($3,230 billion). These categories do not match the categories in the consolidated report.

So I've taken the consolidated net total and subtracted the total listed for the restricted funds.

Benefits due and payable, p. 41	129 billion
Insurance program liabilities, p. 41	+ 73 billion
Federal employee and veteran benefits payable, p. 41	+ 4,679 billion
Other liabilities, p. 41	+ 234 billion
CONSOLIDATED "OTHER" TOTAL	$5,115 billion
Liabilities due and payable to beneficiaries by the restricted funds, p. 87	- 120 billion
Other federal liabilities belonging to the restricted funds, p. 87	-96 billion
Other non-federal liabilities belonging to the restricted funds, p. 87	-3,230 billion
OTHER LIABILITIES BELONGING TO THE OPERATING FUND	$1,670 billion

It's important to note that the consolidated numbers are nets (combined funds). To subtract the restricted funds liabilities from these totals is not really accurate. It is likely that if we could see the separate fund reports that have been consolidated, we would find that the Operating Fund liabilities are actually higher and in balance the restricted fund assets are also higher. These accurate numbers are inaccessible, so again, Part I goes with what we have for now. It is ballpark accurate.

RESTRICTED FUND LIABILITIES

The restricted fund liabilities in Part I of this book lists "Current liabilities due and payable to beneficiaries" ($3,350 billion). This is the sum of the "Liabilities due and payable to beneficiaries" ($120 billion) and the "Other Non-federal liabilities" ($3,230 billion). According to the financial report, the liabilities due and payable to beneficiaries listed only includes monies currently owed. It does not include future obligations. Current laws do not require that the latter be included as a liability on the books. This represents bizarre irresponsibility, as discussed in Chapter 10.

The proposed format in Part I puts these long-term social insurance responsibilities on the books where they belong. The projected total is given in the Executive Summary of the 2006 USFR, p. 3. I have used the total for the "Closed Group of current participants"- $44,147 billion. The closed group "includes current participants (i.e., receiving and/or are eligible to receive benefits) ages 15 and over at the start of the period."

The task of sorting out these numbers from previous year's financial reports is beyond me, so I have not completed the historical information for the restricted funds. Help is welcome.

THE INCOME & EXPENSE STATEMENT

There are several issues with the income and expense statement which were resolved by using the consolidated expense statement on p. 37 of the USFR and comparing it with the individual agency financial reports which are all available from the websites of the various departments. The issues are:

1) **Separating the Operating Fund agencies from the Restricted Fund agencies and the Independent Agencies.** The list of expenses in the USFR (2006, p. 37) includes all major government agencies. Some of these agencies are funded totally from the Operating Fund. Some have funding from the Operating Fund for some of their programs, but also manage the programs that are funded by restricted

funds. Some of the agencies listed are essentially independent; they neither contribute to, nor draw from the Operating Fund except in emergencies.

The proposed format assumes that it is most useful to see the Operating Fund income and expenditures together, and to see the restricted and independent funds separately.

I looked at the financial reports of every agency, which beginning in 2006 are also required to separate their expense summary into "Earmarked Funds" (restricted funds) and "All Other" (Operating Fund monies). Using the allocation from these agency reports, the following agencies belong as restricted fund agencies:

> **Social Security Administration** (92% restricted fund expenditures). The other 8% is a total of $44.8 billion dollars. Since the SSA has more than adequate funding as a restricted fund to cover all of the program expenses–at least for a few more years, it is unclear why it uses $44.8 billion in "Other funds." This requires more research to determine whether the Operating Fund should have another line item that is Operating Fund "Support for the Social Security Program." Until we have this additional information, I have put the SSA in under restricted funds. This may or may not be fully accurate.

> **The Office of Personnel and Management,** the **Railroad Retirement Board,** the **National Credit Union Administration**, and the **Pension Benefit Guarantee corporation** all show in their agency financial reports that 100% of their expenditures are "Earmarked" or restricted fund expenditures, so these agencies have been put in the restricted fund group and removed from the Operating Fund expense list.

The following agencies have also been removed from the Operating Fund list and put in a separate category of "Independent Agencies." These agencies neither draw from, nor contribute to the Operating Fund. When included in the Operating Fund report, they skew the results. For example, the Post Office has been making money for the past few years. In 2006 they earned $71.6 billion and spent $58.9 billion on operations, leaving them with a net income of $12.7 billion. It is most useful to see these agencies that we expect to make it on their own, on their own; that is how we get the information that we need for oversight.

2) **Should income be reported as gross income or net income?** (Chapter 11). I have argued that we get the most accurate picture of the full cost of government and the full revenues available to pay the costs by reporting the gross revenues and expenses, instead of the net. So the suggested draft format in Part I does that. The gross income is reported on page 37 of the 2006 USFR.

3) **Show Intra-agency costs in the summaries.** I wanted the intragovernmental transfers which are expenses to the Operating Fund and income to the restricted funds to show up on both the income side and in the expenses for each department, so I needed to know what share of the $344 billion belonged to each agency. I also wanted to know what share of the "earned revenue," currently found on both the income and expense side, belonged to the Operating Fund and separately to the restricted funds. To guesstimate this separation of the funds, I prepared a spreadsheet listing all the agencies and dividing them into three categories (Operating Fund, Independents and restricted funds), with the following columns:

A.   2006 USFR, p. 37: Gross expense for each department

B.   2006 USFR, p. 37: "Earned revenue"

C.   2006 USFR, p. 37: Net cost

D.   2006 individual agency financial reports: "All Other expenses" which I assumed belong to the Operating Fund. Note: the sum of agency "All Other Expenses" totals $1,701.1 billion, which is $66 billion more than the summary total of $1,635.1 given for "Non-Earmarked expenses" on page 38 of the 2006 USFR.

E.   2006 individual agency financial reports: "Earmarked" expenses which I assumed belong to restricted funds. This total for all agencies (Operating Fund, Independent and restricted funds) of $1,119.4 billion is $146.8 less than the $1,266.2 billion on page 38 of the 2006 USFR.

F.   2006 individual agency financial reports: Total Consolidated net agency expenses–the sum of the net totals from the individual agency financial reports (each available on their respective websites). This total comes to $2810.6 which is $90.7 billion less than the $2901.3 net total given in the financial report.

G.   2006 individual agency financial reports: Internal agency discrepancies - the difference, if any, between the agency's sum total and total of the fund's allocated by the agency to the Operating Fund and the restricted funds. The total discrepancy was $-9.4 billion.

H.   COMPARISON of the USFR and the individual agency reports: Discrepancy, if any, between the agency's sum net expense total and the net expense total reported on page 37 in the 2006 USFR. The sum of the discrepancies is $160.7 billion. The biggest discrepancies were DoD-$52.5 billion and Treasury-$67.4 billion. I was unable to find anyone who could explain the enormous difference in Treasury's reporting, so I just went with the lower figure to keep my final numbers as close to the consolidated financial report as possible.

I.   SUM FORMULA: Gross Operating Fund Expenses. The sum of the Operating Fund expenses listed by the individual agencies PLUS the "earned revenue" given in the 2006 USFR, p. 37. The following exception was made: Health and Human Services-all of the earned revenue was assumed to be for the restricted funds that HHS manages. This assumption may or may not be valid.

J.   GUESSTIMATE FORMULA: An apportionment of intra-agency transfers to each depart-ment. The total intragovernmental transfers for all government agencies listed on page 37 of the 2006 USFR is $344.3 billion. This comes out to roughly 21.75% on top of each agencies net total. This assumes that each department spends an equal percentage of their total spending on intragov-ernmental transfers. It is unlikely that this is true, but it seemed like the best way to make a best guess at the apportionment of this significant cost of government.

K.   SUM FORMULA: The sum of column I (gross operating fund expenses) plus column J, each agencies apportioned intragovernmental transfers.

L.   CORRECTION: In order to get my totals to more closely match the totals in the USFR, I took $11.5 billion off the Department of Defense, with no justification other than expedience. Again, this means that accuracy is ballpark.

M.   BEST GUESSTIMATE of GROSS OPERATING FUND EXPENSES.

N.   This column shows what percent of the Operating Fund Revenue each department's expenses represent.

Column M and N are what I used in Part I.

3. The change in Net worth does not make sense. For example in 2006, we overspent by $622 billion. According to my calculations from the official reports we diminished our assets by $28 billion and increased our debts by $672 billion, for a net change in net worth of $700 billion. Where did that extra $78 billion in reduced net worth come from. I have clearly missed something here, which I am inclined to say is well hidden. If you can help us get to a fully clear picture, do so. Thanks.

THE OPERATING FUND: Statement of Net Worth
4. The official report uses a *net* for property, plant and equipment. This means that the asset values have been net with liabilities against asset properties and the reports of assets and liabilities are diminished by an unknown amount.

5. This sum disappears from view in the consolidated report formats (as asset to the restricted funds / debt to the Operating Fund).

6. **Other.** The descriptors do not match up on the Operating Fund and restricted fund reports. So, separating them is difficult and required throwing some that are described more specifically in one report or the other, into this general "other" category.

This report subtracts the restricted funds' liabilities (USFR, p. 87) from the consolidated liabilities to arrive at a fair reporting of the liabilities that belong to the Operating Fund. This is probably a ball park guesstimate. With your feedback to GAO and Treasury, we'll do better next year.

THE OPERATING FUND: Income and Expense Statement
I wanted the income and expenses separated into those that are income to the general Operating Fund and those that are income to the restricted funds. For this first time in 2006, the Statements of Operations and Changes in Net Position (2006 USFR, p. 38) breaks down the revenue and net costs into those belonging to "Non-Earmarked Funds" (Operating Fund) and "Earmarked Funds" (restricted funds). I used these totals for 2006 and then extrapolated a percentage that I applied to 2002-2005, for which no such breakdown is available.

7. **Forfeited Income** also known as "Tax expenditures," are preferential tax exemptions that let some people off the hook for taxes that others pay. In effect these are a form of spending and should be out in front on the table so that we can be clear about our values and priorities in spending. I was able to find GAO estimates for 2002-2005, and just extrapolated a percentage of revenue for 2006. An estimate for 2006 may become available at a later date. See GAO-05-690 Government Performance and Accountability: Tax Expenditures: www.gao.gov/new.items/d05690.pdf

8. Marketplace Sales and Services, a.k.a. "Earned Revenue." The current official format includes some earned revenue on the income side and some as a debit against the expense side. This is misleading; we lose sight of the full cost of government and the full revenues available to pay for it. The format in Part I rectifies this; it uses the gross expenses from p. 37 and from the individual agency reports as described in the process above, and it adds the "earned revenues" net out on the expense side back onto the revenue side for both the Operating Funds and restricted funds. The breakdown is taken from page 38.

9. Federal Reserve receipts. The official financial report does not break out these receipts; they are included under "Other," and detailed in Note 16 on page 74. This is a substantial sum–greater than the revenues for estate and gift taxes, custom duties and excise taxes–making it worthy of its own line. We have a federal banking system that is privately owned; unidentified private shareholders are guaranteed a 6% profit off the top of our federal banking, before the U.S. Government makes its $30 billion dollars. The federal revenues from this system and the system itself deserve to be part of an engaged public discourse on our values and our operations.

Expenses

10. The official report format does not break out the funding for the Legislative and Judicial branches of government. It lumps them into the "Other" category. As an interested citizen I would like to know what they spend and how they spend it. Currently the best we can do is note a line item, not in the U.S. Government Financial Report, but in Table 21-1 Total Outlays, Gross and Net of Offsetting Collections and Receipts from the Public, By Agency, 2006-2008 of the Budget from the OMB (2006, p. 339). This table sets out the net and gross expenses for the Legislative and Judicial branches of government on a cash-basis. I've set these totals out separately, deducted the totals from the "Other" category, and adjusted them from cash-basis to accrual.

11. There is an enormous discrepancy between Treasury's agency reports and the report of their spending in the consolidated financial report. An explanation has not yet been forthcoming. I went with the lesser amount reported in their agency financial report on the assumption that the balance is likely to be funds that they hold and manage for a restricted fund. This assumption may or may not be valid.

12. The Executive Office of the President is also not broken out of the "Other" category in the current official financial report format. From information in the Budgets from OMB, Table 4.1 Outlays by Agency 1962-2012, we can see that up until 2003, the Executive Office of the President's expenses were under $450 **m**illion– $.4 billion–an insignificant amount in comparison to the size of the other agency budgets, and a reasonable reason for lumping them into "Other."

However, in 2004 the Executive Office of the President made a giant leap in funding to $3.3 **b**illion– roughly 10 times its historical funding level. In 2005, Congress again doubled down on the President's budget and gave him $7.6 billion. In 2006, this dropped to $5.4 billion, which with a guesstimate share of the allocated $344 billion in intragovernmental transfers comes out to a total of roughly $7 billion. This unsupervised Presidential spending in the years leading up to an election was ostensibly for "Iraqi Reconstruction."

Keep this sum in perspective. A three year average annual budget of roughly $6 billion is comparable to half of the total US Agency for International Development Budget. USAID has hundreds of experienced staff and systems in place that have been developed over nearly 50 years. The Executive Office of the President had no such staff or systems in place to manage this magnitude of money or contracting.

This increase also gave the Executive Office of the President **direct control** over a sum **equal to the total spent by each of the other *branches* of government–Legislative and Judicial**.

This enormous increase raises issues about the balance of power intended by the Constitution and about Republican values in practice. What did your Congressman have in mind when he/she decided it made sense to give the Executive Office of the President–which did not have any staff or experience in reconstruction–this huge sum to manage under "emergency" funding conditions where speed, efficiency and transparency were critical to our national security? The Republican controlled Congress also went along with the Bush II administration's blocking of auditing and oversight of this spending until well into the spending cycle. Audits begun in 2006 are finding that there was "inadequate" oversight over most of these funds. How can that be a surprise to anyone? It was surely predictable and deliberate, and as such, a high crime heist of taxpayer money? It is difficult to see an honorable justification for overriding all Executive branch agencies (which are also under the President's control, but have Congressional oversight), to put this extra $6 billion into coffers in the Executive Office of the President (where unprecedented secrecy would make timely oversight nearly impossible). Eliminating and minimizing oversight is a sure recipe for corruption and profiteering. All outcomes point to a greedy lust for power at the expense of performance.

As in most government actions, the policies and decisions have life and death impacts. Criminally negligent performance in the occupation and reconstruction of Iraq have cost many lives, fueled international terrorism, reduced our international prestige, set a precedent in Iraq for profiteering and corruption, and made the world a more dangerous place. Making extending your power base a higher priority than national security is surely treason, and grounds for impeachment. Find out how your Congressman voted and if they voted in support of this travesty, then hold them accountable at the next election.

13. The average annual interest on U.S. debt is from the 2006 USFR, p. 61, "Federal Debt Securities Held by the Public and Accrued Interest."

THE RESTRICTED FUNDS
14. The information for the restricted funds can be found on page 87 of the 2006 USFR.

15. Gregory Cohen, President of the American Highway Users alliance estimates that $75 billion is needed each year just to keep highways and bridges from further deterioration. This information was published in a variety of sources following the collapse of the bridge in Minnesota in 2007.

16. Every financial report of the U.S. Government has a section by the Comptroller General of the United States. All statements by the Comptroller General are from these reports.

PART TWO

Chapter 1: Basic accounting & government accounting
The history of U.S. Government accounting was gleaned from the GAO websites, "History of the GAO, http://www.gao.gov/about/history/splash.htm, as well as the historical perspective sections of the annual Budgets available from the White House.

Chapter 3: Government accounting
17. The Coalition Provisional Authority (CPA) ruled Iraq from April 2003-June 2004, under the direction of the Office of the President and/or the Department of Defense. There are a variety of reports

conflicting reports about the chain of command. When the CPA was established by President G.W. Bush, no system of monitoring the spending of taxpayer (or Iraqi money we held in trust) was put in place.

This story of the San Diego firm was most recently reported in Vanity Fair in an article by Pulitzer Prize winning contributing editors Donald Bartlett and James B. Steele (October 2007). A history of the steps leading up to the appointment of the San Diego firm can also be found at http://www.cooperativeresearch.org/context.jsp?item=UNSecCounRes1483. This story was reported at least two years earlier, because it has been in my notes for that long. I have misplaced my source, however. If you can remind me which of the media were doing there job and reported on this in a timely manner I would be happy to give them credit.

18. *Use of Contractors by State Department Has Soared* by John M. Broder and David Rohde, New York Times, October 24, 2007. It is also worth remembering the story of Ms. Bunnitine Greenhouse, an employee with the U.S. Army Core of Engineers. During her day to day duties, she discovered that Halliburton, Vice President Dick Cheney's former company, received billions of dollars in no-bid contracts for work in Iraq. She asked why one company received over half of the business in Iraq without competition or competitive bids. For this, she received "poor performance" ratings and was demoted from an executive position to middle management. Piles of similar and significant evidence leads to the conclusion that the failure of oversight has been a deliberate policy. It is clear from the actions of this administration that protecting friends' booty is a higher priority than protecting the nation.

19. The most recent and egregious example of this is Blackwater. Erik Prince, the Chairman of this private security company has been a substantial supporter of G.W. Bush and the Republicans. The company has a no-bid contract to guard State Department employees and V.I.P.s in Iraq. It took the dramatic killing of 17 Iraqi civilians in September 2007, to bring longstanding complaints about their swaggering, belligerent, aggressive 'defensive' posture, which has been alienating Iraqis and creating blow back on U.S. troops, to the attention of the American public. If they have any smidgen of competence, the Executive Office of the President, his Secretary of Defense, and Secretary of State, all had to be aware of the mixed outcome from Blackwater's performance–safe V.I.P.s and an angry and hostile civilian population. No action was taken by the Administration until this received public attention, suggesting clearly where their loyalties lie.

20. The International Institute for Strategic Studies issued a report in September 2007, which makes the case that the incompetent execution of the Iraqi Occupation and Reconstruction has seriously compromised U.S. standing in the world, and this loss of prestige has security consequences. www.iiss.org.

21. When Congress passed Public law 108-106, the Emergency Supplemental Appropriations Act for Defense and for the Reconstruction of Iraq and Afghanistan, 2004, it appropriated $18 billion to create the Iraq Relief and Reconstruction Fund (IRRF) which it put under the direct control of the Executive Office of the President (instead of USAID, which might have made more sense). This law established the Inspector General of the Coalition Provisional Authority (CPA-IG) to start work in March 2004–11 *months after* spending of Iraqi reconstruction funds began.

The 2004 assignment of control over $18 billion in Iraqi Reconstruction Funds to the Executive Office of the President, spread out over the 2004-2006 fiscal years was an unusual move that got negligible public attention. This sum appears in the 2004 financial report in the "Actual" column. The line item is titled "Iraq relief and reconstruction fund." In the Appropriation, discretionary category it lists $18.42 billion, with $3 billion in outlays. The presence of this sum contradicts a report in *CongressDaily* on April 16, 2003, which states, *"Nixing the administration's request to put the Executive Office of the*

President in charge of the fund, the supplement calls for the money to be dispersed according to the Foreign Assistance Act while enabling the president to directly fund several domestic agencies and the Defense Department." It is way more difficult than it should be to find any discussion of the management and oversight of this fund, whether the President actually had control of it, as his financial reports suggest (available at www.whitehouse.gov) , or whether his control was more indirect through existing Executive Branch agencies.

When the CPA ostensibly turned governance over to the Iraqis in June 2008, the CPA-IG was out of business. Our Republican-controlled Congress waited another three months, until October 2004, before creating the position of Special Inspector General for Iraq Reconstruction (SIGIR-created by a congressional amendment to Public law 108-106. Evidently your Congressman was OK with no one at the check, balance and anti-fraud post from April 2003 to March 2004 and from June 2004 through October 2004. The SIGIR website speaks about relationships with the DoD, USAID and some other agencies, but I could find nothing whatever about its relationship to the Executive Office of the President and its direct control of a huge chunk of Iraqi reconstruction change.

22. *Imperial Life in the Emerald City* by Rajiv Chandrasekaran (2006) and *Fiasco: the American Military Adventure in Iraq* by Thomas E. Ricks (2006) each provide a litany of examples of crony incompetence, malfeasance and profiteering.

23. Information on improper payments is from the reports found at http://www.whitehouse.gov/omb/financial/fia_improper.html

Chapter 5: More than one fund
24. The information on the ownership of the Federal Reserve is available on their website, as is the statement that this ownership is not really ownership (http://www.federalreserve.gov/generalinfo/faq/faqfrs.htm#5): (emphasis is mine)

Who owns the Federal Reserve?
The **Federal Reserve System is not "owned" by anyone and is not a private, profit-making institution**. Instead, it is an independent entity within the government, having both public purposes and private aspects.

As the nation's central bank, the Federal Reserve derives its authority from the U.S. Congress. It is considered an independent central bank because its decisions do not have to be ratified by the President or anyone else in the executive or legislative branch of government, it does not receive funding appropriated by Congress, and the terms of the members of the Board of Governors span multiple presidential and congressional terms. However, the Federal Reserve is subject to oversight by Congress, which periodically reviews its activities and can alter its responsibilities by statute. Also, the Federal Reserve must work within the framework of the overall objectives of economic and financial policy established by the government. Therefore, the Federal Reserve can be more accurately described as "independent within the government."

The twelve regional Federal Reserve Banks, which were established by Congress as the operating arms of the nation's central banking system, are **organized much like private corporations-possibly leading to some confusion about "ownership."** For example, the Reserve Banks issue shares of stock to member banks. However, owning Reserve Bank stock is quite different from owning stock in a private company. The Reserve Banks are not operated for profit, and ownership of a certain amount of stock is, by law, a condition of membership in the System. The stock may not be sold, traded, or pledged as security for a loan; **dividends are, by law, 6 percent per year.**

The highlighted statements from the Federal Reserve contradict each other. When private shareholders own stock that provides a guaranteed 6% interest rate, that is a "profit" on their investment, and certainly does represent ownership, however qualified and restricted that ownership may be.

While the Bank of Canada was founded as a privately owned corporation in 1934, in 1938 it became a "Crown Corporation" owned by the government. http://www.bank-banque-canada.ca/en/about/are.html

Chapter 8: Be consistent or PAY ATTENTION

25. This is another reference to the story most recently reported in the October 2007 Vanity Fair article, "Billions over Bagdad," previously referenced. The U.S. Government sent C-130 cargo planes full of the largest cash shipments in U.S. history to CPA Head, Paul Bremer. His team were playing football with the cash, stashing the money in rooms with the keys on a hook by the door, and calling contractors to bring in duffle bags to pick up their loot. Minimal paperwork was done. If this is not criminal negligence, I do not know what is. The New York Times story by James Glanz, "Audit describes Misuse of Funds in Iraq Projects" (1/25/06) gives additional information.

26. http://en.wikipedia.org/wiki/United_States_housing_bubble

27. The New York Times has a mind-blowing chart that shows the percentage of all mortgages that are subprime in every county in the nation. Those with "low" percentages are up to 20%. It is very difficult to understand where the adults were when this mess was created. http://www.nytimes.com/interactive/2007/11/03/weekinreview/20071103_SUBPRIME_GRAPHIC.html

Chapter 9: Separate reports for separate funds

28. This was bill HR. 1088 Investor and Capital Markets Fee Relief Act, which can be found at http://www.cbo.gov/ftpdoc.cfm?index=2778&type=0&sequence=0. I sent my Senator, Gordon Smith (R-OR) a request for information on his reasons for voting for this bill. He sent me a copy of the bill, which he referred to in the cover letter as the "Investor and Capital Markets Free Relief Act" and zero information about his reasons for his vote. I wondered if the "free" relief was a Freudian slip.

Chapter 10: Book all the assets and all the debts

29. Taxpayers for Common Sense has a good summary of this fiasco: http://www.taxpayer.net/TCS/wastebasket/budget/2006-03-03bigerror.htm

30. This construction of this bridge was finally removed from consideration in late 2007.

31. There is a Bureau of Public Debt at the Treasury department. This data is from their historical tables. http://www.publicdebt.treas.gov/

32. These estimates are from a Business Week article, *Uncle Sam: Up To His Neck in the Risk Pool; The government is the Insurer-of-last-resort for a mind-boggling array of catastrophes.* June 6, 2005.

Chapter 11: If it's income, call it income

33. There are several quotes in the text about this. Another reference can be found at USA Today for 12/19/2005, "College loans take biggest cuts in budget:"...As Congress moves to slash $40 billion in spending, no program will take a bigger hit than college loans, where almost $13 billion would be cut over five years." The word "slash" should be banned from discussions about the budget unless your talking at least, what? – 1% of the Operating Fund ($14 billion per year), – 3% (42 billion). When does a cut become a slash in responsible journalism?

34. These "earned revenue" figures are from the USFR for the respective years, and have been adjusted for inflation.

35. *Power in America; Wealth, Income, and Power* by G. William Domhoff, September 2005 (updated December 2006): http://sociology.ucsc.edu/whorulesamerica/power/wealth.html.

Chapter 12. Tell the truth, the whole truth and nothing but the truth

36. There is an excellent discussion of supplemental spending history at www.ombwatch.org/budget/supplementalbackgrounder.pdf.

37. British Broad Casting (BBC)'s *Newsnight* reported on this 201-document planning Iraq's economic "recovery"–essentially a candy-jar of privatization and corporate rule. American journalist, Greg Palast, now working in Great Britain has reported extensively on this document, and further information can be found at GregPalast.com. However, the story and all its policy issues and ramifications has been ignored by our mainstream media. Hey Frontline, how about addressing this? In the first 4 pages of Google responses to a search for "101-page plan Iraq," or "101 page plan Paul Bremer," I only found one brief reference on money.cnn.com/2007/08/31/... The existence of this plan does not appear to be in question. The contents and what they say about Bush II's intentions in Iraq have yet to be addressed by our mainstream media. This document, which was evidently fully implemented by Paul Bremer, accounting for his Presidential Medal of Honor, has far-reaching implications. This plan set the stage for an insurgency by placing American corporate interests–and particularly the oil and defense industry interests closest to the Bush II administration–well-above any considerations for democratic rule in Iraq. Again, when does perfidious self-interest over national interest become treason?

38. Testimony on Estimated Costs of U.S. Operations in Iraq and Afghanistan and of Other Activities Related to the War on Terrorism, Congressional Budget Office, July 31, 2007. A link to the PDF file can be found at http://www.cbo.gov/ftpdoc.cfm?index=8497&type=1

Chapter 14. Use consistent terms

39. I took this information from http://www.nationalcenter.org/TPSocialSecurity9.html ...

"The U.S. Supreme Court decided this in 1960 in the case of Fleming v. Nestor. Bulgarian immigrant Ephram Nestor was deported in 1956 for being a Communist in the 1930s. After Congress prohibited Social Security benefits for deportees in 1954, Nestor sued. He claimed title to his FICA tax payments between 1936 and 1955, the year he retired. The Supreme Court disagreed: "To engraft upon the Social Security system a concept of 'accrued property rights' would deprive it of the flexibility and boldness in adjustment to ever-changing conditions which it demands.""

* The Court added: "It is apparent that the non-contractual interest of an employee covered by the [Social Security] Act cannot be soundly analogized to that of the holder of an annuity, whose right to benefits is bottomed on his contractual premium payments."5
* This decision reflected the Court's precedent in Helvering v. Davis. In 1937, it ruled: "The proceeds of both the employee and employer [Social Security] taxes are to be paid into the Treasury like any other internal revenue generally, and are not earmarked in any way."6

40. There is an interesting discussion about foreign aid here: *U.S. and Foreign Aid Assistance* by Anup Shah: http://www.globalissues.org/TradeRelated/Debt/USAid. asp#MoreMoneyIsTransferredFromPoorCountriestoRichThanFromRichToPoor ; and here: *How U.S. dollars disappear in Afghanistan: quickly and thoroughly* by Ann Jones, September 3, 2006: http://www.sfgate.com/cgi-bin/article.cgi?file=/chronicle/archive/2006/09/03/INGR0KRGMF1.DTL

Chapter 15. Include the value of the dollar

41. Up through the 1990s the United States dollar retained its position as the dominant global currency. As the Euro gained in strength, with the Yen surely to follow, a natural inclination to diversify for both economic and political reasons followed. Iraqi President Saddam Hussein converted Iraq's reserve currency and oil trading to Euros in September 2000. North Korea did so in December 2002. By October 2007, 85% of Iran's oil trading was taking place in Euros or Yen. It is no coincidence that these three countries have been in the bulls eye for an administration filled with oil executives and their friends. The policy of the Bush II administration has been to bully, intimidate, and use violent force to keep countries in the dollar fold. After our invasion, Iraq's oil trading and reserves were promptly switched back to Dollars to U.S. benefit and at a cost of 13% of their value to the Iraqis. A basic understanding of how people respond to force would predict that securing Iraqi reserves and oil trading in the dollar camp by invasion and occupation would increase the likelihood that other nations would be more inclined to follow suit, not less. And, that is what is happening...Mexico, China, Russia...the list of nation's dumping some or all of their Dollars is growing, and the Dollar may very well be approaching a crisis in 2008.

Chapter 16. Add a statement of borrowing

42. By the end of fiscal year 2007 the actual, cash-based cost was $456 billion (National Priorities Project- http://www.nationalpriorities.org/index.php?option=com_content&task=view&id=297&Itemid=7). The ratio of accrual-based (real cost) to cash-based has been running at about 120%, which would put the current accrual-based spending on the Iraqi Occupation at roughly $ 550 billion. This does not include associated costs of equipment depreciation and replacement, veterans increased health care costs, et cetera, which some, including a nobel-prize winning economist, are estimating will be at least $2 trillion (http://www.guardian.co.uk/Iraq/Story/0,2763,1681119,00.html). The money borrowed for just the simple out-of-pocket Iraqi War costs through September 2007, at 4.7% average interest, equals $26 billion per year.

Compare my number to the interest estimate in the report issued on November 14, 2007 by the Democratic staff of the Joint Economic Committee of Congress. According to this report, the administration has requested $607 billion by October 2007, and they estimate the interest costs on Iraq-related debt to be more than $23 billion for fiscal 2008. I've used $25 billion as a compromise.

43. Your share is calculated by taking 65% (individual income tax share of federal operating fund income) of the total interest, which equals $16.5 billion. Then, this is divided by the roughly 100 million individual taxpayers, for the $163 dollar 2008 share.

44. The information on the debt incurred by the Reagan administration is from the Treasury Department's Bureau of Public Debt, schedules of debt and interest at http://www.treasurydirect.gov/govt/reports/pd/pd.htm.

45. More Reagan debt information in the story *Economic Legacy; Reagan Policies Gave Green Light to Red Ink* by Jonathan Weisman, Washington Post, June 9, 2004.

46. At a fundraising dinner President G.W. Bush said, "This is an impressive croud. The haves, and the have mores. Some people call you the elite. I call you my base." You can see this for yourself on YouTube.   http://www.youtube.com/watch?v=mn4daYJzyls

47. http://en.wikipedia.org/wiki/United_States_public_debt

48. *"Using a government filing cabinet as a prop, President Bush yesterday played to fears that the Social Security Trust Fund is little more than a stack of worthless IOUs."* Bush portrays Social Security fund as worthless paper, Knight Ridder News Service, April 6, 2005.

Chapter 17. Summarize
49. *Road Bill Reflects the Power of Pork; White House Drops Effort to Rein in Hill* by Jonathan Weisman and Jim VandeHei, Washington Post, August 11, 2005.

50. This AP article can be found on Public Broadcasting http://www.pbs.org/moyers/journal/blog/congress/.

INDEX

Virginia Hammon, MS, TE, is a mediator, group facilitator and educator dedicated to improving the quality of our democracy.

The Great Democracy project brings together her experience, expertise and passions: human development, intercultural communication, collaborative decision-making and bringing order to chaotic information overload. She is a businesswoman, entrepreneur, educator, mediator, community facilitator and trainer.

Life experiences—seven years working and living in Paris, Teheran and Kish Island in the Persian Gulf, founding and directing a private school, raising venture capital for a .com, and parenting four children, now adults— have given her practical wisdom in the art of moving groups toward satisfying positive outcomes.

Your questions and comments are truly welcome - virginia@greatdemocracy.net.

Great Democracy Projects

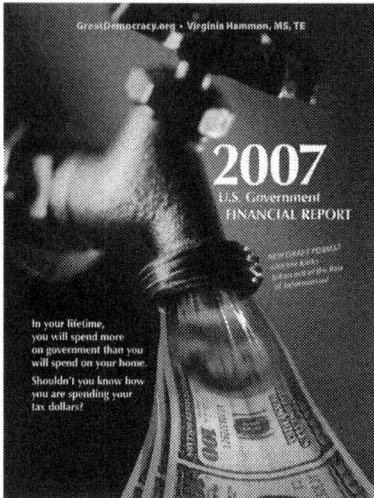

Short & Sweet

The 2007 U.S. Government Financial Report comes out in mid December 2007.
We transform this 160 page report into an illustrated, simple, clear and honest report. Please help distribute it to every citizen.

Full color, 8.5"x11"
Available: January 2008

Pre order your copies now.
Bulk purchases are easy and inexpensive.

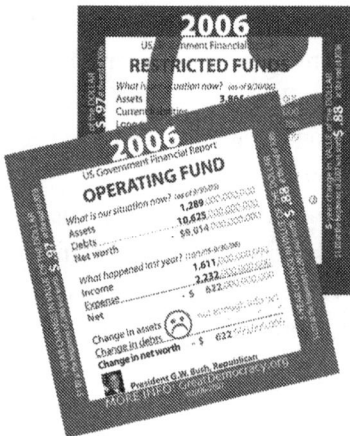

Drink coasters

Conversation starters! Start your collection now with 2006, add 2007 in January 2008.

The short summaries of the U.S. Government Operating Fund and Restricted Funds fit on two sides of a coaster.

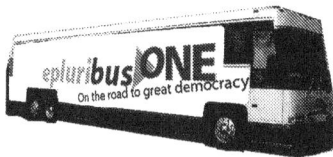

3-dimensional, hands-on exhibits

It's always easiest to understand when you can experience quantity and size in three dimensions. Online, visit greatdemocracy.org for ideas on how you can present the financial report to your church, social or civic organization–
"Let them eat cake!"

On the road – literally

In 2008, the 3-D exhibit, presentation and discussion will go on the road. The goal is to engage at least 5,000 people, online and in person, to perfect the report format and a 3-D exhibit that can be presented at State Fairs every year by volunteer groups.

You can help put the gas in our tank!

To contribute to building a prototype traveling exhibit, funding our presentations to community groups, enhancing the website, and distributing financial reports as widely as possible, please go to greatdemocracy.org or send your check to:

Great Democracy, Inc.,
PO Box 6440,
Portland, Oregon 97228.

Non-profit status is in process. We intend, but cannot guarantee, that your donations will be tax deductible.